Constructing the Responsibility to Protect

This volume examines the ongoing construction of the Responsibility to Protect (R2P) doctrine, elaborating on areas of both consolidation and contestation.

The book focuses on how the R2P doctrine has been both consolidated and contested along three dimensions, regarding its meaning, status and application. The first focuses on how the R2P should be understood in a theoretical sense, exploring it through the lens of the International Relations constructivist approach and through different toolkits available to conventional and critical constructivists. The second focuses on how the R2P interacts with other normative frameworks, and how this interaction can lead to a range of effects from mutual reinforcement and co-evolution through to unanticipated feedback that can undermine consensus and flexibility. The third focuses on how key state actors – including the United States, China and Russia – understand, use and contest the R2P. Together, the book's chapters demonstrate that broad aspects of the R2P are consolidated in the sense that they are accepted by states even while other, specific aspects, remain subject to contestation in practice and in policy.

This book will be of much interest to students of the R2P, human rights, peace studies and international relations.

Charles T. Hunt is Vice-Chancellor's Senior Research Fellow and Australian Research Council DECRA Fellow at the Social & Global Studies Centre, RMIT University, Australia.

Phil Orchard is an Associate Professor of International Relations at the University of Wollongong, Australia.

Global Politics and the Responsibility to Protect

Series Editors:

Alex J. Bellamy
University of Queensland

Sara E. Davies
Griffith University

and

Monica Serrano
The City University of New York.

The aim of this book series is to gather the best new thinking about the Responsibility to Protect into a core set of volumes that provides a definitive account of the principle, its implementation, and its role in crises, that reflects a plurality of views and regional perspectives.

International Organizations and the Rise of ISIL
Global responses to human security threats
Edited by Daniel Silander, Don Wallace and John Janzekovic

Reviewing the Responsibility to Protect
Origins, Implementation and Controversies
Ramesh Thakur

Ethics, Obligation and the Responsibility to Protect
Contesting the Global Power Relations of Accountability
Mark Busser

Implementing the Responsibility to Protect
A Future Agenda
Edited by Cecilia Jacob and Martin Mennecke

The Responsibility to Protect in Darfur
From Forgotten Conflict to Global Cause and Back
David Lanz

Constructing the Responsibility to Protect
Contestation and Consolidation
Edited by Charles T. Hunt and Phil Orchard

For more information about this series, please visit: www.routledge.com/Global-Politics-and-the-Responsibility-to-Protect/book-series/GPRP

Constructing the Responsibility to Protect

Contestation and Consolidation

Edited by Charles T. Hunt and Phil Orchard

Routledge
Taylor & Francis Group
LONDON AND NEW YORK

First published 2020 by Routledge

2 Park Square, Milton Park, Abingdon, Oxon OX14 4RN
605 Third Avenue, New York, NY 10017

Routledge is an imprint of the Taylor & Francis Group, an informa business

First issued in paperback 2021

Publisher's Note

The publisher has gone to great lengths to ensure the quality of this reprint but points out that some imperfections in the original copies may be apparent.

British Library Cataloguing-in-Publication Data
A catalogue record for this book is available from the British Library

Library of Congress Cataloging-in-Publication Data
Names: Hunt, Charles T. editor. | Orchard, Phil, 1976- editor.
Title: Constructing the responsibility to protect : contestation and consolidation / Edited by Charles T. Hunt and Phil Orchard
Description: Abingdon, Oxon ; New York, NY : Routledge, 2020. | Series: Global politics and the responsibility to protect | Includes bibliographical references and index.
Identifiers: LCCN 2019049101 (print) | LCCN 2019049102 (ebook) | ISBN 9780367370343 (hardback) | ISBN 9780429352430 (ebook)
Subjects: LCSH: Responsibility to protect (International law)
Classification: LCC KZ4082 .C66 2020 (print) | LCC KZ4082 (ebook) | DDC 341.4/8–dc23
LC record available at https://lccn.loc.gov/2019049101
LC ebook record available at https://lccn.loc.gov/2019049102

ISBN: 978-0-367-37034-3 (hbk)
ISBN: 978-1-03-217474-7 (pbk)
DOI: 10.4324/9780429352430

Typeset in Times New Roman
by Wearset Ltd, Boldon, Tyne and Wear

Contents

Illustrations

Figure

Tables

Contributors

Sara E. Davies is an Associate Professor at the School of Government and International Relations, Griffith University, Australia; and an Adjunct Associate Professor at the Gender Peace and Security Initiative, School of Social Sciences, Monash University. Sara's research career has been devoted to identifying the political conditions that deny humans access to civil, economic and social human rights. She has published in *Foreign Policy Analysis*, *International Affairs*, *Review of International Studies*, *Medical Law Review*, and *International Relations*. Sara is co-editor of the *Australian Journal* and *International Affairs and the Global Responsibility to Protect.*

Luke Glanville is a Fellow in the Department of International Relations at the Australian National University. He is the author of *Sovereignty and the Responsibility to Protect: A New History* (Chicago: Chicago University Press, 2014) as well as articles in journals including *International Studies Quarterly*, *Ethics & International Affairs*, *European Journal of International Relations*, and *European Journal of International Law*. Luke co-edited the quarterly journal, *Global Responsibility to Protect*, for ten years (2010–2019).

Sassan Gholiagha is a postdoctoral Research Fellow at the WZB Berlin Social Science Center, where he works in a German Research Foundation (DFG) funded project on norm collisions. He has published his work in several edited volumes and international journals, writing among other things, about norms, R2P and drones.

Sarah Hewitt is a PhD candidate at Monash Gender, Peace and Security Centre in the School of Social Sciences at Monash University, Australia. Her doctoral research focuses on women's participation during peace processes, the inclusion of gender provisions in peace agreements, and how this affects women's participation in post-conflict societies concentrating on Nepal and Kenya. Sarah's PhD research is funded by the Australian Research Council Linkage Project *Towards Inclusive Peace: Mapping Gender Provisions in Peace Agreements,* partnered with the Australian Department of Foreign Affairs and Trade in which Associate Professor Sara Davies is one of the chief investigators, among others. Sarah has published articles on the Women, Peace and Security (WPS) agenda in *International Feminist Journal of Politics and the Global Responsibility to Protect*, as well as co-authored chapters on the WPS agenda in the *Oxford Handbook on Women, Peace and Security* (2018) and *Feminist International Relations in the Sage Handbook of the History, Philosophy and Sociology of International Relations* (2018).

Charles T. Hunt is Vice-Chancellor's Senior Research Fellow and Australian Research Council DECRA Fellow at the Social & Global Studies Centre, RMIT University, Australia. He is co-Editor-in-Chief of the quarterly journal, *Global Responsibility to Protect* and author/editor of numerous titles including *UN Peace Operations and International Policing* (Routledge, 2015) and *Exploring Peace Formation* (Routledge, 2018).

Bastian Loges is a lecturer for International Relations at the Technische Universität Braunschweig, Germany. His research focuses on global norms, with an emphasis on human rights and environmental politics. He graduated with a PhD thesis on protection as a new global norm, analyzing the responsibility to protect narrative within the United Nation Security Council's debates on the protection of civilians. Currently, he is co-leader of a project on norm emergence and the global governance of plastics.

Phil Orchard is an Associate Professor of International Relations at the University of Wollongong and a Senior Research Fellow at the Asia Pacific Centre for the Responsibility to Protect. He is the author of *Protecting the Internally Displaced: Rhetoric and Reality* (Routledge, 2018) and of *A Right to Flee: Refugees, States, and the Construction of International Cooperation* (Cambridge University Press, 2014).

Sarah Teitt is an Australian Research Council DECRA Senior Research Fellow and Deputy Director of the Asia Pacific Centre for the Responsibility to Protect in the School of Political Science and International Studies at The University of Queensland. Sarah's research focuses on Chinese foreign policy in relation to international intervention, peacebuilding and humanitarian emergency response, and on the prevention of widespread and systematic sexual and gender-based violence in Southeast Asia.

Heather Rae was Senior Lecturer in Politics and International Studies in the School of Political Science and International Studies at the University of Queensland in Brisbane, Australia until 2019. Her current work focuses on state violence, political identity and liberalism, and their complex interrelationship. She is best known for her book on ethnic cleansing, genocide and state formation, State Identities and the Homogenisation of Peoples (Cambridge University Press, 2002).

Wesley W. Widmaier is an Associate Professor in the Department of International Relations at the Coral Bell School of Asia Pacific Affairs in the ANU College of Asia & the Pacific. His research addresses the interplay of ideas, crises and change – and the ways in which ideational stability can paradoxically cause instability and crisis. He has engaged these concerns across a range of publications, most recently in two books: *Economic Ideas in Political Time: The Rise and Fall of Economic Orders from the Progressive Era to the Global Financial Crisis* (Cambridge University Press, 2016) and *Presidential Rhetoric from Wilson to Obama: Constructing Crises, Fast and Slow* (Routledge, 2015). His published work has also appeared in such journal outlets as *International Studies Quarterly*, the *European Journal of International Relations*, *Review of International Political Economy*, *New Political Economy*, and *International Relations*.

Shannon Zimmerman is a Research Fellow at the Asia Pacific Centre for the Responsibility to Protect at the University of Queensland. Her research investigates the intersections of civilian protection and terrorism in peace operations and their impact on state-building.

Acknowledgments

The year 2020 marks 15 years since the Responsibility to Protect (R2P) doctrine was institutionalized at the international level through the World Summit Outcome Document (WSOD). Its evolution has been impressive. It reframed what had become an entrenched debate around the legality and legitimacy of humanitarian intervention. It has been operationalized within the UN through strong leadership by consecutive Secretaries-General, first under Kofi Annan, then under Ban Ki-moon, and now under António Guterres. It has been referenced in almost every major humanitarian crisis and has been used by the UN Security Council to authorize military action without the consent of the concerned state for the first time in Libya in 2011. Nonetheless, its rapid emergence has also been problematic. The failures of the UN Security Council to take effective action in Syria and issues with the outcome of the intervention in Libya have led to suggestions by commentators that the R2P doctrine may have suffered grave or even irreparable damage. Governments, too, have questioned how it should be applied, proposing new codes of conduct or challenging aspects of the doctrine such as its Pillar Three.

This book began with a common concern: that while alongside R2P's policy growth there has also been sustained academic interest, how the R2P doctrine has been understood in a theoretical sense has been less developed. While this may sound dry, we focus on this issue because these theoretical issues have direct, real world effects in two senses. Focused on the R2P doctrine itself, they can lead to conclusions we argue are incorrect that the R2P is indeterminate or too complex to be successful. Further, stand-alone accounts neglect how the R2P interacts and competes with a range of other normative agendas and practices at both the international and domestic levels. These are the issues we seek to address.

This book has had a long gestation, and we wish first to thank the contributors for their ongoing involvement. It began with an ISA sponsored Catalytic Workshop in 2015, which Phil Orchard convened along with Jason Ralph to examine the Responsibility to Protect at Ten. It then continued with a 2016 workshop at the Oceanic Conference on International Studies in which the authors presented their first drafts of papers and which was supported by the University of Queensland and the Asia Pacific Centre for the Responsibility to

Protect. We would like to extend our thanks to Alex Bellamy, Shahar Hameiri, Cecilia Jacob, Jacinta O'Hagan and Jacqui True, who participated as discussants and provided valuable feedback on this project in its early stages. We would also like to extend our thanks to Brian Job and Anastasia Shesterinina, and to Kai Kenkel and Cristina Stefan, who presented papers at the workshop but were unable to continue with the volume; even so, their papers helped to inform the overall project. We are grateful to the anonymous reviewers for their constructive criticism that helped to improve the manuscript. Finally, we would like to thank Andrew Humphrys and Bethany Lund-Yates at Routledge for their encouragement and support of the project.

Charlie is awfully grateful to Sofia, Amina and Alessia who have helped him to see the world quite differently since this project began. He would also like to recognize the support he has received across this period from the Australian Research Council through Discovery Project [DP160102429] and Discovery Early Career Researcher Award [DE170100138].

Phil would like to extend his personal thanks to his colleagues at Wollongong for their feedback, to Charlotte and Kate for putting up with daddy finishing another book, and to Victoria for everything, always.

Melbourne and Wollongong

Introduction

Consolidation and contestation of the Responsibility to Protect

Charles T. Hunt and Phil Orchard

Introduction

This introduction proceeds in four parts. First, it provides a brief overview of the history and trajectory of the Responsibility to Protect (R2P). Second, it argues that while it is uncontroversial to say the R2P has normative properties, its normative status is much more disputed. That is to say, whether the R2P should be understood as a single coherent norm, a composite norm, an international regime or some other formation or structure operating in the international system is itself contested and one of the central arguments within the rest of the book. Third, the chapter engages with the intersection, interaction and interpenetration of the R2P doctrine with other normative agendas, principles and practices in the international peace, security and human protection realm. Finally, the chapter outlines and links together the chapters in the volume, presents the major themes and threads that run throughout the volume and identifies a series of potential research questions and agendas that flow from this set of engagements.

The Responsibility to Protect: realization or retreat?

In a remarkably short space of time, the R2P doctrine has become established within the international peace and security architecture and has significantly transformed practices at the international level. As of today, the R2P constitutes a framework for action in cases of mass atrocities based on the full array of measures prescribed and proscribed under the United Nations (UN) Charter – including the use of military force as a last resort. The possibility for and pathways to the non-consensual use of force remains the most controversial component of the R2P toolbox, yet it is deeply rooted in the evolution and development of the R2P.

The UN Charter establishes only two situations when the use of force is permitted. Under Article 51, it establishes that there is an inherent right of individual or collective self-defense if an armed attack occurs against a member state; while Article 42 within Chapter VII establishes that the UN Security Council may take any actions it considers necessary in order to maintain international peace and security. Short of that, and as established in Article 2, all members are required to refrain from the threat or use of force against the territorial integrity or political independence of any state and nothing contained in the Charter allows for the UN to intervene in the domestic jurisdiction of any state. This required, however, that states would respect and protect their own populations. If a state failed or was unable to do so, there was no clear mechanisms by which the international community could take action. Even the Genocide Convention established that contracting parties who sought to prevent or suppress acts of genocide could only "call upon the competent organs of the United Nations to take such action under the Charter of the United Nations as they consider appropriate."[1]

Yet, beginning in the 1970s, individual states did undertake a series of interventions which, they argued, were for humanitarian reasons – India in East Pakistan, Vietnam in Cambodia, Tanzania in Uganda (Wheeler, 2000; Orchard, 2013). Then, with the end of the Cold War, we began to see a process of multilateral humanitarian intervention, bookmarked by the US, UK and France going into Northern Iraq in 1991 to protect the Iraqi Kurds; and by the NATO-led intervention in Kosovo in 1999 to protect the majority ethnic Albanian population. These actions, both designed to protect domestic populations under attack, did not fit into the bifold architecture the UN Charter had created. As the Independent International Commission on Kosovo famously noted, the NATO intervention there was "illegal but legitimate" (The Independent Commission on Kosovo, 2000). At the same time, the 1990s saw remarkable failures on the part of the international community – from the failure of the US-led peacekeeping mission in Somalia, to the fall of the Srebrenica safe area, to the Rwandan genocide, crises were occurring which required a response that was not forthcoming.

As UN Secretary-General, Kofi Annan made a provocative argument to the global community. In his 1999 speech to the General Assembly, he noted that in the wake of the Rwandan genocide and the Kosovo intervention, the inability of the international community to reconcile "two equally compelling interests – universal legitimacy and effectiveness in defence of human rights – can only be viewed as a tragedy" (Annan, 1999). Then, the following year, he argued: "if humanitarian intervention is, indeed, an unacceptable assault on sovereignty, how should we respond to a Rwanda, to a Srebrenica – to gross and systematic violations of human rights that offend every precept of our common humanity?" (Annan, 2000: 48). The first answer to that question was introduced the following year, when the International Commission on Intervention and State Sovereignty (ICISS) presented two basic principles:

> State sovereignty implies responsibility, and the primary responsibility for the protection of its people lies with the state itself. Where a population is suffering serious harm, as a result of internal war, insurgency, repression, or state failure, and the state in question is unwilling or unable to halt or avert it, the principle of non-intervention yields to the international responsibility to protect.
>
> (ICISS, 2001: xi)

As Thakur noted the following year, these two principles were deliberately designed to alter the debate around humanitarian intervention, moving it away from "the claims, rights and prerogatives of the potentially intervening states" toward the "urgent needs of the intended, putative beneficiaries of a given action." In so doing, the responsibility to protect acknowledged that "responsibility rests primarily with the state concerned" (Thakur, 2002: 327–328; Evans, 2008). This evolution in language from 'right' to 'responsibility' has been held as a central achievement of the ICISS, even if this shift echoed the ideas of 'responsible sovereignty' earlier introduced by Francis Deng (Deng, 1998; Welsh et al., 2002: 493).

And yet, while the ICISS introduced the language of the "responsibility to protect," retrospectively it had three main limitations. The first was that it framed its notion of serious harm around large-scale loss of life and ethnic cleansing brought about by deliberate state action or inability to act (ICISS, 2001: xii); yet it did not define a threshold or other criterion for 'large scale' and it failed to link these issues to established international human rights, humanitarian and criminal law. The second was that while it sought to create three 'responsibilities' – to prevent, react and rebuild – its focus was very much on the responsibility to react (Bellamy, 2011a). And, finally, the third was that as a Commission, the ICISS had little power itself. With the report being introduced in the wake of the September 11, 2001 attacks in the United States, even its proponents doubted how effective it would be, while the US invasion of Iraq in 2003 was used as justification to both critique the concept and question its applicability to situations such as Darfur (Weiss, 2004; Bellamy, 2005: 39).

Because of this, it was surprising when the R2P was taken up by the UN in its World Summit Outcome Document (WSOD) in 2005, (UN General Assembly, 2005). The WSOD endorsed the concept while modifying it significantly from its ICISS origins. In an expansion from the ICISS report, states accepted that they have a responsibility to protect their own populations from four identified mass atrocity crimes: genocide, war crimes, ethnic cleansing and crimes against humanity. Further, they have accepted responsibilities to help protect other populations from atrocity crimes and to take collective action when other national authorities are manifestly failing to protect their populations. As the WSOD noted, in Paragraphs 138–140:

> 138. Each individual state has the responsibility to protect its populations from genocide, war crimes, ethnic cleansing and crimes against humanity. This responsibility entails the prevention of such crimes, including their incitement, through appropriate and necessary means. We accept that responsibility and will act in accordance with it. The international community should, as appropriate, encourage and help States to exercise this responsibility and support the United Nations in establishing an early warning capability.
>
> 139. The international community, through the United Nations, also has the responsibility to use appropriate diplomatic, humanitarian and other peaceful means, in accordance with Chapters VI and VIII of the Charter of the

> United Nations, to help protect populations from war crimes, ethnic cleansing and crimes against humanity. In this context, we are prepared to take collective action, in a timely and decisive manner, through the Security Council, in accordance with the Charter, including Chapter VII, on a case-by-case basis and in cooperation with relevant regional organizations as appropriate, should peaceful means be inadequate and national authorities manifestly fail to protect their populations from genocide, war crimes, ethnic cleansing and crimes against humanity. We stress the need for the General Assembly to continue consideration of the responsibility to protect populations from genocide, war crimes, ethnic cleansing and crimes against humanity and its implications, bearing in mind the principles of the Charter and international law. We also intend to commit ourselves, as necessary and appropriate, to helping States build capacity to protect their populations from genocide, war crimes, ethnic cleansing and crimes against humanity before crises and conflicts break out.
>
> 140. We fully support the mission of the Special Adviser of the Secretary-General on the Prevention of Genocide.
>
> (Ibid.)

Following the WSOD, in his 2009 Secretary-General's Report on the Responsibility to Protect, Ban Ki-moon offered a three-pillar formulation of the R2P as reflecting three distinct patterns of practice. The first pillar reflects "the enduring responsibility of the State to protect its populations, whether nationals or not, from genocide, war crimes, ethnic cleansing and crimes against humanity, and from their incitement" (UN General Assembly, 2009: 8). The second pillar reflects the "commitment of the international community to assist States in meeting those obligations" (ibid.: 9). Finally, the third pillar articulates "the responsibility of Member States to respond collectively in a timely and decisive manner when a State is manifestly failing to provide such protection" (ibid.).

Framing the R2P within these three pillars, Ed Luck, the former Special Adviser to the Secretary-General on R2P, has argued, allows "for an early and flexible response tailored to the circumstances of each situation." Its clear preference, he argues, "is for preventive action" (Luck, 2010b: 351–352). Indeed, prevention has become the focus of a great deal of R2P debate in the decade since 2009. For instance, some have argued that prevention should be the core business of R2P and point to cases such as Kenya, Guinea and Kyrgyzstan to evidence the value add of R2P providing an atrocity prevention lens (Sharma and Welsh, 2015; Davies and Teitt, 2012; Crossley, 2013; McLoughlin, 2014). Others, however, have pointed to the dilution of the intervention elements of the R2P and argue that this may constitute a paradox in the doctrine – stating but simultaneously reducing in significance the responsibility to react in timely and decisive ways (Chandler, 2015).

However, as Luck also noted, the need to respond effectively to the failure to prevent "is every bit as integral and essential …" (Luck, 2010b: 351–352). And the third pillar, it is important to note, does not only reflect the use of force. Bellamy argues that it consists of two components:

> (a) a generic and ongoing responsibility to use lawful and peaceful measures, consistent with Chapter VI and VIII of the UN Charter, to protect populations from atrocity crimes and, (b) when these measures are judged inadequate, a commitment to take "timely and decisive action" through the UN Security Council.
>
> (Bellamy, 2015a: 4)

This version of the R2P appears to now be widely recognized within the UN and also, increasingly, in regional organizations (below, we suggest it has been institutionalized in the theoretical sense). This can be seen through several indicators. The first is that since 2009 there has been a formal pattern of behavior within the UN Secretariat, with annual Reports by the Secretary-General on the R2P and linked informal interactive dialogues of the General Assembly (Luck, 2018: 34). The ten Secretary-General's Reports issued over this time frame have each focused on different aspects of the R2P doctrine, including early warning (in 2010); on the involvement of regional and sub-regional organizations (in 2011); on the challenges of timely and decisive responses (in 2012); on state responsibility and prevention (in 2013), which led to the subsequent development of the UN Framework of Analysis for Atrocity Crimes; on international assistance (in 2014); on implementation (in 2015); on mobilizing collective action (in 2016); on improving accountability (in 2017); on linking early warning to early action (in 2018); and on prevention (in 2019). In 2018, the General Assembly also shifted to holding a formal plenary meeting on R2P at which 79 states and the European Union spoke (Global Centre for the Responsibility to Protect, 2018).

But, beyond this yearly process, UN bodies routinely invoke the R2P doctrine within resolutions. The UN Security Council, as of April 2019, had referred to the R2P in some 81 resolutions and presidential statements,[2] while the General Assembly has referenced the R2P 15 times in resolutions[3] and the Human Rights Council 42 times.[4] The language of R2P is routinely invoked in statements and speeches by both the Secretary-General and other key figures within the UN. Two roles – special advisers to the Secretary-General on R2P and on genocide prevention – have been created within the UN system (Thakur, 2016). And individual states have signaled a range of commitments. The Group of Friends of R2P includes 50 states and the European Union,[5] while 61 states as well as the European Union and Organization of American States have appointed their own national R2P focal points, a step taken by "governments with differing levels of capacity in mass atrocity prevention to demonstrate their commitment to R2P."[6] However, as Jacob (2018: 399) notes, "there is still a lack of consensus as to how the existing mechanisms could, or should, be mobilized to realize the preventive capacity of R2P...."

The doctrine also has deepening ties at the regional level, though here the record is more mixed. In the Asia Pacific, for example, intergovernmental bodies such as the Association of Southeast Asian Nations (ASEAN) have begun to mainstream R2P considerations into their visions for a shared security community (Morada, 2018). Elsewhere, regional bodies have become key actors in particular cases such as the Arab League vis-à-vis Libya (Azzam and Hindawi, 2016), the Economic Community of West African States (ECOWAS) in relation to Mali, Guinea and the Gambia (Aning and Edu-Afful, 2016), or the Organization of Islamic Cooperation's efforts to refer Myanmar's human rights violations against the Rohingya to the International Court of Justice.[7] Among the more vocal proponents have been the European Union and the African Union. The EU and its member states "have been united in endorsing the norm…" though slower to implement it (De Franco et al., 2015: 996–996). In 2016 at the UN, the European Union noted it was "a strong supporter of the Responsibility to Protect and its three reinforcing pillars … we are committed to implement this important principle through better use of the full range of our diplomatic, political, development, human rights and humanitarian instruments and our partnerships across the globe."[8]

On the African continent, the R2P has had significant traction. In the March 2005 Ezulwini Consensus – a common position on UN reform – African states through the African Union (AU) voiced clear support for the formulation in the Secretary-General Report emerging from the High-level Panel on Threats, Challenges and Change. The statement outlined a willingness to take proactive regional action in line with the doctrine and opined that "authorization for the use of force by the Security Council should be in line with the conditions and criteria proposed by the Panel, but this condition should not undermine the responsibility of the international community to protect."[9] The R2P has also become increasingly embedded in the continent's institutional frameworks (Hunt, 2016a). For instance, the AU Constitutive Act specifically underlines in Article 4(h) "the right of the Union to intervene in a Member State pursuant to a decision of the Assembly in respect of grave circumstances, namely: war crimes, genocide and crimes against humanity." The doctrine has also influenced the development of the AU's Peace and Security Architecture more generally including the operational concepts of the African Standby Force (Dersso, 2010; Hunt, 2013) This institutionalization at the continental level has been accompanied by significant resonance at the local level. Many have pointed to the communitarian and cosmopolitan ethics that undergird traditional forms of social and political order across Africa and the R2P (Murithi, 2008). While the African continent has also been a site of contestation for the R2P, it has found strong support at multiple levels (Hunt, 2018: 155).

Equally, the doctrine has found resonance in both civil society and academia, including through the Non-Governmental Organization (NGO) International Coalition for the Responsibility to Protect, the Global Centre for the Responsibility to Protect, and two regional focused Centers – the Asia Pacific Centre for the Responsibility to Protect and the European Centre for the Responsibility to Protect.

More generally, there appears to be positive advances associated with the R2P, most notably a decline in the past two decades with respect to the "overall number of civilians deliberately killed in any given year" (Bellamy, 2012: 8).

And the R2P doctrine has provided an important focus for how the international community should respond. Alex Bellamy argues that it has created "a collection of shared expectations" (Bellamy, 2011a: 84) while Jennifer Welsh suggests it has created a "duty of conduct" for members of the international community: "to identify when atrocity crimes are being committed (or when there is threat of commission) and to deliberate on how the three-pillar framework might apply" (Welsh, 2014: 136). By any measure the evolution of the R2P has been impressive. It has reframed what had become an entrenched debate around the legality and legitimacy of humanitarian intervention. As Thomas Weiss has argued, with the possible exception of post-Second World War genocide prevention, "no idea has moved faster or farther in the international normative arena than the Responsibility to Protect" (Weiss, 2011).

At the same time, how successful the R2P doctrine has been remains open to question along four dimensions. The first, most notably, has been its application or non-application in the cases of Libya and Syria. The Libyan intervention marked the first time the UN Security Council had authorized non-consensual military action for humanitarian reasons without the consent of the state. It followed the violent crackdown by the Qaddafi regime against protesters which had seen between 500 and 700 civilians killed, but also harsh rhetoric from Qaddafi – who described protesters as rats and cockroaches and pledged to "cleanse Libya house by house" (Adams, 2016: 707). In the debates around Libya, Dunne and Gelber argue that we can see the use of both explicit language reflecting the R2P, as well as implicit signifiers "such as the use of Charter VII authority, and the description of events as atrocities and international crimes" (Dunne and Gelber, 2014: 339). And yet, Libya was a somewhat unique case for a range of reasons. The initial consensus was "enabled by several exceptional factors, in particular a putative regional consensus and the poor international standing of Qaddafi's regime, as well as the clarity of the threat and short timeframe for action" (Bellamy and Williams, 2011: 825). Further, significant questions have been raised about how the Security Council resolution was implemented, reigniting questions about when intervention should occur (Kuperman, 2013), how the use of international military action should be used to avert atrocities (Paris, 2014), whether R2P is actually having an effect (Hehir, 2013) and even whether the Libyan intervention had "done grave, possibly even irreparable, damage to R2P's prospects of becoming a global norm" (Rieff, 2011).

In the case of Syria, the Security Council has failed to definitively halt mass atrocities during the long running civil war which has seen as many as 560,000 people killed.[10] And yet the UN Security Council did allow UN-based humanitarian assistance to enter the country with the notification only, and not the consent, of the government: "Clearly underpinning this shift was a view that the Syrian authorities were not fulfilling their responsibilities toward their own population …" (Orchard, 2017: 179). Some analysts have argued that these efforts in Syria should be understood as R2P in practice as efforts to prevent mass atrocities that are consistent with the goals of the R2P (Bellamy, 2016: 262). However, critics continue to see this as the archetypal example of the doctrine's failure and ability to "legitimise inaction" rather than a case of partial success in extremely unfavorable political conditions in the Security Council (Hehir, 2016: 173).

Second, there have been renewed contestations over how the R2P should be applied, with governments proposing codes of conduct around so-called third pillar interventions such as the Brazilian government's "Responsibility While Protecting" – which sought to emphasize non-military means, limit the recourse to force and strengthen accountability to the Council (Welsh, 2014; McDougall, 2014) – and the Chinese government's semi-official "Responsible Protection" proposal (Li and Chen, 2013; Evans, 2014; Garwood-Gowers, 2016). But there have also been questions raised as to whether the Security Council is even the appropriate venue for considering R2P given the power dynamics within the Council. Moses, for example, has argued that because of this the R2P merely removes the "sovereign immunity" of weaker states, not the more powerful (Moses, 2013: 134).

Further, with the WSOD, any language with respect to a 'responsibility to rebuild' was removed. This became a critical issue with respect to the Libyan intervention, following which the main intervening states – the United States, the United Kingdom and France – did little to ensure a positive transition to a post-conflict state. This led to President Obama identifying the failure to plan for the aftermath of the intervention as the worst mistake of his presidency.[11] And, consequently, it has also led to academic arguments that a 'jus post bellum' – an international duty to rebuild – is needed as, otherwise, future interventions may have subsequent destabilizing effects even if successful in averting a mass atrocity (Paris, 2014: 577–577; Pattison, 2015; Doyle, 2016: 23).

Third, there have also been questions raised around how the UN Security Council actually uses R2P language. Gifkins, for example, suggests that R2P has been referenced by the Council more times since the Libya intervention than it was before it took place (Gifkins, 2016: 157–160). Accounts such as these (see also Bellamy, 2015b) hold that the focus on decision-making and implementation of military intervention masks the wide range of actions occurring under the holistic three-pillar conception of R2P. Other commentators temper that view – Hehir, for example, suggests that while eight resolutions dealing with the Arab Spring have mentioned R2P, each reference "is exclusively to Pillar I of R2P, relating to the host state's responsibility to protect its population. There is no mention in any of these resolutions of Pillar III or the international community's responsibility to protect" (Hehir, 2016: 170).

Notwithstanding its persistent appearance in UN Security Council resolutions, some of the momentum that Weiss speaks of has been lost in recent years. Advocates in civil society and among UN member states have struggled to leverage the R2P in established and emerging cases of mass atrocities – in part due to the perceived toxicity of the R2P after the Libya intervention. The UN, too, has had difficulties using R2P in specific situations. This includes places where the UN already has a strong presence and history of engagement (such as the Democratic Republic of Congo, South Sudan, the Central African Republic and Burundi) as well as places that have arrived on the Council's agenda more recently (such as Syria, Yemen, Myanmar and the Chad basin).

Consequently, the relevance of the R2P in debates and action in response to mass atrocities through the UN is perhaps more open to question than at any time since its endorsement in the WSOD.

Fourth, and finally, there is the remaining question of how global – versus Western – R2P really is. One criticism is that R2P remains premised on "a supposedly universalist Western enlightenment ethos" (Ziegler, 2016: 268) and thereby linked to a form of "pragmatic liberal interventionism" where the United States and allied Western states "exert a disproportionate influence in decision-making and implementation"(Graubart, 2013: 70). The role of the US, UK and France within the Council remains problematic in several senses including their attempt to combine R2P with a discourse around regime change, as Orchard lays out in Chapter 1.

However, there has been growing engagement with the R2P from the developing world. This has not been about simply accepting the R2P wholesale, but rather there has been important engagement and even contestation with its core elements. This has included Brazil's Responsibility While Protecting (RWP) proposal, But India has also engaged with the R2P, initially seeking to argue that R2P's three pillars have a set sequence and to link R2P implementation with Security Council reform (Aneja, 2014), but then, following Libya, increasingly arguing against Pillar Three in favor of a more restrictive interpretation of the sovereignty norm (Bloomfield, 2015).

At the same time, the rise of neo-nationalism, illiberalism, and populism across the world has precipitated retreat from – and at times outright hostility toward – multilateralism and the idea of a rules-based international order that the R2P fits into. In parallel, international humanitarian law is being violated in the world's conflict zones with worrying regularity and horrifying consequences at the same time as powerful states in the international system walking back on commitments to the promotion the protection of human rights or seeing an opportunity to further weaken key international bodies that work to support these efforts. This comes at a time when the redistribution of power in the international system from west to east challenges the status quo and prevailing norms, including those around human protection. The rise of China and the resurgence of Russia creates points of tension and friction that can shape dynamics between the permanent members of the Security Council and therefore the potential for realization of R2P goals.

Though it may also be more accurate to speak in terms of evolving implementation than growing irrelevance, the ebb and flow of the R2P's relative traction and popularity with scholars and practitioners alike raise questions about the precise nature of the R2P. As a result, questions remain about how the doctrine should be used but also what it actually means in practice. In fact, at this stage, the R2P doctrine would appear to be both contradictory and indeterminate in practice.

The nature of the R2P

The central contention of this book is that these debates reflect the fact that the nature of the R2P doctrine remains contested in how it is understood and applied by individual states and in how it is linked to other issue areas. Since its inception, the status of the R2P has been the subject of perennial debate and argument. Particularly in academic literature, there have been widespread efforts to use labels from international relations theories – norms, principles, concepts and so on – to describe a doctrine that does not easily fit within any of these categories.

In its early years, it was usually referred to as either a concept, a principle or an emerging norm. UN member states tended to use the term 'concept' – alluding to their position that the R2P was an idea deserving of further deliberation but not yet something that should shape or trigger action (Bellamy, 2009: 4). The ICISS (2001), for instance, referred to the R2P as a 'principle' connoting a stronger consensus and agreed status than a concept – something that could guide praxis.

The R2P has also long been referred to as an 'international norm.' Within the UN's official discourse, for example, the High-level Panel on Threats, Challenges and Change, released the year prior to the WSOD, argued that meeting the challenge "posed by large-scale, gross human rights abuses and genocide is a normative challenge to the United Nations" (UN, 2004: 18). As a solution to this, the Panel's report argued that both the UN Security Council and the wider international community needed to recognize that there was an "emerging norm of a collective international responsibility to protect" (ibid.: 66).

Similarly, at the policy level, key R2P proponents also use the language of norms, in part as a way of reflecting the R2P's legal potential.[12] Gareth Evans, one of the co-chairs of the ICISS, the commission which first coined the 'Responsibility to Protect' term, albeit under a different definition from the WSOD, argues throughout his 2008 book that the R2P is a "new international norm," one with the "potential to evolve further into a full-fledged rule of customary international law" (Evans, 2008: 3, 52). Louise Arbour, the former UN High Commissioner for Human Rights and Canadian Supreme Court Jurist, similarly refers to it as a new norm, one "anchored in existing law, in institutions and in lessons learned from practice." For her, "the norm asserts a broad international public interest predicated on universal human rights, while appealing to the practical wisdom of confronting threats and ongoing abuses before a crisis unravels and cascades with unforeseeable consequences" (Arbour, 2008: 447–448). Lloyd Axworthy and Allan Rock, the former Canadian Foreign Minister and Ambassador to the UN at the time of the WSOD respectively, refer to the 2009 debate around R2P at the UN General Assembly[13] as representing a moment of reaffirmation: "R2P had indeed emerged as a new norm, resetting limits on sovereignty, and a robust one at that" (Axworthy and Rock, 2013: 184).

Claims to R2P's status as a norm are also frequently made within the academic literature, though these are more likely to identify it more circumspectly as a norm in the process of emerging or under challenge. Thus, one set of arguments see it as an emerging norm which is having or has the potential to have a clear effect. For Badescu and Weiss, the R2P is "at a preliminary stage of its normative trajectory" but still "has the potential to trigger compliance and thus increase protection on the ground" (Badescu and Weiss, 2010: 355). Edward

Luck argues that while R2P has not in a formal and technical sense achieved "the status of a binding legal norm" this "need not condition its effectiveness in terms of affecting the behaviour of states and armed groups and the decisions of international bodies" (Luck, 2010a: 109). Alternatively, the R2P is seen as an emerging norm which remains subject to feedback from the local or regional levels (Prantl and Nakano, 2011; Negrón-Gonzales and Contarino, 2014: 256; Capie, 2012; Job and Shesterinina, 2014). Not surprisingly, within this literature there is always a certain caution in claiming normative status for the R2P. As Bellamy notes, using the language of norms to describe R2P "both helps and complicates efforts to understand it" and that "we should see the question of whether or not R2P is a norm, and what sort of norm it might be, as *parallel* to, but separate from, the question of whether it is a concept or principle" (Bellamy, 2009: 7).[14]

Those more critical of the R2P doctrine have also used a language of norms. Reinold (2010: 65), for example, argues that the R2P as a norm:

> is currently missing: a) conceptual clarity, and thus an intersubjective consensus on the implications of R2P (in particular regarding the military aspect); and b) the consistent application of R2P in state practice. In the absence of these two factors, norm internalization cannot occur.

Alternatively, Hehir suggests that R2P is "commonly presented as a key causal factor, a 'norm' that changed the decision-making calculus" (Hehir, 2013: 146). However, he suggests R2P was not a causal factor in the decision to intervene in Libya because the architects did not publicly acknowledge it (ibid.: 148).

In its language, much of this literature – supportive and critical – is making two assumptions. The first is to assume that the R2P either has or should have (if it is to be effective) normative properties. The second is to assume that the R2P, like other international norms, should follow Finnemore and Sikkink's (Finnemore and Sikkink, 1998) norm life-cycle model. The following section challenges the veracity of these assumptions.

Norm emergence

There is no question that norms are important. In the most widely cited definitions, norms are shared understandings of appropriate behavior for actors with a given identity which isolates a single strand of behavior (Jepperson et al., 1996: 52; Finnemore and Sikkink, 1998: 891). Accepted norms should be viewed as "'binding,' as having qualities of 'oughtness'" (Finnemore, 2000: 702–703; Deitelhoff, 2009: 34). But norms are part of a broader constructivist claim that structures and agents need to be to be treated in a mutually constitutive manner whereby interests and even identity are created through interactions with these structures (Wendt, 1987, 1999; Checkel, 1998).

The norm life-cycle model represents an early attempt to explain how norms in particular emerge and replace other norms. In brief, the life cycle begins when new norms are actively built by norm entrepreneurs; early adopting states then socialize other states to follow them through a variety of mechanisms including legitimation effects, self-esteem effects and pressure for conformity. Once a critical mass of states adopts a new norm, it passes a threshold or tipping point (Finnemore and Sikkink, 1998: 896–906). But, in order to reach this point, in most cases an emergent norm "must become institutionalized in specific sets of international rules and organizations." Such a process of institutionalization, while not a necessary condition:

> contributes strongly to the possibility for a norm cascade both by clarifying what, exactly, the norm is and what constitutes violation (often a matter of some disagreement among actors) and by spelling out specific procedures by which norm leaders coordinate disapproval and sanctions for norm breaking.
>
> (Ibid.: 900)

Following this, the norm enters a third state, where international or regional demonstration effects occur and "international and transnational norm influences become more important than domestic politics for effecting norm change" (ibid.: 902). Following this, norms are so widely accepted that they "are internalized by actors and achieve a 'taken-for-granted' quality that make conformance with the norm almost automatic" (Risse and Sikkink, 1999: 15). This focus on institutionalization as an international level process (see also Keck and Sikkink, 1998; Risse and Sikkink, 1999) sees the new norm gaining precision as states clarify their understandings (Percy, 2007b: 389; Lutz and Sikkink, 2000). Thus, institutionalization is viewed as leading to precision and conceptual clarity of a new norm.

And yet, a range of newer scholarship has questioned whether this actually occurs. One strand focuses on norms which might still lack clarity even after institutionalization. In this view, norms are works in progress, which "tend to be vague, enabling their content to be filled in many ways and thereby to be appropriated for a variety of different purposes" (Krook and True, 2012: 104). They are exposed to ongoing contestation and "co-optation, drift, accretion and reversal of a norm – including disputes over whether it a norm at all – are constant possibilities" (ibid.). Thus, Wiener (2008: 4) argues that a norm's meaning is "constituted through an interactive process. Interpretation is thus derived from the social practice of enacting meaning that is used in a specific context." Sandholtz similarly notes that this is a process driven by the tensions generated between what a norm states and the specific actions it is ascribed to, tensions which "ceaselessly casts up disputes, which in turn generate arguments, which then reshape both rules and conduct" (Sandholtz, 2008: 101; see also Sandholtz and Sweet, 2004; Sandholtz, 2009). As Kratochwil (1989: 61) argues, "actors are not only programmed by rules and norms, but they reproduce and change by their practice the normative structures by which they are able to act, share meanings, communicate intentions, criticize claims, and justify choices." Hence, interpretation and reinterpretation of norms is actually an ongoing process.

A second strand argues that how individual states and other actors understand norms is also subject to variance. This can be seen in Acharya's (2004) concept of norm localization, which "describes a complex process and outcome by which norm-takers build congruence between transnational norms ... and local beliefs and practices. In this process, foreign norms, which may not initially cohere with the latter, are incorporated into local norms" (Acharya, 2004: 241). Localization, however, reflects a one-sided process with international norms being sent down to the local level. This process, as argued by Betts and Orchard, can actually be viewed as significantly more complex. They argue that a process of implementation should be seen as a parallel process to that of norm institutionalization, with norm implementation drawing "attention to the steps necessary to introduce the new international norm's precepts into formal legal and policy mechanisms within a state or organization in order to routinize compliance" (Betts and Orchard, 2014: 2). While institutionalization may bring precision to a norm, clarifying key issues, the implementation process creates an interpretative space around any norm as it is subject to contestations at the domestic level. Through these contestations, actors within and outside of government effectively debate what an international norm means for the state. This also means, as Cortell and Davis (2005: 9) note, "a range of policy choices can be consistent with a given norm." Similarly, Zimmermann (2016) suggests that as norms are brought down to the domestic level, first in discourse, then in law, and finally through implementation into policy, they can go through processes of reinterpretation and reshaping.

A third set of contributions to these debates have further problematized the prevailing wisdom of norm life-cycle thinking and attempted to find ways of better reflecting the continuity of change of norms in the international system. For instance, in more recent work, Acharya has developed a norm circulation model. This constitutes a "two way process" whereby global norms

> are contested and localized to fit the cognitive priors of local actors (localization), while this local feedback is repatriated back to the wider global context along with other locally constructed norms and help to modify and possibly defend and strengthen the global norm in question (subsidiarity).
>
> (Acharya, 2013: 469)

This approach reflects the ongoing and more cyclical nature of sense-making when it comes to norm acceptance and, in doing so, privileges a more evolutionary understanding of norm development. However, his model still assumes the prior emergence of the global norm in question. Pushing beyond this, Hunt (2016b) has developed an approach that conceptualizes bouts of contestation and adaptation as part of a continuous and iterative process of norm evolution in complex international society. The model draws on insights from complexity thinking to eschew the diffusionist linear logics commonplace in the life-cycle orthodoxy.

The dynamic process captured by these implementation-based and evolutionary models can add to the problem of normative ambiguity. Ambiguity has generally been defined as "the ability of a norm to be interpreted in varied ways" (Widmaier and Glanville, 2015: 368). As the flip side to precision, "ambiguity and open-endedness of international standards," as Shelton (2000: 14) notes, can limit efforts to secure compliance, because states may be unsure of the required conduct or unwilling to move beyond minimal efforts to implement the perceived norm." The domestic contestation process can lead actors to have a range of different understandings of the norm, understandings which may then be transmitted back up to the international level and thereby triggering a new process of norm interpretation and contestation (Job and Shesterinina, 2014).

The content also affects a norm's application. Normative ambiguity may make it unclear if a norm applies in a given situation and, if it does, what actions it may require (Percy 2007a, 2014). Thus, Deitelhoff and Zimmermann have suggested that two types of normative contestation occur. Justificatory contestation focuses on clarifying whether a norm is appropriate for a given situation, while applicatory contestation focuses on what actions the norm requires in a specific situation (Deitelhoff and Zimmermann, forthcoming: 55). Applicatory contestation, not surprisingly, is particularly likely during crises in which the application of international norms is vague or ambiguous given the intense nature of the ideational contestation (Milner and Keohane, 1996: 16; Orchard, 2014). In such circumstances, ambiguity surrounding how the norm should be applied can reinitiate the implementation process and trigger a process of re-contestation of the norm at the domestic level leading, to a clarification of how the norm should be applied. In this sense, therefore, R2P could be a norm, but it is a norm that remains subject to contestation.

At a deeper level, however, the argument that R2P is a *single norm* may be difficult to sustain due to its sheer complexity for two reasons. First, a norm as noted above isolates a single strand of behavior. By assuming R2P to be a single norm, there is a tendency to conflate it with Finnemore and Sikkink's norm life-cycle model. This in turn has meant it is either conceptually unclear, and hence should not be treated as a norm, or that it remains an emerging norm with a high level of indeterminacy. As we have argued, norm emergence needs to be viewed as a dynamic process, featuring contestations at both the international and domestic levels. Hence, a lack of precision should not be used to deny a norm's existence. As we have also argued, contestations over understandings of a norm are actually part of the process of its emergence and hence is not necessarily an issue.

The second, and more problematic, issue is that treating R2P as a single norm creates an alternative form of indeterminacy: simply put, we are expecting too much from it given the range of duties and responsibilities it creates. Most norms proscribe behaviors which states should not undertake (Price, 1997; Percy, 2007a), while fewer are prescriptive, requiring a *positive* duty or action on part of states (Glanville, 2006: 154–156). A prescriptive norm, by contrast, requires a positive duty or action on part of states; the norm requires not only for the individual actor to not engage in the injuncted behavior, but to sanction in some way other actors if they do so.

In this sense, by requiring a positive duty, prescriptive norms also create a responsibility for actors who follow the norm. To be responsible for some act, following Erskine (2003: 7), is "to be answerable to for it." But responsibilities can vary. Actors may accept a direct responsibility in internalizing the prescriptive norm. Alternatively, it may be a diffuse responsibility, where such responsibility "can make it easier for states and international organizations to shirk their obligations" (Welsh and Banda, 2010: 219).

Not only do some – but not all – elements of the R2P appear to be binding, but the R2P also mixes proscriptive and prescriptive elements. As Ralph notes, R2P has both a proscriptive element with legal obligations, "which insists that acts of atrocity are wrong" but also a prescriptive element minus a similarly equivalent and separate legal obligation which provides a less clear insistence that "states as members of an international community have a responsibility to protect foreign populations" (Ralph, 2018: 187; Welsh, 2014). The responsibilities held by states are direct, reflecting longer running practices as defined in specific bodies of international law (and in their own domestic law). But the responsibilities of the international community are diffuse. One responsibility is to assist individual states to prevent or avert mass atrocities occurring within their own territory; the second is that, in extreme cases, the international community through the Security Council needs to take a range of direct actions to prevent or avert mass atrocities.

As articulated here, these responsibilities reflect closely the three-pillar structure introduced by the Secretary-General in 2009 (UN General Assembly, 2009). This is a view that Welsh (2014: 133) has supported, arguing that the three-pillar form of R2P reflects a 'complex' norm:

> containing more than one prescription. This complex structure also creates a situation in which the breach of one of the components of R2P (failure on the part of a national government to protect its population) is meant to act as a trigger for fulfillment of another component (the international community's role in protection).

As such, she argues that while a catalyst for debate, the R2P does not provide for a particular type of action to take upon its invocation. That, rather, "will depend on a host of factors, *including* other important international norms" (ibid.: 136). Instead, she suggests the R2P demands 'a duty of conduct' by members of the international community: "to identify when atrocity crimes are being committed (or when there is threat of commission) and to deliberate on how the three-pillar framework might apply" (ibid.). In a similar vein, Job and Shesterinina (2014: 147) have argued that because R2P cannot, by its very nature, be articulated in a straightforward or singular fashion, it instead "functions as a composite norm, a rubric under which interpretations of its various subcomponents are 'nested'."

Alternatively, there is a growing acceptance that while R2P may reflect more than one norm, there is a critical, single, 'R2P norm.' Thus, Glanville (2016: 186) suggests this norm has established "the international community has the responsibility to do what it can to ensure that populations are protected from atrocity crimes." Similarly, Bellamy argues that the core element of the "established international norm" of R2P reflects:

> shared expectations within international society that (1) governments and international organizations do, in fact, exercise this responsibility; (2) they recognize both a limited duty and a right to do so; and (3) failure to fulfill this duty should attract criticism.
>
> (Bellamy, 2015b: 163)

Because of this, he suggests that "R2P is not a single norm but a collection of norms" (Bellamy, 2015c: 62). He has therefore developed his formulation and argued that the R2P should at least be understood as relating to two sets of norms – one around the responsibilities of states to protect their own populations, and another regarding the roles and responsibilities of the international community to assist and respond (ibid.: 63).

Orchard, Chapter 1 in this volume, goes further, arguing that these positions continue to reflect a narrow reading of R2P based principally on the consensus developed with the WSOD, while the original ICISS Report provided a much more expansive view of the responsibilities inherent in the doctrine. He suggests that the evolution of R2P represents a series of negotiated normative positions and that a new norm of practice around R2P that has been successfully grafted onto a longer tradition of the Council having full authority over peace and security issues within the UN. He therefore argues that R2P should be viewed as an international *regime* – one which bundles together a series of norms, some new and some old – and be understood as a linkage mechanism between what might otherwise be a series of disparate norms around international responses to mass atrocities.

The question of whether the R2P has emerged as a composite norm, a norm regime or some other form of constellation or ecosystem of norms – and the extent to which this is settled and consolidated versus under constant renegotiation and contested – is a central concern for all the authors in what follows. Regardless of the precise formation in play (whether it is a composite norm, a regime complex or a regime), we are united in a view that elements of the R2P remain contested by states and other actors, particularly around the responsibilities they create and their applicatory nature.

R2P in conjunction with other norms, regimes and agendas

While the normative status of the R2P remains unclear, the best way to talk about and analyze the R2P is further complicated due to its relative infancy and the way it interacts and competes with a range of other normative agendas, thematic issues and practices. For instance, the R2P has significant interactions with other norms and regimes at the international level. Therefore, the R2P also needs to interrelate to a range of alternative responses to humanitarian crises, themselves rooted in their own shared understandings based on their history, practice and institutional alignment. Too often, the R2P is assumed to be a stand-alone issue – either inadvertently in academic debate or deliberately in policy debates – in order to avoid its politically contentious elements. And yet the R2P would not exist without the prior development of robust human rights norms, the emergence of individual accountability for atrocity crimes (Sikkink, 2011) or without human security presenting a clear alternative doctrine to traditional (and state-focused) security. This leads to an alternative history that can be told around R2P – not just its origins and links to humanitarian intervention, but also how it fits in with much wider and continuous reinterpretations and re-understandings of sovereignty (Glanville, 2011) and of international practices (Adler-Nissen and Pouliot, 2014) as a novel concept, per se.

But this also opens up the question of how the norms within the R2P doctrine interoperate with other norms and regimes outside of it, including the Protection of Civilians (POC) agenda within peacekeeping, the Women, Peace and Security (WPS) agenda, or international efforts to respond to terrorism. Despite stove-piped or siloed depictions in the mainstream literature, the R2P is subject to cross-fertilization and interpenetration in a normative arena and has come to the fore through a process of co-evolution. Therefore, there is a dynamical quality to the system of norms that the R2P sits within. First, the norms that the R2P encompasses are changing in relation to each other and will be shaped by ongoing international responses to individual crises. Second, and moreover, the R2P norm(s) are all adapting in the relation to other norms and practices that sit below, above and alongside side the R2P in an international arena that can be understood as an emergent normative ecosystem (Hunt, 2016b).

Unlike the majority of the academic debate that treats the R2P doctrine as a self-contained consideration, this book examines the R2P in a theoretically informed sense that acknowledges when, where, how and with what consequences it is directly linked to a range of other issues. Therefore, as well as drawing on long-standing constructivist theories about different types of norms (regulatory, constitutive, proscriptive, prescriptive, etc.) and norm development (Finnemore and Sikkink, 1998) the volume will also make use of novel (critical) constructivist approaches and contribute to the development of interdisciplinary theoretical approaches to understanding norm evolution.

Structure of the book

This volume explores the R2P doctrine along three axes. The first focuses on the R2P in a theoretical sense, exploring it through the lens of the international relations constructivist approach and, in particular, through different toolkits available to conventional and critical constructivists, including the roles played by contestation and ambiguity in normative development, intersections between norms and regime theory, and how very specific narrative 'stories' have been constructed around the emergence and use of the R2P. The second focuses on how the R2P interacts with other normative frameworks, and how interaction can lead to a range of effects from mutual reinforcement to co-evolution through to unanticipated feedback which can undermine consensus and flexibility. The third focuses on how key state actors – including the United States, China and Russia – understand, use and contest the R2P. Using a variety of different theoretical frameworks, together the chapters not only demonstrate that wide aspects of the R2P are consolidated in the sense that they are accepted by states even while other, specific aspects, remain subject to contestation in practice and in policy. Overall, the chapters demonstrate that the core principles underpinning the R2P are widely, even unquestioningly, accepted today. States routinely accept that they have a responsibility to protect their own populations from mass atrocity crimes, and to assist other states in doing so. Contestation does continue along a number of axes: how and when Pillar Three interventions should occur; how the Security Council should regulate interventions and the broader use of the R2P; and the capacity for the R2P to align positively with other normative frameworks, but also its capacity to create unanticipated feedbacks and undermine prior consensus. But these challenges, to use Deitelhoff and Zimmermann's framing, reflects three forms of applicatory contestations, rather than direct challenges of the basics of the R2P.

In the first chapter, Phil Orchard argues that the R2P doctrine should be viewed as a regime which encompasses a bundle of norms, some new and some old. R2P, he suggests, provides a linkage mechanism between what might otherwise be a series of disparate norms around international responses to mass atrocities. At the same time, he highlights the critical role played by a new norm, one which specifically assigns to the UN Security Council the primacy of addressing R2P issues. He argues that this norm remains contested, even by Council members themselves, by exploring the response by the Security Council to the use of chemical weapons in Syria. In his view, what this suggests is that elements of the R2P remain contested – particular over questions of how the Council should conduct R2P intervention and the use of the veto – but that these contestations reflect the limited nature of the agreement in the WSOD. In other words, these debates are around the application of R2P, rather than around the substantive nature of the doctrine.

In Chapter 2, Luke Glanville and Wesley Widmaier focus on how norm ambiguity, which is usually thought to be an impediment to norm development, has actually facilitated the development of R2P because it allows the doctrine to be interpreted in varied ways. They suggest that ambiguity matters because it feeds back into how norms are understood, helping to both generate initial consensus and to then facilitate incremental adjustment. They demonstrate these benefits of ambiguity by examining three key moments in the history of the R2P. The first was in efforts to respond to the Rwandan genocide, and in particular the view that it was a moral failure, which led to the creation of the R2P by ICISS in 2001. The second was that ambiguity provided support for the R2P during the World Summit negotiations Finally, in reviewing the United States' actions in the lead up to and during the Libyan intervention, they conclude that Obama's stance of 'leading from behind' helped to lessen both international and domestic concerns about R2P potentially being used for 'hegemonic crusading.' Thus, in their view, ambiguity in the R2P has helped to "enable consensus and flexibility over time, enabling adjustment as a 'feedback loop' extends the life of a norm" and that it is ambiguity, rather than clarity or precision, that has "enabled the establishment and incremental development of the R2P norm."

Chapter 3 sees Sassan Gholiagha and Bastian Loges examine the contestation of R2P from the perspective of narrative creation and storytelling, focusing on how members of the UN Security Council have sought to craft specific stories of R2P during diplomatic debates. As with the Orchard and Glanville and Widmaier's chapters, they too focus on touchstone moments for the R2P – the ICISS Report, the WSOD, and the 2009 Secretary-General's Report on R2P – as well as the arguments around the intervention in Libya. Each of these narratives, they argue, have told different 'stories,' focusing on how R2P is both to be understood but also how agency and even the central purpose of the doctrine has changed. They suggest that these different narratives have directly affected how R2P is understood – "members facilitate contestation when referring to different public narratives but further consolidation by using the same narrative collectively." When it comes to specific cases therefore, like with the intervention in Libya, different actors refer back to these established public narratives, but they will also pick out specific elements from these different narratives and from their own national narratives in order to support their position. These actors are, however, drawing on internationally legitimate public narratives to amplify their positions. Thus, they see the central element of R2P, "the acknowledgment that people are entitled to essential protection," as uncontested across these narratives.

Beginning with Chapter 4, different authors shift to focusing on how R2P interacts with other normative agendas. In that chapter, Charles T. Hunt analyzes R2P in conjunction with the Protection of Civilians (POC) in peace operations – investigating where and how the two concepts have challenged, altered, led to reinterpretations and had feedback effects on each other. Through an examination of their institutionalization at the UN, deployment in UN Security Council practices; and, influence on the activities of field operations, Hunt illustrates how R2P and POC in peace operations have cross-fertilized in discourse and practice at the UN regarding the prevention and response to egregious of human rights abuses. Based on this analysis, he posits that the R2P is more accurately depicted as a bundle of norms that intersect with, and sometimes rely on, other norms, regimes and agendas. Hunt argues that clarifying the normative status of the R2P in these ways will be important for its implementation.

In Chapter 5, Sara E. Davies and Sarah Hewitt focus on the R2P and the WPS agenda. They argue that both agendas share the goal of prevention in complementary ways, and that there is an opportunity "for the two agendas to create normative consensus on the prioritization of preventing conflict, preventing atrocities and preventing gender discrimination as essential to achieve protection." Moreover, they argue that much of this discussion needs to take place outside of the Security Council, focusing in particular on the Human Rights Council including through the Universal Periodic Review process. Finally, in examining the case of Nepal, they argue that alongside UN efforts it is also critical to support sustained efforts to ensure the implementation of progressive legislation at the domestic level. These efforts can be critical to not only prevent violence and build capacity but also to ensure more effective early warning systems.

In Chapter 6, Shannon Zimmerman focuses on the ways in which the R2P coincides with the evolving counter-terrorism agenda. Using the theoretical frame of 'norm regimes,' she explores how both of these regimes have a strong basis in international law and in the primacy of the sovereign state as a first responder. To examine these linkages, she uses the cases of Sri Lanka and the Islamic State, and concludes that ongoing contestation within both of these regimes has actually increased their congruencies: "Growing similarities stem from a renewed emphasis on human rights within counter-terrorism and the growing acknowledgment that leveraging the overlaps between counter-terrorism and R2P help both regimes to be more effective." These increased congruencies, she finds, are directly addressing key tensions between the short-term, often kinetic, focus of the counter-terrorism regime and R2P's longer-term focus on prevention.

The final two chapters focus specifically on how the R2P is today understood by two critical state actors: China and Russia. With this focus, these chapters pick up strands already discussed in other chapters, including Glanville and Widmaier's focus on how US approaches to the R2P evolved under President Barack Obama, and on how individual states have understood both the intervention to Libya, highlighted in Gholiagha and Loges' chapter (Chapter 3), and to chemical weapons use in Syria, highlighted in Orchard's (Chapter 1). Chapter 7 sees Sarah Teitt argue that there is a central contradiction in how China approaches the R2P, divided between its support for the principle and its views that R2P "should be implemented with respect to sovereignty and national ownership." She argues that this contradiction is not a paradox per se, but rather reflects a deliberate norm-shaping strategy through which China has sought to "to recalibrate the meaning and scope of R2P away from its human rights and human security-oriented origins to a sovereignty-centered and state-led implementation agenda." While such efforts are ongoing, China is increasingly being forced to frame these positions as ensuring responsibility to local populations and to global norms, which in turn is forcing China to be seen as being constructively and proactively engaged. The key challenge, she concludes, is how this becomes translated "into policy action that provides actual remedies to ongoing and emerging atrocity situations."

Finally, Chapter 8 sees Phil Orchard and Heather Rae argue that Russian behavior toward the R2P is at odds with commonly held understandings of the doctrine, to the point that it has been suggested that Russia is a norm antipreneur with respect to R2P, seeking to block the formation of new norms that challenge existing understandings around sovereign equality. Instead, they argue that Russia's behavior toward the R2P reflects issues in how Russian national identity is currently conceived at the domestic level, in which both domestic and international factors play a role. These include Russia's understandings of itself as a great power, its commitment to a strict interpretation of state sovereignty and, at the same time, to a contradictory view that Russia has a privileged role in protecting Russians outside its borders. Viewing Russia's understanding of R2P through the prism of identity, this chapter illuminates the aspects of R2P which have been internalized, those which remain contested and – particularly with respect to Ukraine and Syria – those elements the Russian state seeks to violate.

The core concern of the volume is that the R2P doctrine has key ideational aspects which remain contested along multiple dimensions: how the doctrine should be understood and applied; how it functions in conjunction with other norms and regimes; and how specific states continue to challenge it. Because of these contestations, the R2P remains in flux and aspects of it remain contingent and subject to reinterpretation. Therefore, it cannot be presumed that all aspects of the R2P are currently fixed, nor that they are independently consolidating. This book presents a series of arguments for why this is currently the case, and why it is likely to continue to be the case in the future. Understanding these contestations is important, not just for academic reasons, but because they have important ramifications for how these ongoing debates – around the normative status and evolutionary trajectory of the R2P doctrine – will progress. The R2P doctrine has traveled a very long way since the ICISS Report 19 years ago, and its endorsement by the global community 15 years ago. Ongoing contestations, however, mean that it continues to face an uncertain future.

Notes

1 Convention on the Prevention and Punishment of the Crime of Genocide, 1948, Art. VIII.
2 Global Centre for the Responsibility to Protect, "R2P References in UN Security Council Resolutions and Presidential Statements." www.globalr2p.org/publications/232
3 Global Centre for the Responsibility to Protect, "UN General Assembly Resolutions Referencing the R2P," www.globalr2p.org/resources/1133, which includes 13 resolutions and was last updated on July 31, 2018. Since then, the General Assembly has passed two more resolutions invoking R2P with respect to the situation of human rights in the Syrian Arab Republic (A/RES/73/182, January 24, 2019) and with respect to the situation of human rights in the Democratic People's Republic of Korea (A/RES/73/180, January 23, 2019).
4 Global Centre for the Responsibility to Protect, "UN Human Rights Council Resolutions Referencing R2P," www.globalr2p.org/resources/977
5 "Group of Friends of R2P Geneva: Statement on Item 2," June 19, 2018. https://dfat.gov.au/international-relations/international-organisations/un/unhrc-2018–2020/statements/Documents/38th-hrc-joint-statement-gof-responsibility-to-protect.pdf
6 Global Centre for the Responsibility to Protect, "Global Network of R2P Focal Points," n.d. www.globalr2p.org/our_work/global_network_of_r2p_focal_points
7 The Daily Star, "OIC Okays Legal Action Against Myanmar at ICJ," March 6, 2019. www.genocidewatch.com/single-post/2019/03/06/OIC-okays-legal-action-against-Myanmar-at-ICJ
8 European Union Delegation to the United Nations "EU Statement – United Nations General Assembly: 10 Years of the Responsibility to Protect," February 26, 2016. www.globalr2p.org/media/files/european-union-26-feb.pdf

9 Executive Council, 7th Extraordinary Session (March 7–8, 2005). The common African position on the proposed reform of the United Nations: 'The Ezulwini Consensus' (Report). African Union, p. 6, para. B.i.
10 Syrian Observatory for Human Rights, "Syria: 560,000 killed in seven yrs of war, SOHR," December 12, 2018. www.syriahr.com/en/?p=108829
11 BBC, "President Obama: Libya aftermath 'worst mistake' of presidency," Apr 11, 2016. www.bbc.com/news/world-us-canada-36013703
12 As Brunnée and Toope note (Brunnée and Toope, 2010b: 193), legal norms are social norms grounded in shared understandings, but they must also share specific criteria of legality, including "generality, promulgation, non-retroactivity, clarity, non-contradiction, not asking the impossible, constancy and congruence between rules and official action," which the R2P has not yet met. On the legitimacy of legal norms more generally see (Brunnée and Toope, 2010a; Finnemore, 2000).
13 For a detailed discussion of these debates, see (Bellamy, 2011a: 43–44).
14 Elsewhere, Bellamy has identified it as an "established international norm" which has moved in its first decade "from being a controversial and indeterminate concept seldom utilized by international society to a norm utilized almost habitually" (Bellamy, 2015b: 161, 2011a, 2011b) but also as reflecting two distinct sets of norms, as is discussed below (Bellamy, 2015b: 162).

References

Acharya, A. (2004). How Ideas Spread: Whose Norms Matter? Norm Localization and Institutional Change in Asian Regionalism. *International Organization,* **58,** 239–275.

Acharya, A. (2013). The R2P and Norm Diffusion: Towards a Framework of Norm Circulation. *Global Responsibility to Protect,* **5,** 466–479.

Adams, S. (2016). Libya. *In:* Bellamy, A.J. and Dunne, T. (eds.) *The Oxford Handbook of the Responsibility to Protect*, 768–785. Oxford: Oxford University Press.

Adler-Nissen, R. and Pouliot, V. (2014). Power in Practice: Negotiating the International Intervention in Libya. *European Journal of International Relations*, 20(4), 889–911.

Aneja, U. (2014). India, R2P and Humanitarian Assistance: A Case of Norm Containment. *Global Responsibility to Protect,* **6,** 227–245.

Aning, K. and Edu-Afful, F. (2016). African Agency in R2P: Interventions by African Union and ECOWAS in Mali, Côte d'Ivoire, and Libya. *International Studies Review,* **18,** 120–133.

Annan, K. (1999). *Secretary-General Presents his Annual Report to General Assembly: Press Release* [Online]. New York: United Nations. Available from: www.un.org/press/en/1999/19990920.sgsm7136.html

Annan, K. (2000). We, the Peoples: A UN for the 21st Century. United Nations, New York.

Arbour, L. (2008). The Responsibility to Protect as a Duty of Care in International Law and Practice. *Review of International Studies,* 34, 445–458.

Axworthy, L. and Rock, A. (2013). Making R2P Work: Now and in the Future. *In:* Knight, A.W. and Egerton, F. (eds.) *The Routledge Handbook of the Responsibility to Protect.* Abingdon: Routledge.

Azzam, F. and Hindawi, C.P. (2016). The Arab Region. *In:* Bellamy, A.J. and Dunne, T. (eds.) *The Oxford Handbook of the Responsibility to Protect*, 451–468. Oxford: Oxford University Press.

Badescu, C.G. and Weiss, T.G. (2010). Misrepresenting R2P and Advancing Norms: An Alternative Spiral? *International Studies Perspectives,* **11,** 354–374.

Bellamy, A.J. (2005). Responsibility to Protect or Trojan Horse? The Crisis in Darfur and Humanitarian Intervention after Iraq. *Ethics & International Affairs,* 19(2), 31–54.

Bellamy, A.J. (2009). *Responsibility to Protect: The Global Effort to End Mass Atrocities*. Cambridge: Polity Press.

Bellamy, A.J. (2011a). *Global Politics and the Responsibility to Protect: From Words to Deeds.* Milton Park: Routledge.

Bellamy, A.J. (2011b). Libya and the Responsibility to Protect: The Exception and the Norm. *Ethics & International Affairs,* 25, 263–269.

Bellamy, A.J. (2012). *Massacres and Morality: Mass Atrocities in an Age of Civilian Immunity.* Oxford: Oxford University Press.

Bellamy, A.J. (2015a). The First Response: Peaceful Means in the Third Pillar of the Responsibility to Protect. Muscatine, IA: The Stanley Foundation.

Bellamy, A.J. (2015b). The Responsibility to Protect Turns Ten. *Ethics & International Affairs,* 29, 161–185.

Bellamy, A.J. (2015c). *Responsibility to Protect: A Defense*. Oxford: Oxford University Press.

Bellamy, A.J. (2016). UN Security Council. *In:* Bellamy, A.J. and Dunne, T. (eds.) *The Oxford Handbook on the Responsibility to Protect,* 249–266. Oxford: Oxford University Press.

Bellamy, A.J. and Williams, P.D. (2011). The New Politics of Protection? Côte d'Ivoire, Libya and the Responsibility to Protect. *International Affairs*, 87(4), 825–850.

Betts, A. and Orchard, P. (2014). Introduction: The Normative Institutionalization-Implementation ap. *In:* Betts, A. and Orchard, P. (eds.) *Implementation and World Politics: How International Norms Change Practice*, 1–26. Oxford: Oxford University Press.

Bloomfield, A. (2015). India and the Libyan Crisis: Flirting with the Responsibility to Protect, Retreating to the Sovereignty Norm. *Contemporary Security Policy*, 36, 27–55.

Brunnée, J. and Toope, S.J. (2010a). *Legitimacy and Legality in International Law: An Interactional Account*. Cambridge: Cambridge University Press.

Brunnée, J. and Toope, S.J. (2010b). The Responsibility to Protect and the Use of Force: Building Legality? *Global Responsibility to Protect,* 2, 191–212.

Capie, D. (2012). The Responsibility to Protect Norm in Southeast Asia: Framing, Resistance and the Localization Myth. *The Pacific Review,* 25, 75–93.

Chandler, D. (2015). The R2P is Dead, Long Live the R2P: The Successful Separation of Military Intervention from the Responsibility to Protect. *International Peacekeeping,* 22, 1–5.

Checkel, J.T. (1998). The Constructivist Turn in International Relations Theory. *World Politics,* 50, 324–348.

Cortell, A.P. and Davis, J.W.J. (2005). When Norms Clash: International Norms, Domestic Practices, and Japan's Internalisation of the GATT/WTO. *Review of International Studies,* 31, 3–25.

Crossley, N. (2013). A Model Case of R2P Prevention? Mediation in the Aftermath of Kenya's 2007 Presidential Elections. *Global Responsibility to Protect,* 5, 192–214.

Davies, S.E. and Teitt, S. (2012). Engendering the Responsibility to Protect: Women and the Prevention of Mass Atrocities. *Global Responsibility to Protect,* 4, 198–222.

De Franco, C., Meyer, C.O. and Smith, K.E. (2015). "Living by Example?" The European Union and the Implementation of the Responsibility to Protect (R2P). *JCMS: Journal of Common Market Studies,* 53, 994–1009.

Deitelhoff, N. (2009). The Discursive Process of Legalization: Charting Islands of Persuasion in the ICC Case. *International Organization,* 63, 33–65.

Deitelhoff, N. and Zimmermann, L. (forthcoming). Things We Lost in the Fire: How Different Types of Contestation Affect the Validity of International Norms. *International Studies Review*, online first.

Deitelhoff, N. and Zimmermann, L. (2019). Norms under Challenge: Unpacking the Dynamics of Norm Robustness. *Journal of Global Security Studies,* 4, 2–17.

Deng, F.M. (1998). Promoting Responsible Sovereignty in Africa. *In:* Deng, F.M. and Lyons, T. (eds.) *African Reckoning: A Quest for Good Governance*, 1–11. Washington, DC: Brookings Institution Press.

Dersso, S.A. (2010). The Role and Place of the African Standby Force Within the African Peace and Security Architecture. *Institute for Security Studies Papers.* Pretoria: Institute for Security Studies.

Doyle, M.W. (2016). The Politics of Global Humanitarianism: The Responsibility to Protect Before and After Libya. *International Politics,* 53, 14–31.

Dunne, T. and Gelber, K. (2014). Arguing Matters. *Global Responsibility to Protect,* 6(3), 326–349.

Erskine, T. (2003). Making Sense of "Responsibility" in International Relations: Key Questions and Concepts. *In:* Erskine, T. (ed.) *Can Institutions Have Responsibilities,* 1–16. Houndmills: Palgrave Macmillan.

Evans, G. (2008). *The Responsibility to Protect: Ending Mass Atrocity Crimes Once and for All,* Washington, DC: Brookings Institution Press.

Evans, G. (2014). The Consequences of Non-Intervention in Syria: Does the Responsibility to Protect Have a Future? *In:* Murray, R.W. and McKay, A. (eds.) *Into the Eleventh Hour: R2P, Syria and Humanitarianism in Crisis*. Bristol: E-International Relations.

Finnemore, M. (2000). Are Legal Norms Distinctive? *New York University Journal of International Law and Policy,* 32, 699–705.

Finnemore, M. and Sikkink, K. (1998). International Norm Dynamics and Political Change. *International Organization,* 52, 887–917.

Garwood-Gowers, A. (2016). China's "Responsible Protection" Concept: Reinterpreting the Responsibility to Protect (R2P) and Military Intervention for Humanitarian Purposes. *Asian Journal of International Law,* 6, 89–118.

Gifkins, J. (2016). R2P in the UN Security Council: Darfur, Libya and Beyond. *Cooperation and Conflict*, 51(2), 148–165.

Glanville, L. (2006). Norms, Interests and Humanitarian Intervention. *Global Change, Peace & Security,* 18, 153–171.

Glanville, L. (2011). The Antecedents of "Sovereignty as Responsibility." *European Journal of International Relations*, 17(2), 233–255.

Glanville, L. (2016). Does R2P matter? Interpreting the Impact of a Norm. *Cooperation and Conflict,* 51, 184–199.

Global Centre for the Responsibility to Protect (2018). Summary of the UN General Assembly Plenary Meeting on the Responsibility to Protect. New York: GCR2P.

Graubart, J. (2013). R2P and Pragmatic Liberal Interventionism: Values in the Service of Interests. *Human Rights Quarterly,* 35, 69–90.

Hehir, A. (2013). The Permanence of Inconsistency: Libya, the Security Council, and the Responsibility to Protect. *International Security,* 38, 137–159.

Hehir, A. (2016). Assessing the influence of the Responsibility to Protect on the UN Security Council during the Arab Spring. *Cooperation and Conflict,* 51, 166–183.

Hunt, C.T. (2013). The role of the African Standby Force in implementing Article 4(h). *In:* Kuwali, D. and Viljoen, F. (eds.) *Africa and the Responsibility to Protect: Article 4(h) of the African Union Constitutive Act*, 173–192. Oxford: Routledge.

Hunt, C.T. (2016a). African Regionalism & Human Protection Norms: An Overview. *Global Responsibility to Protect,* **8,** 201–226.

Hunt, C.T. (2016b). Emerging Powers and the Responsibility to Protect: Non-linear Norm Dynamics in Complex International Society. *Cambridge Review of International Affairs,* **29,** 761–781.

Hunt, C.T. (2018). Human Protection in Africa's Regional Arrangements: Regional Perspectives and Institutional Expressions. *In:* Hunt, C.T. and Morada, N.M. (eds.) *Regionalism and Human Protection,* 143–168. Leiden: Brill.

ICISS (2001). *The Responsibility to Protect: Report of the International Commission on Intervention and State Sovereignty.* Ottawa: International Development Research Centre.

Jacob, C. (2018). From Norm Contestation to Norm Implementation: Recursivity and the Responsibility to Protect. *Global Governance,* **24,** 391–409.

Jepperson, R., Wendt, A. and Katzenstein, P. (1996). Norms, Identity and Culture in National Security. *In:* Katzenstein, P.J. (ed.) *The Culture of National Security: Norms and Identities in World Politics,* 33–77. New York: Columbia University Press.

Job, B.L. and Shesterinina, A. (2014). China as a Global Norm-shaper. *In:* Betts, A. and Orchard, P. (eds.) *Implementation and World Politics: How International Norms Change Practice,* 144–159. Oxford: Oxford University Press.

Keck, M.E. and Sikkink, K. (1999). Transnational Advocacy Networks in International and Regional Politics. *International Social Science Journal,* 51(159), 89–101.

Kratochwil, F.V. (1989). *Rules, Norms, and Decisions: On the Conditions of Practical and Legal Reasoning in International Relations and Domestic Affairs.* Cambridge: Cambridge University Press.

Krook, M.L. and True, J. (2012). Rethinking the Life Cycles of International Norms: The United Nations and the Global Promotion of Gender Equality. *European Journal of International Relations,* **18,** 103–127.

Kuperman, A.J. (2013). A Model Humanitarian Intervention? Reassessing NATO's Libya Campaign. *International Security,* **38,** 105–136.

Li, Y. and Chen, Z.-N. (2013). From the Responsibility to Protect to the Responsible Protection. *Journal of Shanxi Normal University (Social Science Edition),* **2,** 018.

Luck, E. (2010a). Building a Norm: The Responsibility to Protect Experience. *In:* Rotberg, R. (ed.) *Mass Atrocity Crimes: Preventing Future Outrages.* Washington, DC: Brookings Institution Press.

Luck, E.C. (2010b). The Responsibility to Protect: Growing Pains or Early Promise? *Ethics & International Affairs,* **24,** 349–365.

Luck, E.C. (2018). Why the United Nations Underperforms at Preventing Mass Atrocities. *Genocide Studies and Prevention: An International Journal,* **11(3),** 32–47.

Lutz, E.L. and Sikkink, K. (2000). International Human Rights Law and Practice in Latin America. *International Organization,* **54,** 633–659.

McDougall, D. (2014). Responsibility While Protecting: Brazil's Proposal for Modifying Responsibility to Protect. *Global Responsibility to Protect,* **6,** 64–87.

McLoughlin, S. (2014). *The Structural Prevention of Mass Atrocities: Understanding Risk and Resilience.* Oxon: Routledge.

Milner, H.V. and Keohane, R.O. (1996). Internationalization and Domestic Politics: An Introduction. *In:* Milner, H.V. and Keohane, R.O. (eds.) *Internationalization and Domestic Politics,* 3–24. Cambridge: Cambridge University Press.

Morada, N.M. (2018). Southeast Asian Regionalism, Norm Promotion and Capacity Building for Human Protection: An Overview. *In:* Hunt, C.T. and Morada, N.M. (eds.) *Regionalism and Human Protection,* 7–28. Leiden: Brill.

Moses, J. (2013). Sovereignty as Irresponsibility? A Realist Critique of the Responsibility to Protect. *Review of International Studies*, 39(1), 113–135.

Murithi, T. (2008). African Indigenous and Endogenous Approaches to Peace and Conflict Resolution. *In:* Francis, D.J. (ed.) *Peace and Conflict in Africa*, 16–30. London: Zed Books.

Negrón-Gonzales, M. and Contarino, M. (2014). Local Norms Matter: Understanding National Responses to the Responsibility to Protect. *Global Governance,* 20, 255–276.

Orchard, P. (2013). Humanitarian Intervention and the Legacies of Security Council (In) action: East Pakistan (1971) and East Timor (1975–1979). *In:* Mayersen, D. and Pohlman, A. (eds.) *Genocide and Mass Atrocities in Asia*, 99–116. London: Routledge.

Orchard, P. (2014). *A Right to Flee: Refugees, States, and the Construction of International Society.* Cambridge: Cambridge University Press.

Orchard, P. (2017). Transnational Humanitarian Action and Regime Complexity: The Case of Syria. *In:* Malet, D. and Anderson, M.J. (eds.) *Transnational Actors in War and Peace: Militants, Activists, and Corporations in World Politics*, 168–184. Washington, DC: Georgetown University Press.

Paris, R. (2014). The "Responsibility to Protect" and the Structural Problems of Preventive Humanitarian Intervention. *International Peacekeeping,* 21, 569–603.

Pattison, J. (2015). Jus Post Bellum and the Responsibility to Rebuild. *British Journal of Political Science*, 45, 635–661.

Percy, S. (2007a). *Mercenaries: The History of a Norm in International Relations.* Oxford: Oxford University Press.

Percy, S.V. (2007b). Mercenaries: Strong Norm, Weak Law. *International Organization,* 61, 367–397.

Percy, S.V. (2014). The Unimplemented Norm. *In:* Betts, A. and Orchard, P. (eds.) *Implementation and World Politics: How International Norms Change Practice*, 68–84. Oxford: Oxford University Press.

Prantl, J. and Nakano, R. (2011). Global Norm Diffusion in East Asia How China and Japan Implement the Responsibility to Protect. *International Relations,* 25, 204–223.

Price, R.M. (1997). *The Chemical Weapons Taboo.* Ithaca, NY: Cornell University Press.

Ralph, J. (2018). What Should Be Done? Pragmatic Constructivist Ethics and the Responsibility to Protect. *International Organization,* 72, 173–203.

Reinold, T. (2010). The Responsibility to Protect – Much Ado about Nothing? *Review of International Studies,* 36, 55–78.

Rieff, D. (2011). R2P, R.I.P. *New York Times*, November 7.

Risse, T. and Sikkink, K. (1999). The Socialization of International Human Rights Norms into Domestic Practices: Introduction. *In:* Risse, T., Ropp, S.C. and Sikkink, K. (eds.) *The Power of Human Rights: International Norms and Domestic Change*, 1–38. Cambridge: Cambridge University Press.

Sandholtz, W. (2008). Dynamics of International Norm Change: Rules against Wartime Plunder. *European Journal of International Relations,* 14, 101–131.

Sandholtz, W. (2009). *International Norms and Cycles of Change.* Oxford: Oxford University Press.

Sandholtz, W. and Sweet, A.S. (2004). Law, Politics, and International Governance. *In:* Reus-Smit, C. (ed.) *The Politics of International Law*, 238–271. Cambridge: Cambridge University Press.

Sharma, S.K. and Welsh, J.M. (2015). *The Responsibility to Prevent: Overcoming the Challenges of Atrocity Prevention.* Oxford: Oxford University Press.

Shelton, D. (2000). Introduction: Law, Non-Law and the Problem of "Soft Law". *In:* Shelton, D. (ed.) *Commitment and Compliance: The Role of Non-binding Norms in the International Legal System*, 1–20. Oxford: Oxford University Press.

Sikkink, K. (2011). *The Justice Cascade: How Human Rights Prosecutions Are Changing World Politics*. New York: W.W. Norton & Company.

Thakur, R. (2002). Outlook: Intervention, Sovereignty and the Responsibility to Protect: Experiences from ICISS. *Security Dialogue,* 33, 323–340.

Thakur, R. (2016). The Responsibility to Protect at 15. *International Affairs*, 92(2), 415–434.

The Independent Commission on Kosovo. (2000). *The Kosovo Report: Conflict, International Response, Lessons Learned.* Oxford: Oxford University Press.

UN (2004). A More Secure World: Our Shared Responsibility – Report of the High-level Panel on Threats, Challenges and Change. New York: United Nations.

UN General Assembly (2005). Resolution 60/1: World Summit Outcome. New York: United Nations.

UN General Assembly (2009). Implementing the Responsibility to Protect: Report of the Secretary-General. New York: United Nations.

Weiss, T.G. (2004). The Sunset of Humanitarian Intervention? The Responsibility to Protect in a Unipolar Era. *Security Dialogue,* 35, 135–153.

Weiss, T.G. (2011). RtoP Alive and Well After Libya. *Ethics & International Affairs*, 25(3), 287–292.

Welsh, J. (2014). Implementing the "Responsibility to Protect": Catalyzing Debate and Building Capacity. *In:* Betts, A. and Orchard, P. (eds.) *Implementation and World Politics: How International Norms Change Practice*, 124–143. Oxford: Oxford University Press.

Welsh, J. and Banda, M. (2010). International Law and the Responsibility to Protect: Clarifying or Expanding States' Responsibilities? *Global Responsibility to Protect,* 2, 213–231.

Welsh, J., Thielking, C. and Macfarlane, S.N. (2002). The Responsibility to Protect: Assessing the Report of the International Commission on Intervention and State Sovereignty. *International Journal,* 57, 489–512.

Wendt, A. (1987). The Agent-Structure Problem in International Relations Theory. *International Organization,* 41, 335–370.

Wendt, A. (1999). *Social Theory of International Politics.* Cambridge, NY: Cambridge University Press.

Wheeler, N.J. (2000). *Saving Strangers: Humanitarian Intervention in International Society,* Oxford: Oxford University Press.

Widmaier, W.W. and Glanville, L. (2015). The Benefits of Norm Ambiguity: Constructing the Responsibility to Protect across Rwanda, Iraq and Libya. *Contemporary Politics,* 21, 367–383.

Wiener, A. (2008). *The Invisible Constitution of Politics*. Cambridge: Cambridge University Press.

Ziegler, C. (2016). Critical Perspectives on the Responsibility to Protect: BRICS and Beyond. *International Relations*, 30(3), 262–277.

Zimmermann, L. (2016). Same or Different? Norm Diffusion between Resistance, Compliance, and Localization in Post-conflict States. *International Studies Perspectives,* 17, 98–115.

1 Contestation, norms and the Responsibility to Protect as a regime

Phil Orchard

Introduction

What is the Responsibility to Protect (R2P) doctrine? Obviously on one level, it reflects what was agreed to by the member states of the United Nations in the World Summit Outcome Document (WSOD) in 2005 (UN General Assembly, 2005). In that document, states accepted that they have a responsibility to protect their own populations from four identified mass atrocity: genocide, war crimes, ethnic cleansing and crimes against humanity. Further, they accepted responsibilities to help protect other populations from atrocity crimes and to take collective action when other national authorities are manifestly failing to protect their populations. The R2P doctrine has developed further as it has been operationalized within the United Nations, leading to arguments that it has created "a collection of shared expectations" (Bellamy, 2011: 84).

At the same time, the R2P doctrine remains open to significant questions. With the problematic response to Libya, and the failure of the UN Security Council to take action in Syria, opponents of the doctrine were quick to question it, suggesting that regime change in Libya "has done grave, possibly even irreparable, damage to R2P's prospects of becoming a global norm" (Rieff, 2011). Issues with the Libyan intervention have reignited questions about when intervention should occur (Kuperman, 2013) and whether it is actually having an effect (Hehir, 2013). This variation in practice has led to significant disagreements within academia, focused around the fundamental question of whether the R2P itself is having a clear effect.

In this chapter, I seek to respond to these arguments by contending that what appears to be contradictory forms of practice actually reflect a failure to understand the nature of what the R2P doctrine is. As noted in the Introduction, a range of authors have suggested that the R2P represents a norm and should be understood in line with constructivist theorizing around norm emergence, violation and contestation. Drawing on this same body of theoretical work, I argue instead that we need to understand the R2P doctrine as forming an international regime. This regime bundles together a number of previously existing legal and social norms along with the introduction of three new norms reflecting the acceptances of responsibilities at the domestic and international levels and reflecting the primacy of the UN Security Council in addressing R2P issues.

Treating the R2P as a regime has two significant benefits. The first is that, too often, it has been treated as a stand-alone issue, either inadvertently in academic debate or deliberately in policy debates, in order to avoid its politically contentious elements. And yet the R2P doctrine would not exist without the prior development of robust human rights norms, the emergence of individual accountability for atrocity crimes (Sikkink, 2011) or without human security presenting a clear alternative doctrine to traditional (and state-focused) security. Hence, R2P fits in with much wider reinterpretations and re-understandings of sovereignty (Glanville, 2011) and of international practices (Adler-Nissen and Pouliot, 2014). As a number of the other chapters in this volume make clear, it is critical to understand the contemporary interactions between R2P and other norms and regimes at the international level; at the same time, it is critical to also keep in mind this longer history which underpins a number of the elements of the R2P doctrine.

The second benefit with adopting a view of the R2P as a regime is that this allows us to disentangle discrete elements of it. When we use the WSOD as the basis for understanding the Responsibility to Protect, we are actually accepting a conception that principally reflects the consensus that developed at a particular moment in time – the 2005 negotiations. The original International Commission on Intervention and State Sovereignty (ICISS) Report (ICISS, 2001a) provided a much more expansive view of the responsibilities inherent within the doctrine along three dimensions. The first was to give primary, but not sole, responsibility to the Security Council to decide on the need to action, providing additional and alternative routes through the General Assembly under the 'uniting for peace' resolution system (Orchard, 2010), and through regional organizations. The second was to position any military intervention within broader just war principles, a return to which is reflected by proposals such as Brazil's abandoned "Responsibility While Protecting" (RWP) initiative. The third was a broader set of responsibilities to not only react but also to prevent and to rebuild (ICISS, 2001a: xi).

The evolution of the R2P from the ICISS Report to the WSOD represents a series of negotiated normative positions: that responsibility rests solely with the Security Council rather than other actors; that the R2P should be relatively narrow in what it encompasses; and that the Council's hands should not be tied by criteria. Few question the Council's primacy in R2P decisions, particularly when decisions need to be made without the consent of the concerned state (beyond a few outliers such as Pape [2012]). Not only does this reflect a series of norms, but it also reflects a new norm of practice around R2P that has been successfully grafted onto a longer tradition of the Council having full authority over peace and security issues within the UN.

While some elements of the R2P doctrine are now settled, other elements remain contested, including how the Council itself should respond to situations which fall within the scope of the doctrine, and in particular, when states are 'manifestly failing' in their responsibilities under Pillar Three of the doctrine as laid out in the 2009 Secretary-General's report (UN General

Assembly, 2009). By treating it as a regime which bundles together specific norms, we see a picture in which only one aspect – the specific norm around Pillar 3 action – remains contested, while much of the rest of the regime can be said to have achieved an institutionalized status. As this is a process of contestation, I argue that we can also see a path forward to gain wider support even for this norm.

In this chapter, I begin by exploring what a regime means in a theoretical sense. I then argue that the R2P doctrine can be seen as a regime which bundles together four distinct norms and sets of norms – reflecting the four atrocity crimes – and which creates three other newer norms, around state responsibilities, around the responsibilities of the wider international community and, finally, the norm that the Security Council has the primary role in responding to R2P situations. In the last section of the chapter, I explore this latter norm in three ways. The first is to trace out its evolution from the ICISS Report forward. The second is to examine ways in which the role of the Security Council remains contested. The third is to examine the wider acceptance of this norm, framed through an examination of potential violations.

Regime theory, norms and resilience

The question of whether R2P reflects a single norm or a collection of different norms remains an open one but, as Labonte notes, "despite these nuances … nowhere in the literature is the argument made that R2P is not a norm" (Labonte, 2016: 134–135). One of the strongest critiques of R2P grounded within the normative literature comes from Hehir, who has argued that it is merely "hollow norm," one that is subject both to co-option, instrumental use and which is inherently malleable (Hehir, 2018: 10, 73). In his view, it exists, but it has not had significant effects in part because it has not been implemented by most states at the domestic level (ibid.: 17) Because of this, he argues that as a norm, the R2P is "primarily regulative in nature" and that the R2P has only really been a constitutive norm – actually shaping shared understandings and identities – "for a particular set of states highly unlikely to ever actually engage in the commission of mass atrocities internally." Even this regulative power, in his view, is weak, with states able to circumvent or co-opt it easily and with no clear behavioral prescriptions (ibid.: 72–74).

This reflects a wider critique that R2P as a norm appears to have a high level of indeterminacy: it creates a range of both proscriptive behaviors, actions which states and other actors should not undertake, and prescriptive behaviors, positive duties or actions they should undertake. One solution, as Welsh (2014: 133) argues, is to view R2P as reflecting a complex norm which contains "more than one prescription" and that, as such, it has created 'a duty of conduct' by members of the international community: "to identify when atrocity crimes are being committed (or when there is threat of commission) and to deliberate on how the three-pillar framework might apply" (ibid.: 136). While such an approach solves one issue – the question of prescription – it leaves open a second issue: how do we interpret these different prescriptions and who should play that role? This I see as the critical point in why we need to understand R2P as forming a regime.

Norms rarely exist in isolation. Other structures are needed in order to "emphasize the way in which behavioral rules are structured together and interrelate" (Finnemore and Sikkink, 1998: 891; Donnelly, 2012: 625). Therefore, beyond individual norms, we also need some form of structure which "provides processes to interpret those rules; and … demark who should have a role in interpreting the rules" (Orchard, 2014: 20). These other structures have been marked by a variety of different concepts. A number of authors refer to the concept of norm complexes, "in which behavioural rules are structured together and interrelate" (Finnemore and Sikkink, 1998: 891; Bernstein, 2000). As an alternative, Lantis and Wunderlich have made the case recently for examining "norm clusters" which are "collections of aligned, but distinct, norms or principles that relate to a common, overarching issue area; they address different aspects and contain specific normative obligations" (Lantis and Wunderlich, 2018: 571). Finally, in other work, (Orchard, 2014), I have sought to make the case that regimes can also be understood to play such a role. Let me expand on why this is.

In the initial generation of regime literature, norms were present as one of four discrete components which were understood to make up regimes, alongside principles, rules and decision-making procedures around which actors' expectations converge in a given area of international relations (Krasner, 1982: 186; for critiques of this definition, see Levy et al., 1995: 270; Young, 1986: 106). The function of norms in this scholarship is limited, with them existing only as "external constraints and regulatory mechanisms rather than as expressions of preferred values" (Cronin, 2003: 9). Even so, it was understood that the rules of a regime would convert the norms "into concrete prescriptions or proscriptions, whereby the rule density varies considerably by regime norm" (Hasenclever et al., 1997: 9–10). One strand of this scholarship also argued that regimes could emerge spontaneously – through social convention, convergence, or consensus – rather than solely through formal negotiations. Either form of regime could nonetheless create feelings of legitimacy (Puchala and Hopkins, 1982: 249; Young, 1982: 279; Young, 1986: 107).

More recently, Goertz has argued that regimes can be understood as structures of norms and rules, with norms and rules being counterparts for most purposes (Goertz, 2003: 15), a view that Krasner himself has acknowledged "makes more sense, especially in empirical application" (cited in Betts, 2014: 31). Thus, as a structure, the regime bundles together what might otherwise be disparate norms. In so doing, it provides a clear sense of the scope of international behavior required and how states and other actors *should* deal with a particular problem. Thus, regimes provide a mechanism through which the appropriate standards of behavior suggested by the individual norms are linked together to create a response within the complexity of the issue area. Since a regime provides this linkage, it brings an increased regularity to state practices than would otherwise be the case; they "frame the nature and scope of a given problem and provide potential response scripts" (Orchard, 2014: 241). A regime provides a "web of meaning" by linking together individual norms (Neufeld, 1993: 43; Hasenclever et al., 1997: 165).

Therefore, the existence of a regime may improve how states and other actors understand their normative obligations within a specific issue area. There are also suggestions that the existence of a regime can help to support the individual norms embodied within it. Using the parallel concept of norm clusters, Lantis and Wunderlich (2018: 572) argue that the linkages between individual norms can increase cluster resilience alongside higher levels of institutionalization and legalization. As noted in the Introduction, institutionalization refers to the process by which norms are brought into specific sets of international rules and organizations. Legalization similarly reflects the process by which norms are brought into specific international treaties and is seen as a way to "signal a seriousness of intent that is difficult to replicate in other ways" (Simmons, 2009: 5). For Lantis and Wunderlich (2018: 580), therefore, high resiliency "should be evidenced in clusters with multiple norms that originate and develop in a cohesive manner, and that are embedded in or backed up by a dense institutional network and legal structures."

The normative content of a regime has long been seen as critical to its existence. As Reus-Smit (2007: 159) notes, the broader set of institutions can command legitimacy when "there is a generalized perception that its normative precepts are rightful, that they warrant respect and compliance for more than self-interested reasons, for reasons of their normative standing." Challenges posed by alternative norms can undermine the regime's collective purpose, either by the redefinition of its individual component norms or by the introduction of new norms (see Bernstein, 2000; Donnelly, 1986: 605). But so, too, can inconsistencies between individual norms, logical gaps in their overall structure, and procedural incoherence (Donnelly, 1986: 605). These issues can cause the compliance pull of the regime's individual norms to be undermined (Franck, 1990: 163–180). This would seem to suggest that an R2P regime, given that it is not bound in a specific international treaty (though elements of it are, particularly three of the four atrocity crimes) would be relatively weak.

But is legalization critical to this process? Norms based in treaties are important and have clear strengths. By their nature, they are clearly articulated and their implementation process at the domestic level can be easier to observe (Betts and Orchard, 2014: 8). Is this distinctly because of legalization, or is it, as Finnemore has argued, a process of legitimation? She notes legal norms tend to be powerful "because they have legitimacy. They are viewed as 'binding,' as having qualities of 'oughtness'" (Finnemore, 2000: 702–703; Deitelhoff, 2009: 34). Given that, as Hurd (1999: 381) argues, legitimacy refers to "the normative belief by an actor that a rule of institution ought to be obeyed," any settled norm should bear this property. Therefore, alongside treaty-based norms, other forms of norms can also possess legitimacy, including principle norms which are based on less formal principles that reflect shared understandings which states have not codified (Betts and Orchard, 2014). Such norms can still be institutionalized to a degree as they are accepted through international bodies such as through UN resolutions or declarations, or through customary or soft law processes (Orchard, 2018: 26).

This suggests that norms within a regime help to generate resilience for the overall regime even if they have not been formally legalized or institutionalized because they create shared expectations and are understood to be legitimate, to have that property of oughtness. Institutionalization does not fix a specific understanding of a norm. Instead, it remains open to interpretation and to contestation. Contestation, following Wiener, is a societal practice in which rules, regulations or procedures are critically questioned. This can occur either explicitly, such as through contention, objection, questioning or deliberation, or it can occur implicitly such as through neglect, negation or disregard. It matters, Wiener argues, because it is constitutive: through the process of contestation, legitimacy gaps can be identified and filled (Wiener, 2014: 2–3). It is an interactive process, in which interpretation of the norm is derived through social practice in specific contexts (Wiener, 2008: 4). Because of this, documented language, even for legal norms, indicates only a norm's formal validity, "while its social recognition stands to be constructed by social interaction" (Wiener, 2009: 179). Hence, I have argued in other work (with Alexander Betts), that we need to understand norm implementation as a "parallel process to institutionalization which draws attention to the steps necessary to introduce the new international norm's precepts into formal legal and policy mechanisms within a state or organization in order to routinize compliance" (Betts and Orchard, 2014: 2).

Therefore, three elements are important to understand how the individual norms embodied within a regime help to ensure its overall effectiveness: their level of institutionalization at the international level; implementation at the domestic level; and the overall coherency of the norms embedded within the regime. It is not critical that these norms have been institutionalized or legalized through an international convention provided that we can demonstrate they have taken on a degree of legitimacy through other mechanisms such as domestic implementation or institutional practice.

The Responsibility to Protect as a regime

Given all this, what does the R2P regime look like? I suggest that, as a behavior guide to states and other international actors, it serves three roles. The first is that it links together the four specific sets of atrocity crimes – genocide, war crimes, crimes against humanity, ethnic cleansing. The second is that it establishes a responsibility for all states to refrain from committing atrocity crimes. The third is that it establishes a specific responsibility for the Security Council to consider all cases when a state is manifestly failing to uphold its responsibility, either because it is unable or unwilling to do so.

The four atrocity crimes

The R2P includes genocide, war crimes, crimes against humanity and ethnic cleansing as atrocity crimes. These are linked together by the R2P in a formulation that is now widely accepted. And yet it is important to note that this linkage and the idea that these four sets of acts constituted, and only these acts constituted, a category of 'atrocity crimes' emerged with the WSOD.

Each of these crimes has its own history, and yet only three properly constitute international criminal law. The 1948 Genocide Convention required its signatories to "prevent and punish" the crime of genocide. But the Convention fails to "indicate, let alone clarify, who is to inflict punishment and by what means" (Tatz and Higgins, 2016: 22). Instead, it notes only that the contracting parties could call upon "the competent organs of the United Nations to take such action as they consider appropriate."[1] What this means has remained open to question. The drafters, Nehemiah Robinson noted in 1949, did not mean for this article to deal "with actual prevention and suppression of this crime" but to reflect existing provisions within the UN Charter (Robinson, 1949 [2007]: 33–34). He noted further that the article "grants the parties to the Convention the right to call upon these organs to take action, i.e., it does not impose on them any obligation" and that the drafters considered these organs to include only the General Assembly and the Security Council (Robinson, 1949 [2007]: 37–39). Hurd, similarly, argues that these clauses are generally understood as reflecting the "more limited set of measures described in the rest of the convention, such as prosecuting, punishing, or extraditing suspects found in one's territory" (Hurd, 2011: 299).

Why this hesitancy? When the Convention was proposed, genocide was a new idea. Raphael Lemkin had proposed the term only four years before – prior to that, events such as the Armenian Genocide had been referred to as crimes against humanity (Schabas, 2009: 19–20). Even war crimes and crimes against humanity were new at this time, in the sense that they had only been formally recognized by the International Military Tribunals following the Second World War, with both the Tokyo and Nuremburg Tribunals including crimes against peace, war crimes and crimes against humanity within their charters.[2] Indeed, it was only with the creation of the International Criminal Tribunals for the Former Yugoslavia and for Rwanda, and subsequently the creation of the International Criminal Court, that these crimes were clearly codified.

The fourth crime, ethnic cleansing, is not defined in international criminal law. Instead, a factual definition was provided by a Commission of Experts established by the Security Council in 1994, which defined ethnic cleansing as "a purposeful policy designed by one ethnic or religious group to remove by violent and terror-inspiring means the civilian population of another ethnic or religious group from certain geographic areas."[3] The International Court of Justice has noted "the term 'ethnic cleansing' has no legal significance of its own" (Schabas, 2009: 232).[4] Thus, on the face of it, there is no particular linkage between these four discrete issues as atrocity crimes, with one not constituting an international crime by law in itself.

Instead, this linkage is created as a specific output of the World Summit negotiations. The ICISS Report had originally included three categories of acts that the Commission saw cross a just cause threshold:

> A. Large-scale loss of life, actual or apprehended, with genocidal intent or not, which is the product either of deliberate state action, or state neglect or inability to act, or a failed state situation; or
> B. Large-scale "ethnic cleansing," actual or apprehended, whether carried out by killing, forced expulsion, acts of terror or rape.
>
> (ICISS, 2001b: 12)

The 2004 Report of the High-level Panel on Threats, Challenges and Change (on which Gareth Evans, the ICISS co-chair, was a panel member) endorsed the idea that there was an "emerging norm" around the R2P, but argued that that it included "genocide and other large-scale killing, ethnic cleansing, or serious violations of international humanitarian law which sovereign governments have proved powerless or unwilling to prevent" (UN, 2004: 66). The following year, the Secretary-General's Report "In Larger Freedom," designed to frame the World Summit negotiations, referred simply to the need to embrace and act "on the 'responsibility to protect' potential or actual victims of massive atrocities" (UN, 2005: 35).

Instead, the four atrocity crimes formulation came from two sources. Jean Ping, the Chair of the World Summit negotiations, used the African Union's Constitutive Act Article 4(h) as an explanatory model, which states that member states "shall have the right of the Union to intervene in a Member State pursuant to a decision of the Assembly in respect of grave circumstances, namely: war crimes, genocide, and crime against humanity." But Ping also notes the critical role of the Ambassador of Pakistan, Munir Akram, when the negotiations were facing significant difficulties. He proposed

> to link the responsibility to protect populations to specific crimes, namely, genocide, war crimes, ethnic cleansing, and crimes against humanity. This is what was finally adopted in the Outcome Document during the plenary meeting of the General Assembly in September 2005.
>
> (International Peace Institute, 2009: 12; Luck, 2010: 113)

But while the inclusion of four types of atrocity crimes may have been the product of difficult negotiations, by framing it this way, Brunnée and Toope (2006: 126) note that "the link to international crime is solidified." Linking together these four different issues under the rubric of atrocity crimes, and thereby also creating a clear link to international criminal law, represents one of the important innovations that R2P has made.

The second innovation that R2P has made, following Glanville (2016: 186) and Bellamy (2015: 163), is that it has helped to establish a new set of responses for when such atrocity crimes are either being contemplated or committed. To frame this in another way, R2P has created new norms to interact with this existing normative architecture coming from established international law to create a new form of obligation for the international community.

In effect, this reflects two new norms. As Glanville frames it, the first norm uncontroversially reflects that "each state has a responsibility to protect its population from atrocity crimes." The second norm then holds "that the international community has the responsibility to do what it can to ensure that populations are protected from atrocity crimes," with this second norm reflecting a residual responsibility for the international community (Glanville, 2016: 186). For him, it is this second norm that is the R2P norm.

This form of division of responsibilities has been clearly envisioned within the R2P doctrine from the outset. From the ICISS Report onward, the primary responsibility for taking action has always been viewed as lying with the state (Gholiagha, 2015: 1077). As the ICISS Report established in its basic principles, "state sovereignty implies responsibility, and the primary responsibility for the protection of its people lies with the state itself." It is only when the state is unwilling to halt or avert serious harm, the report argues, that the basic "principle of non-intervention yields to the international responsibility to protect" (ICISS, 2001b: xi). This focus on the primary responsibility of each state to protect its own population, with the responsibility of the international community coming secondary, remains clear in the WSOD (Gholiagha, 2015: 1077).

Beyond this, however, I argue that the R2P doctrine has also created a third new norm: that the international community has vested additional international authority in the UN Security Council to respond to atrocity crimes. This reflects a wider view that R2P has provided a new basis for international authority. Orford notes that the R2P moves away from a vision of authority grounded in the UN Charter in which the "lawfulness of authority over a given territory" became "a matter of both fact and of right." Instead, she argues, the R2P is premised on the notion "that authority, to be legitimate, must be effective at guaranteeing protection, and that the failure to protect a population is a factual matter that can be determined by the international community" (Orford, 2011: 16).

Thus the WSOD created a new international norm when it gave the UN Security Council – and only the Council – the role to decide on collective action, in situations as laid out in the WSOD when "national authorities manifestly fail to protect their populations" from atrocity crimes in accordance with the UN Charter and including Chapter VII (UN General Assembly, 2005: para. 139). In so doing, it reflects a reinterpretation of the Chapter VII provisions to include mass atrocity crimes as a threat to international peace and security. This is, however, not a precise norm. Gallagher has argued that while the 'manifest failing' language necessities a higher threshold for a Pillar Three response, the WSOD provides "little guidance" around what constitutes a 'manifest failing' (Gallagher, 2014: 429). However, this does address a critical issue with the ICISS Report. Cunliffe has argued that the ICISS Report – by diffusing R2P as widely as possible – did "not obligate any specific agent to act in an emergency," or, in other words, it created an imperfect duty which helped to win it support (Cunliffe, 2016: 241). By enshrining a responsibility within the Council – a contingent and limited responsibility, to be certain, and one which reflects Welsh's (2014: 136) duty of conduct – the WSOD did seek to address this issue.

Therefore, as a regime created through the WSOD, the R2P includes seven distinct norms or sets of norms. The first four reflect the four atrocity crimes – genocide, war crimes, crimes against humanity and ethnic cleansing. These are not new, but the way in which they have been bundled together – to form a distinct and coherent category of 'atrocity crimes' – is. The next two norms reflect distinct responsibilities accepted at both the state and the international levels, with the international response norm reflecting a residual duty to be exercised only when the state norm fails. Finally, however, beyond a general international responsibility, it also creates a specific norm enshrining action in the event of manifest failures of responsibility lying with – and only with – the UN Security Council.

Contestations around the role of the UN Security Council

The consensus around the WSOD proved to be durable over the next six years. Following the intervention in Libya, by contrast, we can see three explicit and one implicit forms of contestation occurring: around what Pillar Three really means, around what actions the Council should take under R2P, around the role of the veto, and, finally, around the use of chemical weapons in Syria. It is important to note that in spite of these ongoing contestations, the Council has actually increased its references to the R2P – as of July 2018, it has referred to the R2P in some 75 resolutions and presidential statements,[5] whereas in the first six years following the WSOD the Council referred to it in only four resolutions (Hehir, 2018: 38).

Hehir has been critical of this record, suggesting that the Security Council has actually sought to disavow international responsibilities "by emphasizing the Pillar I, and only very occasionally Pillar II, aspects of R2P, while conspicuously ignoring Pillar III" and by invoking in a manifestly selective manner (Hehir, 2018: 118, 2013). However, there are three issues with this critique. First, as noted above, a state-based responsibility has always been a core element of the R2P as one of its norms; as such, this practice reflects the general understanding of R2P – that international action is necessary but seldom. Second, as Gifkins notes,

> repeated use of phrases in Security Council resolutions is not simple automation, devoid of meaning. Repetitive practices involve reaffirmation of shared meanings … the use of R2P language in Security Council resolutions shows that the Council discusses R2P regularly in its internal negotiations, both in relation to specific conflicts and broader thematic issues.
>
> (Gifkins, 2016: 151; Dunne and Gelber, 2014)

Thus, invoking this language matters irrespective as to which Pillar it specifically refers to. Finally, though, it is also unclear if this pattern actually holds. The Pillar strategy, as noted above, maps on to the WSOD, and, as Glanville has argued, the Council does have a routine pattern of re-endorsing the full content of Paragraphs 138 and 139 (Glanville, Forthcoming).

The first contestation reflects the ongoing questions around the use of Pillar Three but also the decision by the UK, US and France to link the R2P doctrine to regime change in both the cases of Libya and Syria. In the case of Libya, this occurred after the UN Security Council's decision to intervene under Resolution 1973 (see Chapter 3 by Gholiagha and Loges for more detail). David Cameron, Barack Obama and Nicolas Sarkozy argued at the time that while Resolution 1973 had created a mandate to "protect civilians" it was not a mandate to "remove Gaddafi by force." But they also argued that

> it is impossible to imagine a future for Libya with Gaddafi in power.... So long as Gaddafi is in power, NATO and its coalition partners must maintain their operations so that civilians remain protected and the pressure on the regime builds.[6]

Similar statements that Syrian president Bashar al-Assad must "step aside" by Obama and key European leaders occurred in August of that year.[7]

In making these claims, these three permanent members of the Security Council were effectively trying to create a linkage between the R2P and a separate issue – that of regime change – which was not necessarily a requirement to successfully protect the civilian populations of both countries. However, as Ralph and Gifkins note, this move in the case of Libya "alienated key stakeholders and this weakened the consensus behind Resolution 1973 [and] had a profound impact on the willingness of the Council to trust P3 leadership" (Ralph and Gifkins, 2017: 633). Not surprisingly, this contestation is widely seen as having failed (Babbitt, 2017). Western and Goldstein (2013) have argued that in order to ensure R2P retains its legitimacy, it needs to be decoupled from regime change. Fung (2018) has also argued that China was concerned enough by the regime change concept to shift its own position regarding intervention including its successive use of the veto with respect to the Syrian crisis.

The second contestation emerged as an offshoot of this debate and focused on the measures that the Council could use to regulate the use of force once action was undertaken under the R2P. This is not a new debate. The idea of a Security Council Code of Conduct had been proposed in the ICISS Report, but was an element dropped by R2P advocates in the lead up to the World Summit in order to win over reluctant P5 members (Bellamy, 2009: 74). Following the Libyan intervention, however, there was renewed focus on how the Council should deal with R2P resolutions once they were passed. The first proposal, Brazil's "RWP" formula which was first launched in November 2011, sought to respond to these concerns by proposing new Security Council procedures, "equivalent to setting up a monitoring-and-review mechanism to ensure that the implementation of the use-of-force mandates is thoroughly debated" (Stefan, 2017: 99). However, the proposal had an odd life cycle, as the Brazilian government quickly abandoned it even as both Western states and key BRICS countries such as India began supporting the concept (ibid.: 101–103).

This was followed in 2012 with the semi-official Chinese proposal around "Responsible Protection" which similarly sought to reinterpret R2P's third pillar by including decision-making criteria to guide the Security Council.[8] However, as Garwood-Gowers has argued, Responsible Protection draws on both the Brazilian initiative, but also on the ICISS Report and its use of the just war tradition (Garwood-Gowers, 2016: 103; see also Teitt, Chapter 7, in this volume). Both these efforts are in effect positive contestation, exercises "in asking for clarification of R2P implementation" (Kenkel and Stefan, 2016: 46). In neither case have they advanced beyond the proposal stage.

The final explicit contestation has been focused around the role of the veto. This, too, originated with the ICISS Report, which had proposed: "The idea essentially is that a permanent member, in matters where its vital national interests were not claimed to be involved, would not use its veto to obstruct the passage of what would otherwise be a majority resolution" (ICISS, 2001b: 51). While the concept was mentioned in the 2004 High-level Panel Report, Bellamy (2009) notes that it was one of the points that was quickly sacrificed in the lead up to the WSOD, and by 2008 Gareth Evans (2008: 137) noted the proposal had "received little support." However, the issue began to shift after Ban Ki-moon's 2009 Report on Implementing the Responsibility to Protect, which had outlined the need to refrain the use of the veto (Blätter and Williams, 2010: 9).

This new focus has been around two forms of voluntary mechanisms. The Accountability, Coherence and Transparency group of UN member states has proposed a Security Council Code of Conduct whereby signatory states who are elected to the Council would commit not to vote against resolutions aimed to prevent or respond to genocide, war crimes or crimes against humanity.[9] As of January 2019 the Code of Conduct has been signed by 117 member states.[10] In 2013, the French government made a separate declaration to call for permanent members of the Security Council to agree to suspend their right to veto. The French proposal would see the UN Secretary-General investigate situations following a request from at least 50 member states. Where he determined that atrocity crimes were occurring, the permanent members would voluntarily regulate their right to exercise their veto (Fabius, 2013). That declaration has received the support of 96 states, including the United Kingdom.[11] These actions have not restrained Russia's use of the veto, which has cast it 13 times respect to Syria.[12]

The Security Council and the response to chemical weapons use in Syria

We can also see a fourth implicit contestation occurring over this period with efforts by the United States, supported by the United Kingdom and France, to respond to the Syrian government's use of chemical weapons outside of the Council. This is an implicit contestation because none of the major actors have sought to explicitly link their actions – which have included two sets of air strikes without the approval of the UN Security Council – to the R2P. This began with the Red Line debates over Syria in August 2013, following the Assad regime's use of chemical weapons in Ghouta, a Damascus suburb, which killed at least 734 people. Following the release of a US government assessment on August 30, 2013 which asserted "with high confidence that the Syrian government" had carried out the attacks,[13] US President Barack Obama argued that he had:

> decided that the United States should take military action against Syrian regime targets. This would not be an open-ended intervention. We would not put boots on the ground. Instead, our action would be designed to be limited in duration and scope. But I'm confident we can hold the Assad regime accountable for their use of chemical weapons, deter this kind of behavior, and degrade their capacity to carry it out.[14]

These actions, however, were not framed as falling within the R2P. Obama was generally viewed as a strong proponent of the R2P as president (Vaughn and Dunne, 2015). Along with subsequent chemical weapons attacks, these would likely constitute either crimes against humanity (including murder) or war crimes (including willful killing and intentionally directing attacks against the civilian population) under the International Criminal Court's Rome Statute given their widespread and systematic use. However, rather than referring to the R2P, Obama instead framed action around the idea that the prohibition on chemical weapons itself "represents a conclusive international norm" based around the Chemical Weapons Convention, even though Syria was not yet a party (Nahlawi, 2016: 79–80; Price, 2013). At least one reason for this may have been the lack of clear international law. As Ben Rhodes, Obama's Deputy National Security Adviser, stated "our lawyers also had concerns. There was no firm international legal basis for bombing Syria – no argument of self-defense, which justified our actions against al-Qaeda; no UN resolution such as we had had in Libya" (Rhodes, 2018).

The Red Line crisis ended with the Syrian chemical weapons disarmament deal, negotiated between US Secretary of State John Kerry and Russian Foreign Minister Sergei Lavrov, and the ensuing Security Council Resolution 2118. In the Council debate, no actors (either positively or negatively) sought to link these events to the R2P doctrine. Kerry noted that the agreement had placed binding obligations for the first time on the Assad regime, "requiring that it get rid of its tools of terror" and that "the world carried the burden of doing what it must to end mass killing by other means." Lavrov was quick to note that the text had not been passed under Chapter VII nor did it allow coercive measures. Jean Asselborn, the Foreign Minister of Luxembourg, specifically argued that the response was entirely separate from R2P or Protection of Civilians (POC) issues, stating that "for the first time the Security Council has determined chemical weapons use is a threat to international peace." Perhaps the closest linkage was one by Korean Minister of Foreign Affairs Yun Byng-Se, who noted the resolution "showed the Council's unity on the Syrian crisis, fulfilling its over overdue responsibility to the Syrian people."[15]

By contrast, following a further alleged chemical weapons attack by the Syrian government in April 2017 on the town of Khan Shaykhun which killed at least 80 civilians,[16] the United States undertook air strikes against a single Syrian military base. President Trump himself did not reference the R2P, instead arguing the strikes were justified as being in the "vital national security interest of the United States to prevent and deter the spread and use of deadly chemical weapons."[17]

Within the Council, by contrast, three main arguments were made by those in favor of the strikes. The first reflected the idea that this use of chemical weapons was an atrocity crime. US Ambassador Nikki Haley justified the strike by arguing that "the moral stain of the Assad regime could no longer go unanswered. His crimes against humanity could no longer be met with empty words."[18] Matthew Rycroft, the United Kingdom's representative, similarly noted that "impunity cannot be the norm … the United Kingdom supports the United States air strike on the Al-Shayrat air field because war crimes have consequences…."[19] The second argument was that this strike occurred only because the Council itself was unable to take action due to the Russian veto. As Haley argued,

> As I warned on Wednesday … when the international community consistently fails in its duty to act collectively, there are times when States are compelled to take their own action. The indiscriminate use of chemical weapons against innocent civilians is one of those times.[20]

Rycroft argued that the "United States strike was a proportionate response to unspeakable acts."[21] The third argument was that this was a necessary response given the violation of Resolution 2118. François Delattre, the French representative, noted that "the actions of Syria also constitute a clear violation of the resolutions of the Security Council. In that context, the American airstrike constitutes a legitimate response to the chemical attack."[22]

Vladimir Safronkov, the Russian representative, argued that the attack was "a flagrant violation of international law and an act of aggression" but then sought to argue that the US, UK and France "are paranoid about overthrowing the legitimate Government in sovereign Syria,"[23] an argument which was not echoed by other Council members. The Chinese response was much more muted, with Liu Jieyi simply noting that "China has always advocated for dialogue and consultations … a political solution is the only way out of the situation. A military solution will not work."[24] Other representatives, such as that of Bolivia, argued that it was "an extremely serious violation of international law" because the US had acted unilaterally, but also noted that "we unequivocally condemn chemical attacks…."[25]

A second set of strikes were undertaken by the US, UK and France on April 13, 2018 following another chemical attack on the town of Douma which killed more than 40 people. President Trump once again framed the strikes as responding specifically to the use of chemical weapons:

> Chemical weapons are uniquely dangerous … the purpose of our actions tonight is to establish a strong deterrent against the production, spread and use of chemical weapons. Establishing this deterrent is a vital national security interest of the United States.[26]

The Council deliberations following the strikes included the same set of issues as those the previous year. Speaking on behalf of the United States, Haley framed the attacks as limited, legitimate and proportionate designed to deter future chemical weapons use. She also again framed it as a response due to the violation of Resolution 2118.[27] Both the UK and French representatives echoed similar points.[28] The Russian representative stated the attack demonstrated "a flagrant disregard for international law" and suggested that the US, UK and France were refusing "to consult with us, while falsely assuring every one of the opposite. They are undermining the Council's authority."[29] Other responses, however, were more tempered. The Chinese representative simply noted that "any unilateral military action that circumvent the Security Council contravene" the Charter, and China urged all parties to refrain from any actions which might escalate the situation.[30] The representatives from Kazakhstan and Ethiopia simply expressed concerns over escalation and called for restraint.[31] And an effort by Russia to pass a resolution condemning the aggression failed with only three votes (from Bolivia, China and Russia) in favor.[32]

In both cases – and with the abortive steps taken by the Obama administration prior to the disarmament deal – it is unclear how much of a direct contestation of the R2P regime they are. First, neither case replicates the practice of multilateral humanitarian interventions undertaken without Security Council approval in the 1990s, where either ground troops (in Northern Iraq) or a long-term aerial campaign (in Kosovo) occurred. Both strikes against Syria have been strictly limited. As Henriksen has noted, the first operation "does not fit well with our traditional understanding of what a humanitarian intervention is" and should instead be understood as a limited operation which sought to deter the Syrian regime from its use of chemical weapons (Henriksen, 2018: 35).

Second, while the intervening states did raise the issue of atrocity crimes occurring in Syria, they did not explicitly link these to the R2P, even though this could have potentially buttressed claims to legality or legitimacy for the strikes. This suggests that the US, UK and France may not have wanted to undermine the fragile consensus on R2P that the Council possesses. Third, in both cases these same states did explicitly frame their actions as seeking to deter the use of chemical weapons. As such, these states appear to be hierarchically rank-ordering norms, treating the non-use of chemical weapons norm as the primary norm of concern in this case. However, it should also be noted that if the air strikes were designed to deter subsequent use, they do appear to have had some success – while there was no decline in use following the Khan Sheykhoun attacks, the

Global Public Policy Institute found that there was a pause in use following the April 2018 Douma attacks, though the US government has alleged chemical weapons were again used by the Syrian government during attacks in Idlib in May 2019.[33]

Conclusion

The R2P doctrine is not a norm. As a regime, the R2P bundles together a range of existing norms and set of norms around four distinct atrocity crimes as well as enshrining three new norms around state and international responsibilities to respond to these crimes, and the requirement particularly of the UN Security Council to consider action. By treating it as a single norm, a range of authors have pointed to patterns of practice that appear contradictory and indeterminate. And yet these practices do make sense if we presume that some aspects of the R2P doctrine reflect norms that are widely institutionalized and implemented, while other aspects remain subject to contestation at the international level and varied interpretations at the domestic level.

This is not to say that the R2P doctrine itself is not useful. As a regime, it has provided a behavior guide to states to interpret how they should understand mass atrocity events, creating a 'code of conduct' to use Welsh's phrasing. But the actual 'responsibilities' that it has created remain under-defined and will be shaped by ongoing international responses to individual crises. Since the Libyan intervention, the role of the Security Council with respect to the R2P has been contested explicitly in three different ways: whether the R2P should be linked to regime change; whether clearer rules of conduct within the Council are needed; and whether there should be voluntary efforts to restrain the use of the veto. The contestation over regime change which occurred following the passage of Resolution 1973 on Libya has had a significant negative effect on the likelihood of the Council passing new Pillar Three resolutions in part because the idea was layered after the fact on to the resolution and has meant that Russia and – to a lesser degree – China now seek to block any actions within the Council. Both the contestations over conduct by the Council and the use of the veto are different in their orientation. They reflect the limited nature of the WSOD agreement and an effort to add in elements to clarify how the Council's practice should be modified. As such, these are contestations which seek to clarify how Pillar Three will interact with other norms in the regime and have the potential to improve how the R2P doctrine functions in practice and its overall legitimacy.

Finally, there is a fourth, implicit, contestation occurring around how the Council should respond to the use of chemical weapons in Syria. We have now seen three responses, two of which ended in the use of force without Council authorization. As such, this last contestation is a particularly important one, not least because it links back to basic questions around the UN Charter and the use of force. But I have shown this contestation is not directly affecting the R2P doctrine in two senses. The first is that in their statements and rhetoric, the states which have supported this action have identified a separate norm at the core of their response: the norm against the use of chemical weapons. The second is that while atrocity crimes are mentioned, there has been almost unanimous action by all the states within the Council – both those in support or against – to not argue this is an R2P action, or to even mention the R2P by name. As such, it appears that the Council members both accept the role of the R2P and are seeking to not challenge it directly in spite of their actions.

Notes

1 United Nations Convention on the Prevention and Punishment of the Crime of Genocide (1948), Art. VIII; see also (Holzgrefe, 2003: 44).
2 Arts 5 (b) and (c), Charter of the International Military Tribunal for the Far East (IMTFE), January 19, 1946; Charter International Military Tribunal (IMT).
3 UNSC, "Letter Dated May 24, 1994 from the Secretary-General to the President of the Security Council," S/1994/674, May 27, 1994, 33.
4 The International Criminal Tribunal for the Former Yugoslavia, however, did find in the *Simic* Trial Judgement that "deportation and forcible transfer are closely linked to the concept of 'ethnic cleansing'" (International Criminal Tribunal for the Former Yugoslavia, *Simic* Trial Judgement, October 17, 2003, IT-95,9-T, para. 133). Both deportations and forcible transfers can constitute crimes against humanity under the International Criminal Court's Rome Statute.
5 Global Centre for the Responsibility to Protect, "UN Security Council Resolutions and Presidential Statements Referencing R2P." www.globalr2p.org/resources/335
6 Allegra Stratton, "Obama, Cameron and Sarkozy: No Let-up in Libya until Gaddafi Departs." *Guardian,* April 15, 2011. www.theguardian.com/world/2011/apr/15/obama-sarkozy-cameron-libya
7 Chris McGreal and Martin Chulov, "Syria: Assad Must Resign, says Obama." *Guardian,* August 19, 2011. www.theguardian.com/world/2011/aug/18/syria-assad-must-resign-obama
8 In supporting his view that it is a "semi-official" proposal, Garwood-Gowers (2016: 91) notes that "there are indications that R2P has received some degree of official endorsement and can, therefore, be considered to accurately represent the current Chinese position on R2P."
9 ACT Group, "Code of Conduct Regarding Security Council Action against Genocide, Crimes against Humanity or War Crimes," Sep 1, 2015. ww.globalr2p.org/media/files/n1543357.pdf. The group's activities began in 2012 with a draft General Assembly Resolution (A/66/L.42Rev.1, May 3, 2012) which proposed that that Security Council members should explain the reasons for any veto and refrain from using the veto to block action "aimed at preventing or ending genocide, war crimes and crimes against humanity." However, the resolution was withdrawn rather than voted on after the Security Council's permanent members had expressed fears that the proposals could be "divisive or be used against them." United Nations, "Switzerland Withdraws Draft Resolution in General Assembly Aimed at Improving Security Council's Working Methods to Avoid 'Politically Complex' Wrangling," GA/11234, May 16, 2012.
10 Permanent Mission of the Principality of Liechtenstein, "List of Supporters of the Code of Conduct Regarding Security Council Action against Genocide, Crimes against Humanity or War Crimes, as elaborated by ACT," January 1, 2019. www.globalr2p.org/media/files/2019-1-1-coc-list-of-supporters.pdf
11 Global Centre for the Responsibility to Protect, "UN Security Council Code of Conduct." www.globalr2p.org/our_work/un_security_council_code_of_conduct

12 Michelle Nichols, "Russia Casts 13th Veto of U.N. Security Council Action During Syrian war." *Reuters,* September 20, 2019. www.reuters.com/article/us-syria-security-un/russia-casts-13th-veto-of-un-security-council-action-during-syrian-war-idUSKBN1W42CJ

13 The White House, "Government Assessment of the Syrian Government's Use of Chemical Weapons on August 21, 2013," Aug 30, 2013. https://obamawhitehouse.archives.gov/the-press-office/2013/08/30/government-assessment-syrian-government-s-use-chemical-weapons-august-21. While the government's culpability in the attacks has been disputed, including by US reporter Seymour Hersh (Seymour M. Hersh, "Whose Sarin?" *London Review of Books*, December 19, 2013. www.lrb.co.uk/v35/n24/seymour-m-hersh/whose-sarin), other reports came to similar conclusions, with the Independent International Commission of Inquiry on the Syrian Arab Republic concluding the perpetrators "likely had access to the chemical weapons stockpile of the Syrian military, as well as the expertise and equipment necessary to manipulate safely large amounts of chemical agents," and with Human Rights Watch noting evidence strongly suggests it was "carried out by government forces." Human Rights Council "Report of the Independent International Commission of Inquiry on the Syrian Arab Republic," A/HRC/25/65, February 12, 2014; Human Rights Watch, "Attacks on Ghouta: Analysis of Alleged Use of Chemical Weapons in Syria, 2013. In both cases, however, these reports were issued following the United States' initial decision to take action.

14 *New York Times*, "Text of President Obama's Remarks on Syria," August 31, 2013. www.nytimes.com/2013/09/01/world/middleeast/text-of-president-obamas-remarks-on-syria.html?ref=middleeast&_r=0

15 United Nations, "Security Council Requires Scheduled Destruction of Syria's Chemical Weapons, Unanimously Adopting Resolution 2118 (2013)," SC/11135, September 27, 2013.

16 The Leadership Panel of the OPCW-UN joint investigative mechanism subsequently stated that the government was responsible for the attack, noting it "is confident that the Syrian Arab Republic is responsible for the release of sarin at Khan Sheikhun on 4 April 2017" (UN Security Council, "Letter dated October 26, 2017 from the Secretary-General addressed to the President of the Security Council," S/2017/904, Oct 26, 2017. Five days after the air strikes, the White House declassified an intelligence report that stated that the "United States is confident that the Syrian regime conducted a chemical weapons attack, using the nerve agent sarin…." However, it is unclear when the report was prepared. New York Times, "Declassified U.S. Report on Chemical Weapons Attack." www.nytimes.com/interactive/2017/04/11/world/middleeast/document-Syria-Chemical-Weapons-Report-White-House.html

17 Michael R. Gordon, Helene Cooper and Michael D. Shear, "Dozens of U.S. Missiles Hit Air Base in Syria." *New York Times*, April 6, 2017. www.nytimes.com/2017/04/06/world/middleeast/us-said-to-weigh-military-responses-to-syrian-chemical-attack.html?_r=0%3E

18 Haley (United States), UN Security Council, 7919th meeting, April 7, 2017, S/PV.7919, 17.

19 Rycroft (United Kingdom), ibid., 5.

20 Haley (United States), ibid., 17.

21 Rycroft (United Kingdom), ibid., 5.

22 Delattre (France), ibid., 9.

23 Safronkov (Russia), ibid., 10, 11.

24 Liu Jieyi (China), ibid., 10.

25 Llorentty Solíz (Bolovia), ibid., 3,5.

26 *New York Times*, "President Trump on Syria Strikes: Full Transcript and Video," April 13, 2018. www.nytimes.com/2018/04/13/world/middleeast/trump-syria-air-strikes-full-transcript.html. The same day as the strike, the White House issued an assessment which assessed "with confidence that the Syrian regime used chemical

weapons in the eastern Damascus suburb of Duma on April 7, 2018." "United States Government Assessment of the Assad Regime's Chemical Weapons Use," April 13, 2018. www.whitehouse.gov/briefings-statements/united-states-government-assessment-assad-regimes-chemical-weapons-use/. A subsequent investigation by the OPCW concluded that the attacks had included the use of toxic chemicals containing chlorine but did not assign blame. Al-Jazeera, "Chlorine Likely Used in Attack on Syria Town Douma, says OPCW," March 2, 2019. www.aljazeera.com/news/2019/03/chlorine-attack-syria-town-douma-opcw-190302063053270.html

27 See Haley (United States), UN Security Council, 8233rd meeting, April 14, 2018, S/PV.8233, 5.

28 See Pierce (United Kingdom), ibid., 6–7; and Delattre (France), ibid., 8.

29 Nebenzia (Russian Federation), ibid., 3, 4.

30 Ma Zhaoxu (China), ibid., 10.

31 Umarov (Kazakhstan), ibid., 10; Alemu (Ethiopia), ibid., 16.

32 United Nations, "Following Air Strikes against Suspected Chemical Weapons Sites in Syria, Security Council Rejects Proposal to Condemn Aggression," April 14, 2018, SC/13296. www.un.org/press/en/2018/sc13296.doc.htm

33 Global Public Policy Institute, "Nowhere to Hide: The Logic of Chemical Weapons Use in Syria," February 2019. www.gppi.net/media/GPPi_Schneider_Luetkefend_2019_Nowhere_to_Hide_Web.pdf. The report finds find that at least 336 chemical weapons attacks have occurred in Syria with about 98 percent attributed to the Assad regime between December 2012 and January 2019. CNBC, "Pompeo says Syrian Government Used Chlorine in May Chemical Weapon Attack," September 26, 2019. www.cnbc.com/2019/09/26/pompeo-says-syria-government-used-chlorine-in-may-chemical-weapon-attack.html

References

Adler-Nissen, R. and Pouliot, V. (2014). Power in Practice: Negotiating the International Intervention in Libya. *European Journal of International Relations*, 20(4), 889–911.

Babbitt, E.F. (2017). Responsibility to Protect: Time to Reassess. *Journal of Human Rights Practice,* 9, 431–435.

Bellamy, A.J. (2009). *Responsibility to Protect.* Malden, MA: Polity Press.

Bellamy, A.J. (2011). *Global Politics and the Responsibility to Protect: From Words to Deeds.* Milton Park: Routledge.

Bellamy, A.J. (2015). The Responsibility to Protect Turns Ten. *Ethics & International Affairs,* 29, 161–185.

Bernstein, S. (2000). Ideas, Social Structure and the Compromise of Liberal Environmentalism. *European Journal of International Relations,* 6, 464–512.

Betts, A. (2014). From Persecution to Deprivation. *In:* Betts, A. and Orchard, P. (eds.) *Implementation and World Politics: How International Norms Change Practice*, 29–49. Oxford: Oxford University Press.

Betts, A. and Orchard, P. (2014). Introduction: The Normative Institutionalization-Implementation Gap. *In:* Betts, A. and Orchard, P. (eds.) *Implementation and World Politics: How International Norms Change Practice*, 1–26. Oxford: Oxford University Press.

Blätter, A. and Williams, P. (2010). *The Responsibility Not to Veto: A Way Forward.* Washington, DC: Citizens for Global Solutions.

Brunnée, J. and Toope, S.J. (2006). Norms, Institutions and UN Reform: The Responsibility to Protect. *Journal of International Law and International Relations,* 2, 121–137.

Cronin, B. (2003). *Institutions for the Common Good: International Protection Regimes in International Society.* Cambridge: Cambridge University Press.

Cunliffe, P. (2016). From ISIS to ICISS: A Critical Return to the Responsibility to Protect Report. *Cooperation and Conflict,* 51, 233–247.

Deitelhoff, N. (2009). The Discursive Process of Legalization: Charting Islands of Persuasion in the ICC Case. *International Organization,* 63, 33–65.

Donnelly, J. (1986). International Human Rights: A Regime Analysis. *International Organization,* 40, 599–642.

Donnelly, J. (2012). The Elements of the Structures of International Systems. *International Organization,* 66, 609–643.

Dunne, T. and Gelber, K. (2014). Arguing Matters: The Responsibility to Protect and the Case of Libya. *Global Responsibility to Protect,* 6, 326–349.

Evans, G. (2008). *The Responsibility to Protect: Ending Mass Atrocity Crimes Once and For All.* Washington, DC: Brookings Institution Press.

Fabius, L. (2013). A Self-restraint at the U.N. *New York Times*, October 4.

Finnemore, M. (2000). Are Legal Norms Distinctive? *New York University Journal of International Law and Policy,* 32, 699–705.

Finnemore, M. and Sikkink, K. (1998). International Norm Dynamics and Political Change. *International Organization,* 52, 887–917.

Franck, T.M. (1990). *The Power of Legitimacy Among Nations.* New York: Oxford University Press.

Fung, C.J. (2018). Separating Intervention from Regime Change: China's Diplomatic Innovations at the UN Security Council Regarding the Syria Crisis. *The China Quarterly,* 235, 693–712.

Gallagher, A. (2014). What Constitutes a "Manifest Failing"? Ambiguous and Inconsistent Terminology and the Responsibility to Protect. *International Relations,* 28, 428–444.

Garwood-Gowers, A. (2016). China's "Responsible Protection" Concept: Reinterpreting the Responsibility to Protect (R2P) and Military Intervention for Humanitarian Purposes. *Asian Journal of International Law,* 6, 89–118.

Gholiagha, S. (2015). "To Prevent Future Kosovos and Future Rwandas." A Critical Constructivist View of the Responsibility to Protect. *The International Journal of Human Rights,* 19, 1074–1097.

Gifkins, J. (2016). R2P in the UN Security Council: Darfur, Libya and Beyond. *Cooperation and Conflict,* 51, 148–165.

Glanville, L. (2011). The Antecedents of "Sovereignty as Responsibility". *European Journal of International Relations*, 17(2), 233–255.

Glanville, L. (2016). Does R2P Matter? Interpreting the Impact of a Norm. *Cooperation and Conflict,* 51, 184–199.

Glanville, L. (Forthcoming). *Sharing the Responsibility to Protect: Histories and Possibilities.*

Goertz, G. (2003). *International Norms and Decision-making: A Punctuated Equilibrium Model.* Lanham, MD: Rowman & Littlefield Publishers.

Hasenclever, A., Mayer, P. and Rittberger, V. (1997). *Theories of International Regimes.* Cambridge: Cambridge University Press.

Hehir, A. (2013). The Permanence of Inconsistency: Libya, the Security Council, and the Responsibility to Protect. *International Security,* 38, 137–159.

Hehir, A. (2018). *Hollow Norms and the Responsibility to Protect.* Houndmills: Palgrave Macmillan.

Henriksen, A. (2018). Trump's Missile Strike on Syria and the Legality of Using Force to Deter Chemical Warfare. *Journal of Conflict and Security Law,* 23, 33–48.

Holzgrefe, J.L. (2003). The Humanitarian Intervention Debate. *In:* Holzgrefe, J.L. and Keohane, R.O. (eds.) *Humanitarian Intervention: Ethical, Legal and Political Dilemmas*, 15–52. Cambridge: Cambridge University Press.

Hurd, I. (1999). Legitimacy and Authority in International Politics. *International Organization,* 53, 379–408.

Hurd, I. (2011). Is Humanitarian Intervention Legal? The Rule of Law in an Incoherent World. *Ethics & International Affairs,* 25, 293–313.

ICISS (2001a). *The Responsibility to Protect.* Ottawa: International Development Research Centre.

ICISS (2001b). *The Responsibility to Protect: Report of the International Commission on Intervention and State Sovereignty.* Ottawa: International Development Research Centre.

International Peace Institute (2009). *The Responsibility to Protect (RtoP) and Genocide Prevention in Africa.* New York: International Peace Institute.

Kenkel, K.M. and Stefan, C.G. (2016). Brazil and the Responsibility while Protecting Initiative: Norms and the Timing of Diplomatic Support. *Global Governance: A Review of Multilateralism and International Organizations,* 22, 41–58.

Krasner, S.D. (1982). Structural Causes and Regime Consequences: Regimes as Intervening Variables. *International Organization,* 36, 185–205.

Kuperman, A.J. (2013). A Model Humanitarian Intervention? Reassessing NATO's Libya Campaign. *International Security,* 38, 105–136.

Labonte, M. (2016). R2P's Status as a Norm. *The Oxford Handbook of the Responsibility to Protect*, 133–150.

Lantis, J.S. and Wunderlich, C. (2018). Resiliency Dynamics of Norm Clusters: Norm Contestation and International Cooperation. *Review of International Studies*, 570–593.

Levy, M.A., Young, O.R. and Zurn, M. (1995). The Study of International Regimes. *European Journal of International Relations,* 1, 267–330.

Luck, E. (2010). Building a Norm: The Responsibility to Protect Experience. *In:* Rotberg, R.I. (ed.) *Mass Atrocity Crimes: Preventing Future Outrages*, 108–127. Washington, DC: Brookings Institution Press

Nahlawi, Y. (2016). The Responsibility to Protect and Obama's Red Line on Syria. *Global Responsibility to Protect,* 8, 76–101.

Neufeld, M. (1993). Interpretation and the "Science" of International Relations. *Review of International Studies,* 19, 39–61.

Orchard, P. (2010). Regime-Induced Displacement and Decision-Making within the United Nations Security Council: The Cases of Northern Iraq, Kosovo, and Darfur. *Global Responsibility to Protect,* 2, 101–126.

Orchard, P. (2014). *A Right to Flee: Refugees, States, and the Construction of International Society.* Cambridge: Cambridge University Press.

Orchard, P. (2018). *Protecting the Internally Displaced: Rhetoric and Reality.* London: Routledge.

Orford, A. (2011). *International Authority and the Responsibility to Protect.* Cambridge: Cambridge University Press.

Pape, R.A. (2012). When Duty Calls: A Pragmatic Standard of Humanitarian Intervention. *International Security,* 37, 41–80.

Price, R. (2013). No Strike, No Problem. *Foreign Affairs* (online).

Puchala, D.J. and Hopkins, R.F. (1982). International Regimes: Lessons from Inductive Analysis. *International Organization,* 36, 245–275.

Ralph, J. and Gifkins, J. (2017). The Purpose of United Nations Security Council Practice: Contesting Competence Claims in the Normative Context Created by the Responsibility to Protect. *European Journal of International Relations,* 23, 630–653.

Reus-Smit, C. (2007). International Crises of Legitimacy. *International Politics,* 44, 157–174.

Rhodes, B. (2018). Inside the White House During the Syrian “Red Line” Crisis. *The Atlantic*, June 3. Available from: www.theatlantic.com/international/archive/2018/06/inside-the-white-house-during-the-syrian-red-line-crisis/561887/

Rieff, D. (2011). R2P, R.I.P. *New York Times*, November 7.

Robinson, N. (1949). [2007]. The Genocide Convention: Its Origins and Interpretation Reprinted in *Case Western Reserve Journal of International Law,* 40, 315–392.

Schabas, W.A. (2009). *Genocide in International Law: The Crimes of Crimes*. Cambridge: Cambridge University Press.

Sikkink, K. (2011). *The Justice Cascade: How Human Rights Prosecutions Are Changing World Politics*. New York: W.W. Norton & Company.

Simmons, B.A. (2009). *Mobilizing for Human Rights: International Law in Domestic Politics.* Cambridge: Cambridge University Press.

Stefan, C.G. (2017). On Non-Western Norm Shapers: Brazil and the Responsibility while Protecting. *European Journal of International Security,* 2, 88–110.

Tatz, C. and Higgins, W. (2016). *The Magnitude of Genocide*. Santa Barbara, CA: Praeger.

UN (2004). A More Secure World: Our Shared Responsibility – Report of the High-level Panel on Threats, Challenges and Change. New York: United Nations.

UN (2005). In Larger Freedom: Towards Development, Security and Human Rights for All: Report of the Secretary-General. New York: United Nations.

UN General Assembly (2005). Resolution 60/1: World Summit Outcome. New York: United Nations.

UN General Assembly (2009). Implementing the Responsibility to Protect: Report of the Secretary-General. New York: United Nations.

Vaughn, J. and Dunne, T. (2015). Leading from the Front: America, Libya and the Localisation of R2P. *Cooperation and Conflict,* 50, 29–49.

Welsh, J. (2014). Implementing the “Responsibility to Protect”: Catalyzing Debate and Building Capacity. *In:* Betts, A. and Orchard, P. (eds.) *Implementation and World Politics: How International Norms Change Practice.* Oxford: Oxford University Press.

Western, J. and Goldstein, J. (2013). R2P After Syria. *Foreign Affairs*, March 26 (online).

Wiener, A. (2008). *The Invisible Constitution of Politics*. Cambridge: Cambridge University Press.

Wiener, A. (2009). Enacting Meaning-in-use: Qualitative Research on Norms and International Relations. *Review of International Studies,* 35, 175–193.

Wiener, A. (2014). *A Theory of Contestation.* Berlin: Springer.

Young, O.R. (1982). Regime Dynamics: The Rise and Fall of International Regimes. *International Organization,* 36, 277–297.

Young, O.R. (1986). International Regimes: Toward a New Theory of Institutions. *World Politics,* 39, 104–122.

2 R2P and the benefits of norm ambiguity

Luke Glanville and Wesley W. Widmaier

Introduction

Over the past two decades, the notion that states possess a shared Responsibility to Protect (R2P) populations from mass atrocities has evolved into a widely recognized norm, justifying a range of diplomatic practices, sanctions and multilateral interventions.[1] In explaining the successful construction of norms, scholars from a variety of perspectives have tended to stress the importance of norm clarity, defined as entailing the precise definition of standards of behavior. For example, liberal approaches that highlight the potential for "hegemonic socialization" stress that this requires leading states like the US to clarify "a set of normative principles" and to "articulate a clear set of normative claims about the international order" (Ikenberry and Kupchan, 1990: 284, 292; Simmons et al., 2006). Similarly, scholars of legalization write of norm emergence as a process driven by domestic entrepreneurs who "unambiguously define the conduct" that norms "require, authorize, or proscribe" (Abbott et al., 2000: 401; Kahler, 2000). Finally, constructivists highlight the importance of clarity on the part of entrepreneurs who institutionalize norms, or "standards for the appropriate behavior of states," by "clarifying what, exactly, the norm is and what constitutes violation" and identifying "specific … sanctions for norm breaking" (Finnemore and Sikkink, 1998: 893, 900; Reinold, 2011). Despite key differences between them, each approach sees clarity and precision as necessary for the establishment, institutionalization, and internalization of norms, and dismisses ambiguity as an impediment to norm construction and compliance.

In this chapter, we argue that such perspectives obscure the benefits of norm ambiguity, defined as the ability of a norm to be interpreted in varied ways (Best, 2008: 356; Percy, 2007; Mahoney and Thelen, 2010). To be sure, in offering a corrective, we do not deny that *too much* ambiguity can impede norm development. Rather, we argue that *too little* ambiguity can undermine the consensus, flexibility and adjustment necessary for incremental change.[2] We suggest that when scholars overrate the importance of clarity, they obscure the possibility that excess clarity can undermine consensus and flexibility and so, as Skowronek (2011) puts it, efforts to maintain norms or regimes can actually hasten their ends.

We identify conditions under which norm ambiguity can be constructive and suggest that consensus around a norm can sometimes best emerge when the norm is initially articulated in ambiguous and flexible terms and then incrementally adjusted over time by norm entrepreneurs through a process that we call the "norm feedback loop."[3]

Having advanced our framework, we chart the contributions of ambiguity to the incremental construction of R2P across the Rwanda, Iraq and Libya crises. First, we stress the importance of hegemonic and institutional ambiguity in the 1990s, as constructions of the Rwandan genocide as a moral failure of the international community provoked a re-examination of rights and responsibilities for human protection, culminating in the articulation of R2P by the International Commission on Intervention and State Sovereignty (ICISS) in 2001. Second, turning to the acceptance of R2P at the 2005 United Nations (UN) World Summit, despite the abuse of R2P-related ideas in justifications for the Iraq war two years earlier, we stress the contributions of ambiguity in not only attracting wider international support for the principle, but also enabling a wider array of political and legal forms of collective action to prevent and address atrocity crimes. Finally, we argue that the Barack Obama administration's stance of "leading from behind" eased both international and domestic concerns about hegemonic crusading, enabling the Libyan intervention and facilitating incremental compliance in its Presidential Study Directive 10 (PSD-10) on the prevention of mass atrocities. We conclude by contrasting the absolutism and clarity of neoconservative norm entrepreneurs and the tolerance of ambiguity exhibited by R2P supporters to highlight the benefits of ambiguity for norm durability.

Theoretical framework: from norm life cycle to norm feedback loop

International Relations (IR) scholars have tended to stress the importance of clarity for the construction of norms. While not denying that clarity has its virtues, we argue that *too much* clarity can harm the development of a norm and we instead appeal to the constructive effects of norm ambiguity. After outlining the potential problems of excessive clarity, we offer a framework suggesting that actors seeking to promote norms may be most successful when allowing for a constructive ambiguity that facilitates consensus and flexibility, enabling adjustments to interpretive shifts and variation in policy effectiveness over a norm feedback loop.

Rethinking the norm life cycle: the costs of clarity

As we have already noted, scholars from a range of perspectives have tended to stress the importance of clarity and precision for the definition, institutionalization and eventual "taken-for-granted" internalization of norms. We suggest, however, that an overemphasis on norm clarity obscures the contributions of ambiguity in the commencement and continuation of a norm life cycle. First, ambiguity may help to attract a wider array of supporters for a norm by easing concerns of weak actors about potential abuses by hegemonic agents and easing concerns of the powerful about being bound to inflexible expectations. Second, ambiguity may enhance flexibility in implementation at both domestic and international levels, providing room to adjust to interpretive shifts and unexpected events, rather than requiring adherence to formal rules whose strict application compromises the deeper values that underpin the norm.[4] By leaving a degree of discretion regarding implementation to relevant agents – be they governments contemplating the limits and possibilities of responding to distant atrocities or international bodies deliberating what measures to authorize and/or demand – ambiguity may expand the available "toolkit" of policy options, reducing the need for stark choices or trade-offs between, for example, sending in the troops or doing nothing. Finally, a lack of ambiguity may explain norm decline – as scholars across the realms of historical institutionalism (Skowronek, 1993) and IR (Barnett and Finnemore, 1999; Best, 2005, 2008, 2012) have cast efforts to isolate bureaucratic administration from wider political contexts as impediments to policy consensus and effectiveness. Despite their different concerns for domestic and international policies, Skowronek and Best both single out John F. Kennedy-era efforts at reducing political debates to technocratic questions as undermining policy legitimacy and effectiveness. Viewed in this light, the norm life-cycle model may obscure the need for norm entrepreneurs to remain open to interpretive shifts.[5] From this vantage point, a degree of ambiguity may enable norm adaptation to broader feedback, in ways that extend the life of the norm life cycle.

Indeed, in recent years, an increasing range of IR scholars have developed these themes, highlighting the importance of ambiguity in facilitating initial consensus around a norm and allowing ongoing adjustment through interpretive struggles over norm meanings. Van Kersbergen and Verbeek (2007: 221), for example, claim that norms are often "vague and elusive" and suggest that this may facilitate their adoption by a larger number of actors who are able to interpret the norm in a variety of ways that suits their preferences. Wiener (2004: 199) likewise argues that the successful signing of international agreements often depends on imprecision to the extent that "meanings are often left intentionally vague." This vagueness and imprecision, in turn, is said to generate ongoing contestation and adjustment over time (see also Krook and True, 2012; Sandholtz, 2008). Complementing these claims, Percy (2007) argues that excess clarity can perversely undermine a norm by creating loopholes that can be exploited and hindering the adjustment necessary to realize the norm's broad objectives.

To be sure, a norm can suffer from excess ambiguity. Indeed, an excessively ambiguous norm does not warrant the name "norm" at all. All norms must fit into an intersubjective and institutional context. Where they become divorced from any set of institutions, rules and decision-making procedures, then they have become too ambiguous and should no longer be considered norms. Our emphasis, however, is on the problem of excess clarity, in which norms are abstracted away from their ethical context and reduced to inflexible prescriptive rules, undermining the possibilities for consensus contributing to norm breakdown.[6] Building on the insights of the above-mentioned scholars, our contribution is to offer a new framework highlighting the benefits of ambiguity as a source of consensus and flexibility, and so we suggest in the next section that notions of a norm life cycle might be supplanted by that of a more dynamic norm feedback loop.

Toward a norm feedback loop: ambiguity, consensus and flexible adjustment

In this section, we offer a framework that emphasizes the conditions under which ambiguity contributes to consensus, flexibility and adjustment. We stress the contributions of ambiguity both to the initial development of consensus and then to the facilitation of incremental adjustment. Taking these dynamics together, we posit the notion of a norm feedback loop, in which ambiguous societal understandings, mediated by political/norm leaders, shape debate among norm entrepreneurs occupying positions of institutional influence, either domestically of internationally, who operationalize these values by seeking a degree of clarity, while ideally remaining open to input from leaders and publics – in ways that help sustain and extend ostensible norm life cycles.

To the extent that ambiguity provides a basis for interpretive pluralism, the scope for variation can lead agents holding a range of predispositions to accept a common set of norms, thereby providing a basis for wider consensus (Best, 2008, 2012). From this perspective, an insistence on clarity in proscribing or prescribing highly specified behaviors may generate controversy and conflict, forcing interpretive differences "into the open" in ways that increase awareness of disagreements. One might adapt Wendt's (1992) critique of security dilemma reasoning to identify key sources of norm consensus. Wendt argued that agents form inferences regarding cooperation not on the basis of worst-case *possibilities*, but rather with respect to *probabilities*, which must be inferred from a social context. Extending this insight to decisions regarding support for norms, we posit that agents are more likely to reject norms where hegemonic or institutional clarity with respect to behavioral requirements heightens "worst case possibility" concerns for unreasonable expectations or arbitrary enforcement. In this light, to the extent that ambiguity eases such concerns, it can enable the formation of norm consensus among international actors.

Having established a norm consensus, norm life-cycle models stress the importance of the institutionalization and internalization of new standards for behavior (Finnemore and Sikkink, 1998). However, unthinking internalization or unqualified institutionalization can cause norm inflexibility. We argue that ambiguity can limit such tendencies to bureaucratic or epistemic closure. For example, where ambiguity enables agents to flexibly interpret and implement norms, they will more easily sustain consensus by adapting to evolving shared interpretations, as well as enabling compliance by employing a more nuanced "toolkit" of responses. Similarly, we argue that norm ambiguity can enable norm entrepreneurs to adapt and adjust to incremental shifts in standards of acceptable behavior, in ways that stave off norm collapse.[7] In short, ambiguity helps ensure that norms will "bend," but not "break."

First, ideationally speaking, we argue that ambiguity is useful in enabling agents to adapt to evolving interpretations of norms, resisting technocratic (Best, 2005) or managerial (Skowronek, 2011) tendencies to epistemic closure that may undermine responsiveness and consensus. Indeed, even in the immediate context of "tipping points" which set off norm cascades, the concomitant promulgation of formal norms may give rise to changed practices and unintended consequences which require *immediate* adjustment. In this light, we qualify the emphasis placed by Finnemore and Sikkink (1998: 896) on "agents having strong notions about appropriate or desirable behavior in their community," where such "strong notions" may obscure the need to modify their ideas. The ideational costs of clarity and advantages of ambiguity in these regards may be most apparent if one contrasts two similarly situated epistemic communities that arose to prominence over the 1995–2005 period, as advocates of R2P emerged in tandem with foreign policy neoconservatives. Where neoconservatives broadly refused to adjust their ideas and preferences to multilateral or domestic opposition, R2P advocates engaged in constant adjustment, as understandings of human protection responsibilities evolved across two iterations of R2P at the ICISS and World Summit. By the 2010s, neoconservatism had been largely discredited by the misadventure in Iraq, while R2P had gained legitimacy as a focal point of domestic and international debate.

Second, developing institutional implications, we argue for the merits of ambiguity in limiting bureaucratic pathologies, particularly stemming from standard operational procedures that reduce the scope for discretion and intensify formal policy trade-offs – in the case of R2P, between intervening militarily and "doing nothing." To limit such tensions, R2P advocates argue for the use of a variegated "toolkit" spanning diplomatic, economic, legal and military measures. The contributions of ambiguity in this regard were particularly clear in the international response to the disputed 2007 Kenyan elections, which were followed by the killing of over 1,000 people and the displacement of an additional 300,000. While not using force, the UN quickly defined the crisis as an "R2P situation" and urged Kenyan leaders to "meet their responsibility to protect the civilian population," warning they could face later punishment – efforts reinforced as Archbishop Desmond Tutu lauded UN "action on a fundamental principle, the Responsibility to Protect" (Evans, 2008: 51). In this way, the absence of procedural clarity saw ambiguity enable a flexible response and the incremental enhancement of policy possibilities.

Third, given such increased cognitive and institutional flexibility, ambiguity can limit longer-term tendencies to norm decay. Put more formally, where norm life-cycle models emphasize the importance of clarity and precision, they obscure the ways in which these values can give rise to "ambiguity aversion" and lead agents to reduce interpretive differences to subjective risks that "cancel out," leading agents to make inefficient use of information regarding evolving interpretations (Ellsberg, 1961). In other words, where the pursuit of clarity leads agents to abstract away from the value-laden bases of norms, it may engender what Best (2005) terms their "hollowing out," as they are reduced to utilitarian or legal rules, whose inflexibility can contribute to instability and crisis. Given this common need for ongoing norm modification, we argue that the norm life cycle should be re-envisioned as a potentially more open-ended process which acknowledges the scope for "norm feedback." Rather than cast norm entrepreneurs as the initial source of norm clarity, we suggest that ambiguity must precede attempts at clarity, and so the rhetorical appeals of norm leaders to the public might presage the emergence of specific groups of entrepreneurs. Such entrepreneurs must in turn prove willing to adjust norms where shifts in behavior, resource constraints or tensions among values attract attention and require adjustment.

In sum, we posit not a model in which norm entrepreneurs oversee stages of norm emergence, institutionalization and internalization, but rather one in which leaders and publics engage in broad debates, the outcome of which enables specific norm entrepreneurs to assume positions of institutional influence, and in turn requires that they remain open to feedback in terms of public views and policy performance. Viewed in its entirety, the norm feedback loop is marked by the successive interplay of broad debates over constructions of crises, efforts by entrepreneurs to institutionalize norms, and – if a norm is to be sustained – entrepreneurial adjustments to shifts in public debate, institutional resources and policy effectiveness. An aversion to ambiguity, in contrast, risks norm collapse.

The ambiguity of R2P: norm feedback over Rwanda, Iraq and Libya

To highlight such dynamics, the remainder of the chapter addresses the contributions of ambiguity to R2P. It is worth clarifying that R2P, as negotiated by world leaders at the 2005 UN World Summit, entails two distinct, although complementary, norms (noting this bundle of norms, Phil Orchard usefully suggests in Chapter 1 that R2P might be fruitfully described as an international regime). The first norm holds that each state has a responsibility to protect its population from atrocity crimes. This norm is uncontroversial. It is acknowledged by all states, it is firmly established in international law and its violation is commonly subject to condemnation, the imposition of sanctions, and in some cases military intervention or international criminal prosecution. The second norm holds that the international community has a shared responsibility to do what it can to ensure that populations are protected from atrocity crimes. This is understood to involve not only helping and encouraging states to protect their populations but, where necessary, using appropriate diplomatic, humanitarian and other peaceful means and even taking collective action under Chapter VII of the UN Charter should states manifestly fail to protect their populations.[8] This second norm, which accords a residual responsibility to the international community, is of course closely related to the first, which accords a primary responsibility to the host state. But it is distinct and more contested. It is this second norm that we focus on.

In what follows, we explore the contributions of ambiguity to this R2P norm, tracing domestic and international discourses over the Rwanda, Iraq and Libya crises. We suggest that this evolution matters not only as these debates have had an intrinsic historical and policy importance, but also as R2P itself comprises a "crucial case" for the study of systemic norms, as the "high politics" of national security should lead states to focus on relative power concerns. We highlight in each section the state of debate over R2P across varied hegemonic pronouncements by the US in reacting to crises, institutional debates among norm entrepreneurs in adjusting to shifts in the terms of debate and the continuation of such deliberations across recurring crises. More specifically in iterative fashion, we show how prevailing ideas were reshaped in public constructions of Rwanda, Iraq and Libya, as respectively institutionalized in the 2001 ICISS Report, the 2005 World Summit Outcome Document (WSOD) and the 2011 Obama PSD-10 on mass atrocities. We give particular attention to the US, while also taking account of shifts in opinion and consensus in the broader international community, because the US has tended to play a key role both in developing and at times undermining consensus around R2P, as well as in implementing the military intervention aspect of R2P.

The 1990s: from Rwanda to the ICISS

In the early post-Cold War period, US policymakers used precision as a means to limit the scope for humanitarian intervention. In the context of the Somalian intervention, US President Bill Clinton (1993) addressed the UN General Assembly, advancing explicit guidelines to govern the multilateral use of force, suggesting a need to ask "harder questions about proposals for new peacekeeping missions," stressing the need for "clear objectives" in interventions, and arguing that "the United Nations should address these and other hard questions for every proposed mission before we vote and before the mission begins." Clinton stressed the need to be more cautious in committing UN troops, arguing that "[i]f the American people are to say yes to UN peacekeeping, the United Nations must know when to say no." Ultimately, the pursuit of clarity regarding humanitarian intervention lessened the likelihood that such interventions would occur. When Somalia was followed by the Rwandan crisis in 1994, US policymakers initially saw their avoidance of intervention as a success, as Americans were safely evacuated, and a Somalia-style debacle avoided.[9] Justifying the failure to act in May, Clinton (1995: 829) cited the Somalian precedent, arguing that "we learned that it is very difficult to have the forces … go in for any prolonged period of time and say that this is only a humanitarian crisis." Such concerns were not exclusively felt by the hegemon. UN officials also expressed concerns about intervening in Rwanda, fearing that "another 'loss' after Somalia would jeopardize the UN's future" (Barnett, 1997: 561).[10]

Yet, interpretations of Rwanda's lessons evolved, as a pursuit of clarity yielded to efforts at grappling with moral ambiguities.[11] Following Rwanda, the hegemonic certitude of the US gradually gave way to a more flexible understanding of the purposes of US power, while at the same time international fears of potential abuses of a right to intervene that had dominated debate in the early 1990s gradually gave way to concern regarding the failure to intervene. Ensuing years saw a widening of debate over Rwanda, across a series of public apologies, statements and formal pronouncements. Indeed, Clinton (1998) visited Kigali to apologize, conceding the global community's failure to live up to a collective responsibility. Clinton admitted to having failed to "act quickly enough after the killing began" or even to "call these crimes by their rightful name: genocide," and pledged to work "with the international community" to improve "our system for identifying and spotlighting nations in danger of genocidal violence."[12]

Such attitudes were also addressed in multilateral institutional contexts, as UN Secretary-General Kofi Annan (1999) – building on the work of Francis Deng in particular – advanced an integrated view of sovereignty as embodying not only the autonomy of a state, but also its responsibilities to its people, who possessed "individual sovereignty." Regional debates over collective security – for example, in African contexts – further foreshadowed the integration of these views in the construction of R2P, as the emergent African Union affirmed in its Constitutive Act the collective right to intervene "in respect of grave circumstances: war crimes, genocide and crimes against humanity."

These shifts also found expression in evolving debates among entrepreneurs and experts over the meaning of sovereignty – as policymakers sought to navigate between views of sovereignty as residing in states or individuals, and as a right or responsibility.[13] In this manner, Annan used his 2000 *Millennium Report* to pose the question, "if humanitarian intervention is, indeed, an unacceptable assault on sovereignty, how should we respond to a Rwanda, to a Srebrenica – to gross and systematic violations of human rights that affect every precept of our common humanity?" (quoted in ICISS, 2001: vii). In response, the Canadian government sponsored the ICISS which, in December 2001, produced its report, *The Responsibility to Protect.*

The report made deliberate use of ambiguity as it sought to shift the terms of debate from the "right to intervene" to a shared "responsibility to protect" – with co-chair Gareth Evans (2008: 42) trumpeting the importance of the new concept's ability to bridge interpretive gaps, as "new ideas, or old ideas newly expressed [might] … change the behavior of key policy actors." The ICISS (2001: 16) elaborated that the

> traditional language of the sovereignty –intervention debate – in terms of 'the right of humanitarian intervention' or the 'right to intervene' – is unhelpful [as it] … focuses attention on the claims, rights and prerogatives of the potentially intervening states much more so than on the urgent needs of the potential beneficiaries of the action.

Yet, as Bellamy (2011: 18) has noted, highlighting the controversial nature of the ideas under discussion, the report also spent the majority of its focus on intervention rather than prevention or reconstruction, advancing arguments with the intent of making future military operations easier – for instance, in suggestions that the permanent members of the Security Council refrain from exercising the veto "in matters where their vital state interests are not involved," and setting forth the possibility that if the Security Council failed to address a challenge, the General Assembly or regional organizations might step into the breach (ICISS, 2001: xiii).

Moreover, to the extent that it emerged against a backdrop of successes at humanitarian intervention, the ICISS Report arguably reflected a mounting confidence – as US and global fears of Somalian-style quagmires yielded to a new confidence inspired by the perceived success of Kosovo via the use of air power to attack the armed forces of suspect regimes, while largely sparing civilians. Such confidence in the use of force by powerful states to protect the weak was tainted by the policies and attitudes of the administration of US President George W. Bush in the aftermath of the terrorist attacks of September 11, 2001. The emerging certainty of the hegemonic US about the value of neoconservative-styled preemptive military intervention gave rise to further debate and generated the need for a more constructive ambiguity on the part of institutional agents. The 2005 World Summit thus saw the emergence of a new iteration of the R2P.

The 2000s: from Iraq to the World Summit

In the aftermath of September 11, 2001, Bush's (2001) construction of that day's attacks saw any reserve discarded in favor of an unambiguous moral clarity: "Every nation … now has a decision to make: either you are with us or you are with the terrorists." Following the failure to find weapons of mass destruction in Iraq, the administration redoubled its moral case with a renewed stress on democracy promotion. In his second inaugural address, Bush (2005) declared that "it is the policy of the United States to seek and support the growth of democratic movements and institutions in every nation and culture, with the ultimate goal of ending tyranny in our world."

This broad context of crusading unilateralism posed a challenge to R2P advocates from two directions. From one vantage, many states feared that the US would manipulate the concept of R2P to justify excessive interventionism. Their fears were reinforced by the Iraqi invasion, which was at least in part justified in R2P-style language of humanitarianism and the prevention of atrocities.[14] From an alternative perspective, US fears that international organizations might bind it to respond to mass atrocities where it had no interests in doing so also mounted, inspiring US resistance to R2P. Summing up this paradox, Special Adviser to the Secretary-General on R2P Edward Luck (2009: 11) noted that while "weaker states, particularly those that have suffered colonialism, are more prone to interpret sovereignty in territorial terms," major powers, "including most pointedly the United States, tend to see sovereignty in terms of freedom of policy choice and hence are reluctant to accept any interpretation of [R2P] that implies an automaticity of response."

By the mid-decade, the price of broad consensus on the R2P turned out to be a constructive ambiguity regarding both the collective responsibility of the international community to protect populations, and the means by which such protection might be provided. When R2P was put on the agenda of the UN 2005 World Summit of global leaders, claims about obligations to engage in collective action were muted. To be sure, in the Summit outcome document, states formally recognized their responsibility to protect *their own* populations from four crimes which are clearly defined in international law (genocide, war crimes, ethnic cleansing and crimes against humanity), and they also insisted that intervention to enforce this protection must be authorized by the Security Council. On these matters, clarity was precisely what the negotiating states demanded since they refused to agree to a principle that would provide scope for unauthorized interventions that were justified on vague humanitarian grounds, as they had recently seen in Iraq. However, with respect to the responsibilities of the international community, ambiguity was preferred over clarity. States accepted a collective responsibility to protect populations, but through a variety of means, spanning efforts to "encourage and help" states, or to pressure them to protect their populations through "appropriate diplomatic, humanitarian and other peaceful means." The responsibility to take military action was expressed in equally ambiguous terms: the international community was "prepared" to take collective action when states were "manifestly failing" in efforts to protect their populations, and the decision to act through the Security Council was to be undertaken "on a case-by-case basis" (UN General Assembly, 2005: 30). While some advocates of R2P, in particular ICISS co-chair Evans (2005), had lobbied for the endorsement of specific criteria for when intervention was appropriate, this stance was ultimately rejected by states.

Hegemonic and institutional ambivalence provided important sources of subsequent consensus and flexibility. In terms of US policy, the US Ambassador to the UN, John Bolton, ironically wound up enabling a constructive ambiguity at the World Summit – as US wariness helped ease multilateral concerns regarding hegemonic abuses. First, seeking to limit the scope for benchmarks requiring intervention, Bolton (2005) affirmed that "we do not accept that either the United Nations as a whole, or the Security Council or individual states, have an obligation to intervene under international law," elaborating that "a determination as to what particular measures to adopt in specific cases cannot be predetermined in the abstract but should remain a decision within the purview of the Security Council." Second, Bolton's concomitant preference for leaving discretion with the Security Council and not restricting the veto was shared not simply by the permanent five members, but also by a range of states who saw the veto as a source of restraint on great power interventionist tendencies (Luck, 2009: 19–20). Finally, this cognitive flexibility necessitated in turn a bureaucratic pragmatism that had the consequence of providing R2P supporters with a wide array of institutional options. As Luck (ibid.: 18) later noted, the WSOD recognized a "whole panoply of 'diplomatic, humanitarian and other peaceful means … in the [R2P] toolkit" as the international community recognized the need "to 'help,' 'assist,' 'support' and 'encourage' states in meeting their [R2P] obligations." Luck further noted that the Outcome Document stressed as well the "value of preventive measures," efforts to "build state capacity" and to assist "those which are under stress before crises and conflicts break out."

In sum, in the post-Iraq context, the construction of R2P was characterized less by unidirectional norm entrepreneurship aimed at clarity than by negotiation and adjustment to ongoing feedback aimed at securing consensus. Describing the shift from the ICISS to the World Summit, Bellamy (2011: 8–9) argued that eventual "consensus on [R2P] was not a matter simply of norm entrepreneurs selling the principle to states who, by dint of the persuasiveness of the argument, agreed to the new norm." Instead, the World Summit resulted in a norm that was "quite different to the concept proposed by ICISS in 2001 and it was precisely those changes that made consensus possible." To be sure, establishing the norm would only be a first step. Implementing the R2P was abetted by a retreat from hegemonic clarity, as the Obama administration's ambiguous pragmatism eased concerns regarding abuses of the R2P, providing foundations for the Libyan intervention, and domestic efforts at institutionalizing the R2P in US foreign policy practices.

Into the 2010s: from Libya to PSD-10

During the early years of the Obama administration, US foreign policy rhetoric was marked by a shift away from Bush-era crusading, both as Obama recognized the material limits to US power and as he espoused less a utopian vision of human perfectibility than a more pragmatic stress on human imperfections. These shifts eased international concerns regarding US interventionist excesses under the R2P, and so hegemonic restraint again created the space for norm progress, facilitating the Security Council's adoption of Resolution 1973 authorizing intervention to protect Libyan civilians. In domestic contexts, Obama's constructive ambiguity likewise limited domestic tensions. In contrast to prior administrations that were marked by stark divides over intervention, the Obama administration was marked by an interpretive openness that helped enable agreement – particularly among younger administration officials who had less invested in "grand debates" – on the Libyan intervention and provided a basis for a more incremental compliance with R2P norms.

Initially, Obama sought not simply to move away from Bush's crusading tendencies, but to mute traditional crusading-isolationist tensions within his administration, reflecting a broader generational impatience over ideological rigidities. Obama (2006: 37) had voiced impatience with the post-Vietnam calcifying of debate between "hawks" and "doves," observing that "in the elections of 2000 and 2004, I sometimes felt as if I were watching the psychodrama of the Baby Boom generation … played out on the national stage." Within the administration, this predisposition could be seen in a mutual tolerance of realists and idealists, as the former recognized the importance of legitimacy to power, and the latter recognized the importance of force in advancing principles (Mann, 2012: 67–72). Indeed, Obama's own early rhetoric often juxtaposed appeals to promote democratization or human rights with realist warnings. In his Nobel address, for example, Obama (2009) acknowledged that "force can be justified on humanitarian grounds," but emphasized the need for humility, arguing for a focus "on a more practical, more attainable peace, based not on a sudden revolution in human nature but on a gradual evolution in human institutions."

Yet, while Obama sought to maintain a restrained stance, even in the early aftermath of the June 2009 Iranian uprisings, this proved untenable. Over the next year, Obama shifted back to adopt a more assertive stance on democracy and humanitarian concerns. First, within the US, the response to Iran provoked a degree of backlash from supporters who had become disillusioned with the gap between Obama's rhetoric and policies. Mirroring Clinton's concerns from the 1990s that weakness in the face of Bosnian atrocities would undermine his standing, Obama's officials recognized domestic limits to excessive, even if justifiably realist, restraint. Second, the administration increasingly recognized that the Iranian uprisings might speak to regional aspirations and prepared to promote such possibilities. In August 2010, Obama sent a five-page memo to senior members of his foreign policy team, which noted "evidence of growing citizen discontent with the region's regimes" and stressed the need for US efforts to promote "political openness and improved governance" (quoted in Ignatius, 2011). Third, the administration began to shift in its public rhetoric, as Obama (2010) addressed the UN in September 2010, arguing that "we stand up for universal values because it's the right thing to do," condemning those who would "put human rights aside for the promise of short term stability." National Security Council adviser Benjamin Rhodes later argued that the initial restraint had been necessary, on the grounds that if the administration "had just come in, guns blazing on democracy … we'd have been less able to advocate for democracy" (quoted in Mann, 2012: 254). In this way, the administration's initial step back worked to advance an eventual step forward with respect to R2P.

The importance of these shifts intensified with the December 2010 outbreak of the Arab Spring. In key ways during the early Arab Spring, the Obama administration hewed to a cautious line, as it worked with the Egyptian military to engineer the ouster of Egyptian President Hosni Mubarak, tolerated the Bahraini crackdown aided by Saudi forces, and, as Power recalled, initially sought "to convince Gaddafi to act with restraint." However, as the administration came to the view that Gaddafi had "decided to crush this thing," debate intensified (ibid.: 283). In a mid-March 2011 meeting, against a backdrop of regional support from the Arab League and a French announcement that it would push for a Security Council resolution, key Obama officials met to discuss the US response. To some degree, the debate fell along Allison-styled lines, as "where agents stood" reflected "where they sat" – with US Secretary of Defense Robert Gates stressing the lack of vital interests and US Vice President Joseph Biden stressing the domestic political costs. Yet, a more meaningful divide was generational, as unambiguous institutional attachments had been superseded by the above-noted pragmatic integration of realist and idealist predispositions. As Lewis (2012) later described it, while the leading figures were opposed to intervention, "opinion at the fringes of the room … was different," as "several people sitting there had been deeply affected by the genocide in Rwanda." Summing up the meeting, Lewis concluded that "the junior staff made the case for saving the Benghazis."

Even as he supported the intervention, Obama did so in a way that muted concerns about US unilateralism, seeking not only Security Council approval but also – against the backdrop of the global financial crisis – a substantial European strategic and financial role, arguing that while the US "should not be afraid to act … the burden of action should not be America's alone" (Obama, 2011).[15] In advancing these views, Obama was also aware of domestic constraints, where he had to thread a needle by appearing neither too aggressive and prone to squander US resources, nor too passive as he might rely too much on allies. This danger could be seen in the negative reaction to administration claims to "lead from behind" in the Libya campaign (Lizza, 2011). Having implemented R2P in this high-profile manner, the administration then sought to apply it in more incremental ways. In August 2011, the administration issued PSD-10 on the protection of civilians and atrocity prevention (Jentleson, 2012: 407). These shifts were publicly heralded in Obama's (2012) address at the United States Holocaust Memorial Museum, in which he argued that "preventing mass atrocities and genocide is a core national security interest and a core moral responsibility of the United States." In this way, Obama can be seen as advancing R2P within the US domestic context at a deeper level, to enable an array of flexible responses.

The way NATO conducted the Libyan intervention proved deeply controversial. This prompted calls for further clarification of the grounds on which states may resort to military intervention in the name of R2P and for accountability of intervening states to the international community, most notably in a Brazilian proposal that states accept "Responsibility While Protecting" (RWP). Such developments are themselves part of the ongoing process by which norm feedback enables adjustment (see also Hunt, 2016).[16] Controversy about R2P has continued in the years since, particularly in the context of the horrific atrocities witnessed in Syria. However, as lamentable as the international response to the crisis in Syria has been, we tentatively suggest that the absence of a Libyan-style military intervention suggests some of the value of the flexibility incorporated into the 2005 agreement on R2P. While some offer as evidence of the impotence of R2P the fact that the 2005 agreement fails to "affirm the responsibility of international society to intervene in every case where human rights are being abused" (Murray, 2013: 28), such a rigid construction of obligations would have had disastrous consequences if implemented in Syria.[17] Some have asserted that the failure of the US and the broader international community to act with force to protect Syrian civilians shows that the R2P norm is ineffective due to its imprecision. But nothing would be gained from an international norm that locked states into undertaking an intervention that would likely do more harm than good (see Glanville, 2016).

Certainly, the international community is worthy of blame for failing to take various other measures short of military intervention in Syria that are provided for in the World Summit agreement. The international community has plainly failed to discharge its responsibility to protect in this case. Nevertheless, in contrast to the Syrian government's massacres of domestic opponents in the early 1980s – which went unchallenged by the international community – the fact that the UN and its member states have remained closely engaged with the Syrian crisis since 2011 and have continually felt the need to justify, excuse and deflect blame for their failure to resolve the crisis speaks to the importance of R2P in reshaping the behavior of actors.[18] There are observable benefits, therefore, in the fact that R2P is sufficiently ambiguous as to facilitate intervention to end atrocities in Libya, while not requiring an imprudent military intervention in Syria – even if the failure of the international community to orchestrate a concerted non-coercive effort to resolve the Syrian crisis remains deeply regrettable.

Conclusion: theoretical, historical and policy implications

In prevailing debates, IR scholars have widely stressed the benefits of clarity to norm development. Concomitantly, these scholars have cast ambiguity as limiting norm effectiveness. However, in this chapter, while not denying the virtues of clarity, we have suggested that *too much* clarity can impede agreement and necessary adjustment to the extent that it harms the development of a norm. We have argued that where agents accept a degree of ambiguity, this can enable consensus and flexibility over time, enabling adjustment as a "feedback loop" extends the life of a norm. Having advanced these theoretical claims, we argued for the benefits of ambiguity to post-Cold War debates over R2P as it enabled consensus and flexibility. To explain the initial construction of R2P, we first argued that ambiguity eased multilateral concerns regarding hegemonic excesses, and that debates over the meaning of Rwanda spurred a reconstruction of understanding of international responsibilities for the protection of populations. However, we second argued that the increasing resort to unilateral intervention – in Kosovo and Iraq – spurred a partial backlash, leading to efforts at the 2005 World Summit to further reconstruct R2P, clarifying the conditions for the resort to force, but also expressing the collective responsibilities of states in ambiguous terms so as not to deter powerful states such as the US from accepting the norm, as well as emphasizing the importance of efforts short of intervention that might work to protect civilians. Finally, we suggested that the Obama administration's acceptance of this more ambiguous R2P enabled both the Libyan intervention and also the administration's own institutionalization of intermediate measures aimed at atrocity prevention. Taken as a whole, this analysis suggests that it has been less clarity or precision than ambiguity that has enabled the establishment and incremental development of the R2P norm.

To conclude, we stress theoretical implications for approaches to the study of norm development, highlighting the ways in which the pursuit of ideational clarity may be not simply irrational, but may also contribute to the collapse of political orders. Where agents exhibit "ambiguity aversion" and systematically underrate the scope for interpretive variation, this may be seen as an inefficient use of information which may lead to strategically irrational choices and overconfidence in the scope for shaping others' behavior. From this perspective, theories of political development that stress the contributions of norm entrepreneurs to regime maintenance risk failing to recognize that efforts at maintenance and the limitation of debate may – as Skowronek (2011) argues – foreshadow the demise of political orders. Indeed, it is worth contrasting the rise of R2P with the fall of US neoconservatism over the last two decades. US neoconservatives possessed every material and cognitive advantage over advocates of R2P in terms of resources and clarity of purpose, and yet neoconservatives failed to anticipate that unambiguous assertions that "either you are with us, or you are with the terrorists" would undermine any broader consensus in advancing the war on terror (Ikenberry, 2004). In this light, it is not a little ironic that R2P has had more success in the battle of ideas – a contrast which suggests that as ambiguity enables an openness to interpretive differences, it can extend norm life cycles and forestall norm collapse.

Notes

1 This chapter is based on an argument about norm ambiguity developed in Widmaier and Glanville (2015). We explain later in this chapter what we mean when we refer to R2P as a "norm."

2 One might argue that ambiguity also contributes to "norm localization" as "local agents reconstruct foreign norms to ensure the norms fit with the agents' cognitive priors and identities" (Acharya, 2004: 241, 239). To maintain conceptual focus, however, we emphasize here the contributions of ambiguity to consensus, flexibility and adjustment.

3 The notion of a norm feedback loop has also been explored by Prantl and Nakano (2011). Similarities can also be detected in Acharya's (2013) notion of "norm circulation". See also the discussion of dynamic and non-linear norm evolution in the Introduction to this volume.

4 On the relationship between the domestic and international as it pertains to norm implementation, see Betts and Orchard (2014).

5 For a valuable work that grapples with questions of normative coherence, consistency and contestation with respect to R2P, see Welsh (2013).

6 The challenge for scholars, then, is one of interpretation as they seek to juxtapose the broader context of values and expectations with institutional and policy debates that arise from moments of crisis.

7 To put this in language that echoes the framework of Phil Orchard's Chapter 1, a constructive ambiguity can both enable adaptation in the interpreted content of a norm and also allow flexibility in application. To be sure, too much ambiguity can render a norm meaningless or utterly ineffective. But a constructive ambiguity can offer benefits that norm scholars have commonly overlooked.

8 UN Secretary-General Ban Ki-moon (2009) expounded the 2005 agreement in a 2009 report, where he divided R2P into three "pillars." We suggest that the first norm is encapsulated in Pillar One and the second norm entails a combination of Pillars Two and Three.

9 One well-known way in which the emphasis on normative clarity reduced the likelihood of humanitarian intervention in this period was the sharp distinction drawn between situations of genocide, which would generate an obligation on the US and

other powerful states to "do something," and situations short of genocide, which would not. For analysis, see Power (2002) and Glanville (2009).

10 For an R2P-insider's account of the impact of Rwanda and also Kosovo on the development of R2P, see Thakur (2016).

11 A similar story could be told about Srebrenica (Power, 2002).

12 Rwanda also motivated agents across administrations. When Samantha Power interviewed Susan Rice regarding her Clinton-era experiences, Rice recounted to her future Obama administration colleague, "I swore to myself that if I ever faced such a crisis again, I would come down on the side of dramatic action, going down in flames if that was required" (Power, 2001: 107–108).

13 On the historical development of sovereignty, a principle that has been subject to contestation since long before the end of the Cold War, see Glanville (2014).

14 Rice (2010: 51, 54–55), the former US Ambassador to the UN during the Obama administration, later lamented that "some defended the war in Iraq by invoking the Responsibility to Protect, a tactic that still casts a shadow on efforts to deepen the consensus around the R2P concept." Rice countered efforts to "conflate R2P with an unfettered right to intervention" on the grounds that R2P encompassed "a range of responses" spanning "early warning, analysis, and decision-making ... preventive diplomacy ... peacekeeping ... sanctions ... [and] peacebuilding [efforts]," all of which could reduce the need for more costly military intervention.

15 For more on the international normative context of the adoption of Resolution 1973 authorizing the Libyan intervention, see Glanville (2013 and 2016).

16 If our argument about the benefits of norm ambiguity is correct, it may provide grounds for the international community to exercise caution when considering such proposals for further clarification and specificity regarding the legitimate grounds for the resort to force, lest it facilitates a renewal of Rwandan-era debates about criteria that must be satisfied before action takes place, which can perversely hinder the protection of populations.

17 Of course, others might point to the danger of excessive norm flexibility, which can enable actors to shirk their international responsibilities or to reshape a norm in way that undermines its original purpose. For some discussion, see Sarah Teitt's Chapter 7 in this volume.

18 For refutation of claims about the irrelevance or death of R2P post-Libya and defense of its ongoing impact despite the clear failure to protect in Syria, see Bellamy (2014), Glanville (2016).

References

Abbott, K.W., Keohane, R.O., Moravcsik, A., Slaughter, A.-M. and Snidal, D. (2000). The Concept of Legalization. *International Organization*, 54(3), 401–419.

Acharya, A. (2004). How Ideas Spread: Whose Norms Matter? Norm Localization and Institutional Change in Asian Regionalism. *International Organization*, 58(2), 239–275.

Acharya, A. (2013). The R2P and Norm Diffusion: Towards a Framework of Norm Circulation. *Global Responsibility to Protect*, 5(4), 466–479.

Annan, K. (1999). Two Concepts of Sovereignty. *The Economist*, September 16. www.economist.com/node/324795

Ban, Ki-moon. (2009). Implementing the Responsibility to Protect. Available from: www2.ohchr.org/english/bodies/chr/special/docs/17thsession/SG_reportA_63_677_en.pdf

Barnett, M.N. (1997). The UN Security Council, Indifference, and Genocide in Rwanda. *Cultural Anthropology*, 12(4), 551–578.

Barnett, M.N. and Finnemore, M. (1999). The Politics, Power, and Pathologies of International Organizations. *International Organization*, 53(4), 699–732.

Bellamy, A.J. (2011). *Global Politics and the Responsibility to Protect: From Words to Deeds*. New York: Routledge.

Bellamy, A.J. (2014). *The Responsibility to Protect: A Defense*. Oxford: Oxford University Press.

Best, J. (2005). *The Limits of Transparency: Ambiguity and the History of International Finance*. Ithaca, NY: Cornell University Press.

Best, J. (2008). Ambiguity, Uncertainty, and Risk: Rethinking Indeterminacy. *International Political Sociology*, 2(4), 355–374.

Best, J. (2012). Ambiguity and Uncertainty in International Organizations: A History of Debating IMF Conditionality. *International Studies Quarterly*, 56(4), 674–688.

Betts, A. and Orchard, P. (2014). *Implementation and World Politics: How International Norms Change Practice*. Oxford: Oxford University Press.

Bolton, J. (2005). Dear Colleague, Letter, August 30. www.responsibilitytoprotect.org/files/US_Boltonletter_R2P_30Aug05[1].pdf

Bush, G.W. (2001). Text: President Bush Addresses the Nation. *Washington Post*, September 20. www.washingtonpost.com/wp-srv/nation/specials/attacked/transcripts/bushaddress_092001.html

Bush, G.W. (2005). Second Presidential Inaugural Address, January 20. www.americanrhetoric.com/speeches/gwbushsecondinaugural.htm

Clinton, W.J. (1993). Remarks to the 48th Session of the United Nations General Assembly in New York City. *The American Presidency Project*, September 27. https://2009-2017.state.gov/p/io/potusunga/207375.htm

Clinton, W.J. (1995). Public Papers of the Presidents of the United states: 1994 (in Two Books): Book I – January 1 to July 31, 1994. Washington, DC: US Government Printing Office.

Clinton, W.J. (1998). Remarks to the People of Rwanda, March 25. millercenter.org/the-presidency/presidential-speeches/march-25–1998-remarks-people-rwanda

Ellsberg, D. (1961). Risk, Ambiguity, and the Savage Axioms. *Quarterly Journal of Economics*, 75(4), 643–669.

Evans, G. (2005). The Responsibility to Protect: Evolution and Implementation, July 1. www.gevans.org/speeches/speech119.html

Evans, G. (2008). *The Responsibility to Protect: Ending Mass Atrocity Crimes Once and for All*. Washington, DC: Brookings Institution Press.

Finnemore, M. and Sikkink, K. (1998). International Norm Dynamics and Political Change. *International Organization*, 52(4), 887–917.

Glanville, L. (2009). Is "Genocide" Still a Powerful Word? *Journal of Genocide Research*, 11(4), 467–486.

Glanville, L. (2013). Intervention in Libya: From Sovereign Consent to Regional Consent. *International Studies Perspectives*, 14(3), 325–342.

Glanville, L. (2014). *Sovereignty and the Responsibility to Protect: A New History*. Chicago, IL: University of Chicago Press.

Glanville, L. (2016). Does R2P Matter? Interpreting the Impact of a Norm. *Cooperation and Conflict*, 51(2), 184–199.

Hunt, C.T. (2016). Emerging Powers and the Responsibility to Protect: Non-linear Norm Dynamics in Complex International Society. *Cambridge Review of International Affairs*, 29(2), 761–781.

ICISS (2001). *The Responsibility to Protect*. Ottawa: International Development Research Centre.

Ignatius, D. (2011). Obama's Low-key Strategy for the Middle East. *Washington Post*, March 6. www.washingtonpost.com/wp-dyn/content/article/2011/03/04/AR2011030404614.html

Ikenberry, G.J. (2004). The End of the Neo-conservative Moment. *Survival*, 46(1), 7–22.

Ikenberry, G.J. and Kupchan, C.A. (1990). Socialization and Hegemonic Power. *International Organization*, 44(3), 283–315.

Jentleson, B.W. (2012). The Obama Administration and R2P: Progress, Problems and Prospects. *Global Responsibility to Protect*, 4(4), 399–423.

Kahler, M. (2000). Conclusion: The Causes and Consequences of Legalization. *International Organization*, 54(3), 661–683.

Krook, M.L. and True, J. (2012). Rethinking the Life Cycles of International Norms: The United Nations and the Global Promotion of Gender Equality. *European Journal of International Relations*, 18(1), 103–127.

Lewis, M. (2012). Obama's Way. *Vanity Fair*, October. www.vanityfair.com/politics/2012/10/michael-lewis-profile-barack-obama

Lizza, R. (2011). The Consequentialist. *New Yorker*, May 2. www.newyorker.com/reporting/2011/05/02/110502fa_fact_lizza

Luck, E.C. (2009). Sovereignty, Choice, and the Responsibility to Protect. *Global Responsibility to Protect,* 1(1), 10–21.

Mahoney, J. and Thelen, K. (2010). A Theory of Gradual Institutional Change. *In:* Mahoney, J. and Thelen, K. (eds.). *Explaining Institutional Change: Ambiguity, Agency, and Power*, 1–37. Cambridge: Cambridge University Press.

Mann, J. (2012). *The Obamians: The Struggle Inside the White House to Redefine American Power.* New York: Viking.

Murray, R.W. (2013). Humanitarianism, Responsibility or Rationality? Evaluating Intervention as State Strategy. *In:* Hehir, A. and Murray, R.W. (eds.) *Libya: The Responsibility to Protect and the Future of Humanitarian Intervention*, 15–33. Basingstoke: Palgrave Macmillan.

Obama, B. (2006). *The Audacity of Hope: Thoughts on Reclaiming the American Dream.* New York: Crown.

Obama, B. (2009). A Just and Lasting Peace: Nobel Lecture, December 10. www.nobelprize.org/nobel_prizes/peace/laureates/2009/obama-lecture_en.html

Obama, B. (2010). Remarks by the President to the United Nations General Assembly, September 23. www.whitehouse.gov/the-press-office/2010/09/23/remarks-president-united-nations-general-assembly

Obama, B. (2011). Remarks by the President in Address to the Nation on Libya, National Defense University, Washington, DC, March 28. www.whitehouse.gov/the-press-office/2011/03/28/remarks-president-address-nation-libya

Obama, B. (2012). Remarks by the President at the United States Holocaust Memorial Museum, Washington, DC, April 23. www.whitehouse.gov/the-press-office/2012/04/23/remarks-president-united-states-holocaust-memorial-museum

Percy, S.V. (2007). Mercenaries: Strong Norm, Weak Law. *International Organization*, 61(2), 367–397.

Power, S. (2001). Bystanders to Genocide. *The Atlantic*, September, 84–108.

Power, S. (2002). *"A Problem from Hell": America and the Age of Genocide*. London: Flamingo.

Prantl, J. and Nakano, R. (2011). Global Norm Diffusion in East Asia: How China and Japan Implement the Responsibility to Protect. *International Relations*, 25(2), 204–223.

Reinold, T. (2011). The United States and the Responsibility to Protect: Impediment, Bystander, or Norm Leader? *Global Responsibility to Protect*, 3(1), 61–87.

Rice, S.E. (2010). Keynote Address to the 39th International Peace Institute on June 15, 2009. *In:* Winkler, H., Rod-Larsen, T. and Mikulaschek, C. (eds.) *The UN Security*

Council and the Responsibility to Protect: Policy, Process, and Practice, 50–56. 39th IP Vienna Seminar, Favorita Papers 01/2010, Vienna: Diplomatic Academy of Vienna.

Sandholtz, W. (2008). Dynamics of International Norm Change: Rules against Wartime Plunder. *European Journal of International Relations*, 14(1), 101–131.

Simmons, B.A. Dobbin, F. and Garrett, G. (2006). Introduction: The International Diffusion of Liberalism. *International Organization*, 60(4), 781–810.

Skowronek, S. (1993). *The Politics Presidents Make: Leadership from John Adams to George Bush.* Cambridge, MA: Belknap Press.

Skowronek, S. (2011). *Presidential Leadership in Political Time: Reprise and Reappraisal.* 2nd ed. Lawrence, KS: University Press of Kansas.

Thakur, R. (2016). Rwanda, Kosovo, and the International Commission on Intervention and State Sovereignty. *In:* Bellamy, A.J. and Dunne, T. (eds.) *The Oxford Handbook of the Responsibility to Protect*, 94–113. Oxford: Oxford University.

UN General Assembly (2005). *2005 World Summit Outcome*. www.un.org/en/development/desa/population/migration/generalassembly/docs/globalcompact/A_RES_60_1.pdf

Van Kersbergen, K. and Verbeek, B. (2007). The Politics of International Norms: Subsidiarity and the Imperfect Competence Regime of the European Union. *European Journal of International Relations*, 13(2), 217–238.

Widmaier, W.W. and Glanville, L. (2015). The Benefits of Norm Ambiguity: Constructing the Responsibility to Protect across Rwanda, Iraq and Libya. *Contemporary Politics*, 21(4), 367–383.

Wiener, A. (2004). Contested Compliance: Interventions on the Normative Structure of World Politics. *European Journal of International Relations*, 10(2), 189–234.

Welsh, J.M. (2013). Norm Contestation and the Responsibility to Protect. *Global Responsibility to Protect*, 5(4), 365–396.

Wendt, A. (1992). Anarchy is What States Make of It: The Social Construction of Power Politics. *International Organization*, 46(2), 391–425.

3 Telling the story of R2P

The emplotment of R2P in the UN Security Council's debates on Libya

Sassan Gholiagha and Bastian Loges

Introduction

Stories allow us to make sense of the world; it matters who tells a story and how they tell it. Analyzing stories and narratives enables us to understand normative realities of the narrators and to explain differences in perceptions and practices. This chapter takes ideas about narratives, stories, and the way and form a story is told, or short: its emplotment, to cast light on the Responsibility to Protect (R2P), and its simultaneous consolidation and contestation. Although literature on the status of R2P offers a variety of conceptualizations, ranging from R2P as a norm (Bellamy, 2006, 2011) to R2P as a concept (Wheeler and Egerton, 2009), to a doctrine (Arbour, 2008) or even a regime (see Orchard, Chapter 1 in this volume), with our focus on storytelling, these conceptual questions are secondary. However, by looking at the stories actors tell about R2P, we understand it, as many others do, as a "complex norm" (Welsh, 2013). Conceptually, our analysis is situated at the intersection of three different debates on norms and R2P. First, it builds in part on the existing literature on norm contestation (Hofius et al., 2014; Wiener, 2018; Deitelhoff and Zimmermann, 2018) and R2P (Welsh, 2013; Gholiagha, 2015; Labonte, 2016; Hunt and Orchard, the Introduction in this volume). However, this latter literature does not focus on the simultaneous consolidation of R2P that seems to take place at the same time (Hunt and Orchard, the Introduction in this volume). Second, we engage with the growing literature on the role of the UN Security Council (hereafter UNSC or Council) for the (missing) implementation of R2P (Loges, 2013; Morris, 2013; Adler-Nissen and Pouliot, 2014; Gifkins, 2016; Ralph and Gifkins, 2017). Third, we add to the literature on narrative and R2P that deals with strategic narrative, international order, and alliances (Miskimmon et al., 2013; Roselle, 2017; Levinger and Roselle, 2017). Even though we share this literature's empirical focus on the intervention in Libya and R2P, we nonetheless present a different perspective and integrate all three debates by examining R2P's contestation and consolidation as a norm from a storytelling account by asking: How can IR scholars make sense of the simultaneous consolidation and contestation of R2P?

To answer this question, we argue that simultaneous consolidation and contestation becomes analytically accessible through 'storytelling' as a conceptual lens. In narrative scholarship, how we tell a story provides ourselves and others with a specific "sense of purpose and place" (Patterson and Renwick Monroe, 1998: 321). This insight is relevant for diplomatic debates on R2P within the UNSC as well. How Council members craft their individual story and relate it to public narratives is instructive for answering our research question. By focusing on storytelling, we can also address three gaps in recent research on R2P. First, we foreground the interpretation that R2P as a normative prescription has changed considerably from its first installment in the report of International Commission on Intervention and State Sovereignty (ICISS) to Ban Ki-moon's account of R2P as a three-pillared concept. Second, we respond to R2P's status as a norm facing consolidation and contestation by referring to these different narratives as an explanation for its ambiguous status. Third, we underline the potential of a narrative approach in analyzing specific international processes of normative contestation and consolidation. We use the concepts of diplomatic storytelling, emplotment, and public narratives as repertoires to make sense of the consolidation but also the contestation of R2P at the same time via narrative practices. To demonstrate this, we provide a detailed empirical analysis of the deliberations in the UNSC on Resolution 1973, which authorized the use of force in Libya. We are aware of the critical accounts on whether R2P played a decisive role in the Council's decision to act in Libya (Morris, 2013; Hehir, 2018). However, we demonstrate in the following that actors referred – to varying degrees and in different ways – in their statements to public narratives on R2P, thus somewhat questioning these more critical works.[1]

Our analysis consists of two parts: first, we trace different 'public narratives' about R2P as "narratives of institutions or social formations" (Patterson and Renwick Monroe, 1998: 325). Specifically, we engage with the 2001 ICISS Report, the 2005 World Summit Outcome Document (WSOD), and the 2009 Report of the Secretary-General (ROSG), as the three most prominent public narratives on an R2P. Here, we largely rely on literary scholar Kenneth Burke's pentad (Burke, 1945) to analytically access the stories in these different public narratives (see the next subsection). Second, we apply the insights gained from this discussion to the debates inside the UNSC regarding Libya in 2011. Here, we demonstrate that diplomats utilize different public narratives as repertoires to compose their own story about R2P and that their emplotment also differs. Emplotment refers to the form and way a story is told; it means to present stories differently while nonetheless keeping the essence of the story (Abbott, 2007: 43; Fina and Georgakopoulou, 2012: 18). In the end, these stories diplomats tell about R2P in Libya help us to understand its simultaneous consolidation and contestation. Therefore, we also develop a heuristic to guide our analysis in order to observe different patterns of narrative divergence or convergence (see subsection on 'Emplotting R2P' below). A brief conclusion summarises the results of the chapter and provides an outlook on future research.

Narrating realities: story, plot and emplotment in context

We base our analysis on the broad perspective within narrative approaches that "social life itself is storied" (Somers and Gibson, 1994: 38). The narrative is an interaction of text, the narrator and the audience who, ultimately, organise much of their lives in narrative forms by reading, speaking or even thinking about reality. As Patterson and Renwick Monroe note: "We create and use narratives to interpret and understand the political realities around us. We do this as individuals and we do it as collective units, as nations and groups" (Patterson and Renwick Monroe, 1998: 315). For our analysis, the most relevant are so-called social narratives: they are "embraced by a group that also tells, in one way or another, something about the group" (Shenhav, 2015: 19) and relate in specific ways to more individual narratives. In order to address where and how individual stories refer to larger narratives, Somers and Gibson identify four dimensions of narrative: ontological, conceptual, public, and meta-narratives that represent different levels but are interrelated in practice. For our purpose, we are mostly interested in a specific type of social narrative: so-called 'public narratives' that capture the stories that institutions and social formations tell (Somers and Gibson, 1994: 61–63). Therefore, these public narratives are social by default and form potential repertoires for members of a specific social entity like the UNSC to draft their narratives accordingly.

Analytically, narrative approaches distinguish between story and plot: story is what a narrative is about, while plot refers to how this story is specifically told (Abbott, 2007: 39, Abbott, 2008: 16–20; Spencer, 2016: 16–17). In line with most of the literature, story is then primarily about the events, characters, and actions, resulting in a story's progression or its storyline. Implicitly, this assumes that stories usually have a beginning, a middle and an end (Jahn, 2008: 189; Abbott, 2008: 189). In contrast, plot is about the form, "logic or syntax" of narrative (Somers and Gibson, 1994: 60). The act of constructing or choosing a plot as the specific form to tell a story is called emplotment. Emplotment does not change a story as such. It presents stories differently but keeps their essence despite different choices in time, perspective or style. Accordingly, emplotting a story is as much a narrator's skill as it is a choice (Abbott, 2007: 43; Fina and Georgakopoulou, 2012: 18).

To systematically grasp narrative in its story dimension, we apply literary scholar Kenneth Burke's concept of a dramatistic pentad. Every narrative or story needs to rest on five specific elements: an act, a scene and one or more agents equipped with agency and purpose. The 'act' defines what kind of event took place; Burke explicitly includes thoughts or immaterial practices into his account of an act. 'Scene' refers to the situation or context in which the narrated act occurred. 'Agent', 'agency' and 'purpose' relate to the specific person or entity that acts, by naming the instruments used in the act and by presenting the supposed motives of the agents and their actions (Burke, 1945: XV).[2] Every narrative and story evolves round these five elements. Therefore, the following analytical frame that is also frequently applied in IR (Miskimmon et al., 2013: 5; Krebs, 2015: 12–13, 52–54; Miskimmon et al., 2017: 6–7) guides the analysis of the public narratives on R2P.

Table 3.1 Analytical frame based on Kenneth Burke's pentad

Act	What is happening?
Scene	Where is the action taking place? What is the background to action?
Agent	Who is acting?
Agency	What means or instruments do agents employ?
Purpose	What are the agents' motives or reasons for action?

Source: Based on (Burke, 1945).

In analyzing the plot, we focus on three distinct features of a story's form: the sequence or order of the narrative arrangement, the style or tone and, lastly, the relational implications that transcend the story as a pure form of text by bringing in implied audiences. First, stories can be told from different perspectives or angles, chronologically but also in more artificial ways by pausing progress, highlighting specific episodes or even going backward in time. Consequently, how a story is emplotted regarding sequence and order is the more structural dimension of a narrative's formal arrangement (Somers and Gibson, 1994: 59–60). A second important element of emplotment is composition in tone or style. Every text has its specific arrangement since narrators can choose to sound funny or scientific, set their story in a dramatic or a moral tone, or use metaphors or slang (Abbott, 2008: 20, 238; Fina and Georgakopoulou, 2012: 22). Third, plot includes an assessment of the implied audience: Stories are always told to someone and, therefore, implicitly or explicitly imply a relation between narrator and audience. Narratology has addressed this issue by referring to different types of implied, intended or postulated readers that could be found in literary text. Therefore, this relation underlines an anticipation of the different ways an audience could interpret that narrative (Rabinowitz, 2008: 30; Bode, 2014: 344). Thus, for narrative accounts, not only the story but also the form of a narrative – its emplotment – is relevant for our analysis.

Emplotting R2P: three public narratives on responsible action

The history and development of R2P can be described largely with reference to three documents:

a) The 2001 report of the ICISS, initiated by the Canadian government, that came up with the idea to frame the field of mass atrocities, sovereignty and humanitarian intervention as a "responsibility to protect;"
b) The UN's WSOD of 2005 where diplomats and state leaders reformulated the core ideas of the ICISS Report;
c) The first ROSG on R2P that was released by Ban Ki-moon in 2009 and became an annual practice.

In the following, we reconceptualize all three as public narratives with their discrete stories and plots to shed light on their similarities and differences, using the analytical frame developed above. As mentioned before, public narratives are stories and their emplotments, created by collective actors like institutions. Regarding R2P and the international community, we understand these three documents as the most prominent narratives to date. All of them furthered the discourse on R2P and gave it new momentum but also a slightly new direction.[3]

ICISS and the story of three responsibilities

In the 2001 ICISS Report, the authors began with the question of whether there was a right to humanitarian interventions, a question broadly discussed in the literature (Holzgrefe and Keohane, 2003). However, the ICISS explicitly focused not on a possible right to intervene, but on the responsibility of different actors to protect people from suffering. This shift was based on "the idea that sovereign states have a responsibility to protect their own citizens from avoidable catastrophe […] but that when they are unwilling or unable to do so, that responsibility must be borne by the broader community of states" (ICISS, 2001: VII). Furthermore, the report identifies "respect for human rights" as a "responsibility of international relations" (ibid.: 6) and outlines in detail how this responsibility could and should manifest. Arguing from the understanding that the protection of vulnerable populations is of central importance to (international) politics, the objective of the report is to clarify who has a responsibility to do so, in which situations and by which means. It also identifies three distinct but interrelated responsibilities – a

Table 3.2 Analytical frame for the ICISS Report

Act	Human suffering challenges international practice since interventions are problematic when they are carried out (sovereignty) as well as when they were missing (human rights). Explicitly the report refers to Bosnia and Somalia as well as to Rwanda and Kosovo.
Scene	The setting is predominantly international. Although states are of concern as well, the wording, quantity and historical background are more concerned with international responses to human suffering. The appropriate arena for action is the UNSC, but also the GA in its Uniting for Peace capacity as well as regional bodies.
Agent	The international community, especially the UNSC.
Agency	At large, the report separates preventive instruments from reactive instruments and those used for rebuilding. Special emphasis is placed on the agency of the members of the UNSC and here especially the P5 to use their veto responsibly. Moreover, if a reaction in military terms is necessary, it should be precautious and rightly authorized.
Purpose	In general, the report points at responsibility as the reason for action. More specifically, there should be a "just cause" for action (large-scale loss of life or ethnic cleansing). The motive for action is to fulfill "the requirements of those who need or seek assistance" (ICISS, 2001: 18).

Source: Authors.

"Responsibility to Prevent," a "Responsibility to React" and a "Responsibility to Rebuild" – that together represent responses to discrete phases of an ideal-typical conflict cycle (ibid.: 19, 29, 39). From a narrative perspective, the following table summarizes the results of applying the analytical frame of the pentad introduced above to the ICISS Report.

Regarding emplotment, the ICISS Report is chronological as it follows a conflict cycle with its different phases from prevention via reaction to rebuilding. With regard to tone or style, it is largely idealistic in presenting moral arguments and trying to lay out a consensus to reconcile sovereignty and human rights. By focusing on the notion of sovereignty as responsibility, the report engages in ambitious agenda-setting and makes a fundamentally moral argument in favor of a cosmopolitan vision of humankind as a responsive community. We also find an implicit relation between the ICISS as the narrator and the international community as the audience. To sum up: The ICISS Report is emplotted as a moral story, told by intellectuals to humankind, whose focus is on a universal responsibility to stop human suffering and protect vulnerable people.

The 2005 World Summit and the story of two chapters

The literature on R2P has provided an in-depth account of the negotiations during the World Summit in 2005 (Bellamy, 2006; Strauss, 2009) that ultimately led to the inclusion of R2P into the well-known §138 and §139 in the WSOD (UN, 2005). These two short paragraphs tell a story about R2P that differs from the one in the ICISS Report. In general, the focus is on two issues: first, R2P is interpreted from a perspective that stresses a fit between R2P and the UN Charter or other essential elements of international law. It explicitly mentions Chapters VI and VII in the Charter to emphasize that any action to protect vulnerable populations must be in accordance with the Charter. Priority should lie on non-forceful measures, and the importance of regional engagement is emphasized. Moreover, it is cautious about the use of force, which the UN Security Council shall consider on a "case-by-case basis" only (UN, 2005: §139). Second, the WSOD underlines that R2P consists of two respective responsibilities. The primary responsibility lies with each state to protect its population from genocide, war crimes, ethnic cleansing and crimes against humanity. The responsibility of the international community is to take over in case a state "manifestly fails" its responsibility and is "unwilling or unable" to fulfill it (ibid.). The following table presents the WSOD from the narrative perspective of our analytical framework.

The WSOD story of R2P is told not in terms of 'security' but of 'human rights' according to the section under which R2P appears in the document. This is surprising since §139 in particular has very explicit references to Chapters VI and VII of the UN Charter, which is concerned with essential questions of international peace and security. Also, the WSOD story establishes a sequence not based on conflict phases but levels of escalation and forceful reaction by the UNSC due to the legal regulations in the Charter. By referring to international

Table 3.3 Analytical frame for the WSOD

Act	States declare to be bound to protect populations from four specific situations of harm (genocide, war crimes, ethnic cleansing and crimes against humanity). Only if a state "manifestly fails" to protect their population shall the international community be prepared to take responsible action (Chapter VI and VII) on a case-by-case basis.
Scene	The setting is predominantly national as the first paragraph with its focus on nation states and the supportive character of international action in the second column indicates. Thus, only a secondary scene is set internationally that delegates appropriate action (if necessary) to the UNSC and further considerations to the UNGA.
Agent	Individual states are seen as the central agents. The UNSC (where necessary in coordination with regional organizations) may act in a supportive or complementary matter only as a last resort.
Agency	Regarding agency, namely the specific instruments, the WSOD stays rather vague, referring to "appropriate and necessary means."
Purpose	Four specific reasons for national (and to a lesser degree international) action: genocide, war crimes, ethnic cleansing and crimes against humanity. International reactions are only necessary if a state fails manifestly in its responsibility or when peaceful means were unsuccessful. The motive is to act responsibly but also by "bearing in mind the principles of the Charter and international law" (United Nations, 2005: §139).

Source: Authors.

crimes codified in international criminal law, both paragraphs share a very formal, legalistic tone.

At the same time, it is told in a 'we'-narration that leaves open to interpretation whether this 'we' is referring to the international community as a community of independent states or to the UN as a highly organized arena of programs, bureaucracies and states. In our view, these references support an interpretation preferring the national to the international level. Generally, this emplotment streamlines R2P into a UN story by translating the moral ICISS argument into the terminology and logic of the UN as an intergovernmental organization. To sum up: this is the intergovernmental short story, told by states to states with a focus on rather established legal commitments than moral responsibilities.

Ban Ki-moon and the story of the three pillars of R2P

In 2009, then-Secretary-General Ban Ki-moon published the first report on R2P, a practice that has become regular from then on (Ban, 2009). In his report, he tells a story of three pillars of R2P, with the explicit aim of operationalizing R2P for the organization and its human rights, security, and humanitarian institutions, bodies and agencies. However, by aiming for the implementation of R2P into the UN, he gave the concept a new logic: Instead of three responsibilities or Charter references, it is now a story of three distinct pillars on which R2P rests. Pillar One consists of the responsibility of each state to protect its population, as outlined in §138 of the WSOD. Pillar Two assigns responsibility to the international community to support states in their Pillar One responsibility. Finally, Pillar Three enshrines the responsibility of the international community to react, should a state manifestly fail its responsibility (ibid.: 31–32). The table below (Table 3.4) presents the report as a story, relying again on the analytical frame developed above.

The narrative of the ROSG is a story about operationalizing the very condensed story that was told in the WSOD but also mixing it with normative and moral reminders through references to the ICISS Report and the failures of the 1990s. This emplotment takes up the intergovernmental story formulated in the short paragraphs of the WSOD that focuses on states but gives it a new sequence or order: It is neither based on an ideal type of conflict and its phases nor the sequence of different chapters of the Charter but gives the composition a structure based on three pillars. In a requesting, sometimes pleading tone the Secretary-General urges the member states to follow the UN's example and implement the pillars quickly and comprehensively, critically

Table 3.4 Analytical frame for the ROSG on the three pillars

Act	Heads of state committed to the WSOD to support the protection of people facing four specific international crimes. Now the operationalization and implementation of these commitments are needed. The ROSG lays out a roadmap to do so but is also a reminder of the moral contents of the concept.
Scene	The story is set inside the UN as an intergovernmental but also as a transnational organization. Therefore, the first pillar is a nation-state dominated stage. The second pillar involves different fora, bodies and agencies inside or associated with the UN, such as the Human Rights Council, the UN Development Programme or the International Criminal Court. Therefore this draws a rather transnational scene. The third pillar is set inside the intergovernmental politics of the UNSC.
Agent	States are set as the most important actors in two ways: First, as the bearer of their individual responsibility. Second, as part of the intergovernmental UN where they must fulfill their responsibility as well (by assisting other states, acting quickly and decisively). Also, the UN as a transnational organization and thus the UNSG has responsibilities towards better implementation (and is faster in doing so than the states).
Agency	The report names numerous instruments to establish R2P via the three pillars, ranging from inclusive political systems to the collective use of force. However, most of them need better implementation or more consistent application.
Purpose	UNSG aims at bringing the WSOD commitment into reality but also at reminding of the origins of R2P (failure in the 1990s, genocide, etc.). The motives and thresholds for action by the member states remain unchanged: protect people through good national practices and, on a case-by-case basis, assist or even sanction/intervene.

Source: Authors.

referring to missing political will in resources and reliability (ibid.: 32). Here, his tone is more normative than a pure operationalization would require. In short: this is an operational as much as a moral story, told by a bureaucrat to teach states.

Comparing the public narratives on R2P

A comparison of these three narratives indicates that all inform us about R2P as 'the act' but differ by shifting focus between protection and responsibility. Where the ICISS narrative takes a moral R2P for granted in spelling out different aspects of protection in detail, the other narratives clarify who has a (primary) responsibility to protect. Moreover, the setting of their specific story varies: With ICISS it is an international background, whereas WSOD argues predominantly from a national perspective, while the ROSG understands R2P as a common responsibility shared by national state actors and international institutions of the UN system. These differences are mirrored with regard to the importance of specific actors, and the agency outlined: Where the ICISS Report names specific fields of protection and suggests what responsible practice shall look like in different phases of the conflict cycle, the WSOD stays rather vague with regard to specific instruments. In comparison, the ROSG has the most detailed but also the most politically challenging suggestions by outlining how R2P could be implemented and mainstreamed within the organization. With regard to purpose, all R2P narratives share a focus on responsible action but

Table 3.5 Comparison of the stories in the three public narratives

	ICISS (2001)	*WSOD (2005)*	*ROSG (2009)*
Act	Moral responsibility to stop human suffering and protect people	The legal obligation to protect populations from specific international crimes	Implementation of the commitment made by states in the WSOD
Scene	International (UNSC, GA, Regional Organizations)	National, international only on a case-by-case basis when it comes to actions under Chapter VII	National and international, in the form of the UN as an intergovernmental and transnational organization
Actor	International community	Individual states; UNSC as a last resort	Responsible states and the UN
Agency	Some specific instruments with regard to the three responsibilities	Vague instruments	Many specific instruments used by states and UN agencies and bodies
Purpose	Responsible action to protect people	Responsible action in light of the UN Charter and international law	Responsible action regarding the three pillars

Source: Authors.

Table 3.6 Comparison of the plots in the three public narratives

	ICISS (2001)	*WSOD (2005)*	*ROSG (2009)*
Sequence and order	Based on an idealized conflict cycle represented via three responsibilities	Based on the chapters and logic of the UN Charter, especially Chapter VI and VII	Based on the three pillars that were developed to implement R2P
Style and tone	Propulsive/emotional: moral tone to generate acceptance of the new concept	Dispassionate/formal: Legal tone to underline the commitment	Requesting/pleading: Bureaucratic tone to generate support for implementation
Implied relation between narrator and audience	Cosmopolitan: from intellectuals to humankind	Equal: states to states	Admonishing: teacher to students

Source: Authors.

understand reasons and motivations to be based on three different backgrounds: a will to protect people, a need to be in line with international law and practice when doing so, and a division of labor in order to shoulder the responsibility to protect in practice.

The three narratives also differ strikingly in terms of emplotment. All three are sequential but with different backgrounds: from a stylized conflict cycle via the progress of collective measures within the UN Charter to the complexities of a shared responsibility between the national and the international sphere, namely the UN. Their style and tone differ considerably as well: From ICISS's moral and emotional use of language to WSOD's rather formal or legalistic style to Ban Ki-moon's bureaucratic but morally requesting or pleading tone. However, the three do not share a common starting point of narration and hence imagine their audience differently. Whereas the ICISS is not part of the intergovernmental world and thus argues from the narrative point of the international community, the WSOD and the ROSG understand themselves as narrations from the diplomatic realm.

In sum, these three public narratives of R2P not only tell three different stories with their specific emplotment but represent a repertoire to choose from when crafting diplomatic stories inside the UN. To underline our point empirically, we now turn to diplomatic storytelling in the UNSC and the 2011 decision to authorize the use of force in Libya via Resolution 1973.

Diplomatic storytelling as a situated practice: the consolidation and contestation of R2P inside the UNSC

In general, we understand storytelling as a practice navigating between a more structural component (public narratives) and a more individual one (specific emplotment). Our approach is thus rooted in a constructivist ontology, which assumes the co-constitutiveness of agency and structure (Wendt, 1987: 360). We also assume that each narrative representation indicates different degrees of contestation and consolidation by organizing these components in a specific relation. Although public narratives embody alternative stories and emplotments, thereby accentuating different aspects of R2P, they form in sum the general narrative repertoire that is collectively available and will be reactivated whenever an actor tells a story about R2P inside the UNSC. However, the consolidation and contestation of R2P within the Council varies with different emplotments. From a macro-perspective on the Council as a whole, members facilitate contestation when referring to different public narratives but further consolidation by using the same narrative collectively. In this respect, recent IR literature questioned how strategically plotted narratives become dominant in discourse despite a general narrative contestation in the political realm (Miskimmon et al., 2013; Krebs, 2015; Miskimmon et al., 2017). Their findings implicitly underline our reading of consolidation as a situation where a specific narrative is shared widely within a community. Similar patterns of concordance and dissonance appear at the microlevel of rhetoric when Council members emplot their stories. Public narratives need not be applied coherently and totally, sometimes they will be combined creatively. Also, on other occasions, states will not stick to R2P-narratives but mix it with other stories (national ones, professional ones, autobiographical ones) or use different plots. This broadens avenues for contestation in a mosaic of consolidation.

Therefore, we will focus empirically on the different methods diplomats use to craft their R2P story inside the UNSC. By deliberately using public narratives on R2P in strategic ways, diplomats choose their storylines in relation to already established narratives within the international community but also regarding their national interests and identities. In recent IR literature, Subotic (2016), Berenskoetter (2014), as well as Innes and Steele (2014) draw on autobiographical storytelling by states, especially in phases of ontological insecurity. Under these instances, storytelling aims at reaching two interconnected goals: to communicate worldviews, interests or solutions to others but also to assure themselves of their collective identity (Subotic, 2016: 616). These studies share the assumption that when actors emplot a story, they are not restricted to any specific range of content or form. On the contrary, they are free to choose from a repertoire of social narratives in individual and creative ways. Thus, they pick the whole story (act, scene, agent, agency and purpose) or aspects of it, apply the same plot as the public narrative or give it a very different sequence, tone or relation to an audience. Here, the strategic calculation is crucial to a narrative's composition due to its effects regarding the persuasion of others while aiming at a new political consensus (Polletta et al., 2011: 123; Berenskoetter, 2014: 270–274). Therefore, states as storytellers act individually and strategically in the first place. Nonetheless, storytelling remains always situated in a specific setting and is therefore deeply social: By telling their stories people must refer to a "repertoire of available social, public, and cultural narratives" (Somers and Gibson, 1994:

Table 3.7 Consolidation and contestation

Contestation / *Consolidation*	*High*	*Low*
High	Shared Narrative, conflicting Story and Plot	Shared Narrative, Story and Plot
Low	Conflicting Narrative, Story and Plot	Conflicting Narrative, shared Story and Plot

Source: Authors.

39; see also: Gadinger et al., 2014: 19, 27; Spencer, 2016: 32–35). It is the total of ontological, conceptual, meta or public narratives that narrators with their individual stories and plots collectively point to. These resonate with social narratives since the world is "made" of narrations and actors must locate themselves narratively in this world (Somers and Gibson, 1994: 59; Krebs, 2015: 12).

The analytical potential of narratives for the simultaneous contestation and consolidation of R2P lies especially in this interactive account of storytelling: Narratives are found in collective situations of reasoning and decision-making at different levels, with different actors in different roles ranging from narrators to audiences. So, when diplomats present their opinions inside an international forum like the UNSC, we see individual choices made against a collective repertoire in the narrative background. This individual storytelling or emplotment is constituted by collectively held public narratives but also reconstitutes them by establishing new webs of stories, new relations of story and plot, and new forms of emplotment (Fina and Georgakopoulou, 2008: 383; Krebs, 2015: 11). As the table above summarizes, it is that interplay between these three components that is instructive of whether we find high or low consolidation and contestation. This interplay then also can provide us with an analytical frame in which the apparent puzzle of a simultaneous consolidation and contestation is solved.

As we will demonstrate in the following part, the stories diplomats tell in the UNSC chamber help us to better understand the simultaneous consolidation and contestation of R2P. Therefore, we reconstruct the different stories they tell and analyze which narrative(s) diplomats draw on.

Telling the story of R2P and Libya

The development leading to the passing of Resolution 1973 authorizing the use of force against the Libyan government is well documented elsewhere (Bellamy, 2011; Adler-Nissen and Pouliot, 2014; Gifkins, 2016, Puri, 2016: 59–103 for an account of the Indian representative at the UN at the time; in this volume see the chapter by Glanville and Widmaier, Chapter 2), as is the 'Arab Spring' context of the developments in Libya (Wilkens, 2015). Following calls from various regional actors (Arab League, 2011; African Union Peace and Security Council,

2011; Organisation of Islamic Cooperation, 2011) and a UNSC resolution referring the situation in Libya to the International Criminal Court (UNSC, 2011b), the Council met on March 17, 2011 to discuss the situation in Libya again and passed Resolution 1973, with Brazil, China, Germany, India and Russia abstaining (UNSC, 2011a: 4).

As the following analysis demonstrates, different actors refer to different public narratives through the specific story and its emplotment they employ. Methodologically, we used the public narratives as quasi-ideal types, meaning that the empirical analysis below reveals that actors pick elements from different public narratives in specific combinations and also add individual issues to their narrative. In order to illustrate this, we have assessed several statements within the meeting document of the meeting in which the UNSC passed Resolution 1973. We begin with those states that draw on one public narrative as their central repertoire. Then, we present examples of states which draw on different public narratives. We end with those states that instead draw on national narratives and not on the public ones we identified. The states we cover in our analysis include all P5, all states who abstained, and Lebanon as a state from the Arab world. What becomes obvious is that all of these states, regardless of which public narratives they draw on and regardless of which additional narratives they make use of, do not contest R2P in principle. This observation is noteworthy as it indicates that, while contestation exists about R2P, none of the states in the UNSC deliberations about Libya rejects R2P as such.

States who draw on one public narrative: France, Lebanon, and the USA

With regards to the emplotment, France tells a story of change and opportunity that the Arab Spring presents and juxtaposes this with the situation in Libya. It describes how various international actors responded to the situation in Libya through a number of peaceful measures. Because these measures failed, and Libya failed in its responsibility to protect its population, the international community had to take over. The French statement closes with a passionate call to all members of the international community:

> We do not have much time left. It is a matter of days, perhaps even hours. Every hour and day that goes by means a further clampdown and repression for the freedom-loving civilian population, in particular, the people of Benghazi. Every hour and day that goes by increases the burden of responsibility on our shoulders.
>
> (Ibid.: 3)

Furthermore, France tells this as an international story. Here, the international community is a community of humankind. Thus, France's call for a need to react directly links to the idea of the responsibility to react in the ICISS Report. Finally, protection is central and needs to be granted. Overall, we see a clear reference to moral responsibility and the need to fulfill this responsibility as an international community. In its emplotment, France thus relies largely on the public narrative of the ICISS Report.

Lebanon tells the story beginning with Libya and violence committed against civilians. It applauds the UNSC taking action and also refers to the ICC. Furthermore, it points to other UN bodies and their work (UNGA, HRC). Lebanon also reiterates a statement made earlier that calls for the Security Council to "assume its responsibility" (ibid.: 3). Interestingly, Lebanon, in its statement, hopes for a deterrent effect of the resolution, pointing to the idea of prevention. It also emphasizes the importance of regional actors, especially the Arab League. It closes with a statement hoping that the resolution will provide a "better future" for Libya, thus referring to the need to rebuild (ibid.: 4). What we find in this emplotment is several references to the public narrative of the ROSG, including the need to take responsible action in line with the three pillars, and through the UN and its various bodies and agencies.

In its statement, the USA makes clear that the UNSC responds to the Libyan people in need. The US representative Susan Rice outlines how the resolution passed is in line with proper procedures of the UNSC and the Charter. She begins her story with reference to the previous resolution on Libya, detailing how Libya failed to respond to this resolution. Rice then embeds the current resolution in calls of regional actors, namely the Arab League. Also, there is a clear focus on the content of the resolution and what it is supposed to achieve. The way the US representative tells the story, this was the inevitable outcome of the development in Libya and the reasoning is rather bureaucratic-formalistic. This is the UNSC acting, based on the failure of all peaceful means previously employed and using Chapter VII as a last resort. Thus, the US, in its emplotment, clearly follows the public narrative we find in the WSOD and the pathway it lays out for the application of R2P. This becomes especially evident in the US Statement, which refers to the Council acting under Chapter VII. The following quote is a strongly worded version of the "unable or unwilling" phrase we find in the WSOD: "But Colonel Al-Qadhafi and those who still stand by him continue to grossly and systematically abuse the most fundamental human rights of Libya's people" (ibid.: 5).

States who combine creatively: Germany, Russia, Brazil and the UK

Germany refers in its statement to the need for a political solution and argues all judicial and economic measures should be exhausted before turning to force. For Germany, the use of force is always a difficult decision to make, and in the case of Libya, Germany did not support it. Germany thus largely builds its emplotment of the public narrative we find in the WSOD (ibid.). Germany also points to the risk of military intervention, using a more cautious approach to the use of force, which fits its national narrative: "Decisions on the use of military force are always extremely difficult to take. […] We see great risks" (ibid.). This statement also draws on the WSOD idea of first making use of all peaceful means available to fulfill the international community's R2P before employing the use of force. Here Germany especially points to sanctions (ibid.).

Russia chooses to abstain instead of vetoing the resolution because it agrees that the attacks on civilians had to stop and respects the request of the Arab League. However, it could not support the resolution, because in its view it had moved away too far from the request of the Arab League and was not discussed properly: "[…] work on that document [the draft resolution] was not in keeping with standard practice in the Security Council" (ibid.: 8). Here, Russia relies on issues of the proper operationalization of R2P within the UN and thus relies on the RSOG public narrative. At the same time, Russia would have preferred an "immediate ceasefire" (ibid.) and is cautious against any use of force, thus relying on the idea of the use of force as the last resort we find in the WSOD.

Brazil relies on a reference to a national narrative by emphasizing that despite its abstention "it stands in solidarity with all movements in the region expressing legitimate demands for better governance, more political participation, economic opportunities and social justice" (UNSC, 2011a). At the same time, it is very cautious about the use of force, fearing that it would not help to achieve the goal of "[…] the immediate end to violence and the protection for civilians" (ibid.: 6). This statement is in line with the WSOD narrative of using the use of force as a last resort. Brazil also made the same point Russia did, pointing out that the resolution had moved away too far from the call of the Arab League. In addition, Brazil feared that the use of force could be harmful to other popular movements in the region (ibid.). We thus find a mix of a national narrative and the WSOD public narrative.

The UK, in its statement, focuses on the need of the UNSC to act and makes clear that the situation is one the international community had to deal with in order to protect civilians through all necessary means. It also emphasizes that the international community comes together to act. The UK states that they are willing to "shoulder their responsibility" together with "partners in the Arab world" and NATO (UNSC, 2011a: 4). Thus, the UK mostly bases its emplotment on the public narrative we find in the WSOD but also includes elements from the ICISS public narrative.

States who draw on a national narrative: India and China

India argues that there is not sufficient information available and points to lack of clarity on how the mandate will be operationalized. They end with a call to the Libyan authorities to cease fire and protect the civilian population. India's statement includes a reference to a categorical rejection of the use of force, hence referring to their national narrative (UNSC, 2011a: 6; again, see Puri, 2016: 59–103 for a detailed analysis of the situation in Libya from an Indian perspective). China refers to its general position of following the Charter and the relevant norms. It also refers to its general position not to use force. They close with reference to the Arab League's wish of a no-fly zone which they respect (UNSC, 2011a: 10).[4] Both India and China thus refer to national positions and narratives that they apply to the situation at hand.

In conclusion, we see that actors refer to different public narratives, but also draw on additional national narratives. What comes to the fore here are moments of consolidation, as no actor in the UNSC meeting contests R2P on fundamental grounds. The debate does not question whether Libya or the international community has a responsibility to protect as such. Also, there is a consensus that the situation in Libya constituted a threat to international peace and security with grave implications for the Libyan population regarding international law. Thus, the debate instead focuses on thresholds between Chapters VI and VII of the UN Charter and the different pillars of the ROSG, debating the proper actors and means of protection. At the same time, R2P remains contested, as actors cannot settle on a common narrative in the face of a severe humanitarian crisis, as the debate on the proper response to the situation in Libya demonstrates.

Conclusion

Our chapter asked how IR scholars can make sense of the simultaneous consolidation and contestation of R2P? To answer this question, we argued that the concurrence of consolidation and contestation becomes analytically accessible through 'storytelling' as a conceptual lens. A closer look at both the public narratives of R2P and the debates in the UNSC on Libya in 2011 provided us with empirical evidence for this argument. Members of the UNSC compose their story in relation to the repertoire of public narratives in a specific configuration, which discloses a mosaic of instances for the consolidation but also contestation of R2P.

In our two-tiered analysis, we demonstrated that analyzing the development of R2P through the lens of storytelling reveals a first instance for contestation or consolidation. Understood as public narratives, the three key documents, namely the ICISS Report from 2001, the WSOD from 2005, and the Report of the Secretary-General from 2009, clearly outline different stories and different plots with similar and sometimes overlapping storylines, but also with narrative tensions. For example, with regard to 'scene' or the appropriate level of action, these narratives differ, ranging from an international account (ICISS) to rather bottom-up understandings of R2P that favor the national level in answering protection needs (WSOD). Also, the ICISS narrative focuses exclusively on people in need of protection while the other two narratives are concerned with institutional and legal context as well, namely international law or the three discrete pillars of implementation of R2P within the UN. However, we also see common aspects of all three narratives. In particular, the acknowledgment that people are entitled to essential protections, and that sometimes even the international sphere needs to address shortcomings in protection, is central to these public narratives.

Those instances for contestation and consolidation from public narratives were amplified through individual narrative practices as our second tier of analysis indicates. The ways in which diplomats craft their stories within the UNSC in the debates on Resolution 1973 revealed differing versions regarding act, scenes, actors or purposes, implicates alternative plot beginnings and/or endings, and thus disruptions within specific stories but also in the narratives practices of the UNSC as a whole. Explicitly, while some members composed their story based on one specific narrative, others built their story in a pick-and-choose-manner or applied aspects of other narratives, furthering instances for convergence or divergence in storytelling. In the end, the relation between a repertoire of different, but nonetheless internationally legitimate public narrative at the macrolevel and individual agency via storytelling at the microlevel establishes a mosaic of instances for both consolidation or contestation of R2P and helps us make sense of, and analytically grasp, its simultaneous occurrence.

Our chapter contributed to both the literature on R2P and narrative approaches within IR. Future research can apply the analytical framework developed and illustrated here to additional empirical material, to either provide even more detailed insight into single cases of R2P application or non-application or to facilitate across-case comparison. We also believe that the analytical framework is in principle applicable to other debates in the UNSC or in fact to debates in other international fora. Humans have always told stories, and they will continue to do so. IR scholars can – as we demonstrated – learn a lot by focusing their analysis on storytelling. We hope that our story about R2P provides others with the incentive to look for stories in their areas of research.

Acknowledgments:

An earlier version was presented at the 5th open IR Section Conference of the German Political Science Association in Bremen in 2017. We thank the audience, our co-panelists, the chair Katja Freistein, and our discussant Lisbeth Zimmermann for valuable comments. The chapter has also immensely profited from the feedback by the editors, Phil Orchard and Charlie Hunt, as well as the three anonymous reviewers. In addition, the paper profited from an exchange with Siddharth Mallavarapu, who suggested useful Global South perspectives on R2P. Sassan's thinking about narratives benefited from debates on narratives at the University of Hamburg on narratives in the context of the "Constitutionalism Unbound" project and in that context he would like to thank especially Maren Hofius, Antje Wiener, and Jan Wilkens. Finally, we thank Martha van Bakel for careful language editing. We are responsible for any remaining errors of fact or interpretation.

Notes

1 We thank one of the reviewers for asking us to engage with this question. For a critique of Hehir's assessment of R2P also see Orchard's Chapter 1 in this volume.

2 We are aware that this understanding of agency differs from the prevalent definition in IR, but we work with Burke's definition in order to keep his analytical framework conceptually intact. We also believe that Burke's conception is useful for our analysis.

3 It is noteworthy that R2P's history stretches back much further, as Siddharth Mallavarapu has rightly argued: "Interventionism has had a long history" (Mallavarapu,

2015: 306). In this context Amitav Acharya notes, that – next to the ICISS – there are three other sources of R2P: "[....] the [...] idea of responsible sovereignty developed in an African context, evolving human rights policy debates and approaches, and the just war tradition in its classical and contemporary formulations" (Acharya, 2015: 61). For pragmatic and conceptual reasons, we focus our analysis on those public narratives that contain clear references to R2P.

4 For an analysis of China's critique of the implementation of Resolution 1973 see Chapter 7 by Teitt in this volume.

References

Abbott, H.P. (2007). Story, Plot, and Narration. *In:* Herman, D. (ed.) *The Cambridge Companion to Narrative*, 39–51. Cambridge: Cambridge University Press.

Abbott, H.P. (2008). *The Cambridge Introduction to Narrative.* Cambridge: Cambridge University Press.

Acharya, A. (2015). The Responsibility to Protect and Theory of Norm Circulation. *In:* Thakur, R. and Maley, W. (eds.) *Theorising the Responsibility to Protect*, 59–77. Cambridge: Cambridge University Press.

Adler-Nissen, R. and Pouliot, V. (2014). Power in Practice: Negotiating the International Intervention in Libya. *European Journal of International Relations,* 20(4): 889–911.

African Union Peace and Security Council (2011). Communique of the 265th Meeting of the Peace and Security Council. Available at: www.peaceau.org/uploads/communique-libya-eng.pdf

Arab League (2011). The Outcome of the Council of the League of Arab States Meeting at the Ministerial Level in its Extraordinary Session on the Implications of the Current Events in Libya and the Arab Position. Available at: http://responsibilitytoprotect.org/Arab%20League%20Ministerial%20level%20statement%2012%20march%202011%20-%20english%281%29.pdf

Arbour, L. (2008). The Responsibility to Protect as a Duty of Care in International Law and Practice. *Review of International Studies,* 34(3): 445–458.

Ban, Ki-moon (2009). Implementing the Responsibility to Protect. Available at: www2.ohchr.org/english/bodies/chr/special/docs/17thsession/SG_reportA_63_677_en.pdf

Bellamy, A.J. (2006). Whither the Responsibility to Protect? Humanitarian Intervention and the 2005 World Summit. *Ethics & International Affairs,* 20(2): 143–169.

Bellamy, A.J. (2011). Libya and The Responsibility to Protect: The Exception and the Norm. *Ethics & International Affairs,* 25(3): 263–269.

Berenskoetter, F. (2014). Parameters of a National Biography. *European Journal of International Relations,* 20(1): 262–288.

Bode, I. (2014). Storytelling in den Vereinten Nationen: Mahbub ul Haq und menschliche Entwicklung. *In:* Gadinger, F., Jarzebski, S. and Yildiz, T. (eds.) *Politische Narrative. Konzepte – Analysen – Forschungspraxis*, 339–362. Wiesbaden: Springer VS.

Burke, K. (1945) *A Grammar of Motives.* Berkley, LA, London: University of California Press.

Deitelhoff, N. and Zimmermann, L. (2018). Things We Lost in the Fire: How Different Types of Contestation Affect the Robustness of International Norms. *International Studies Review,* 54(3): 421.

De Fina, A. and Georgakopoulou, A. (2008). Analysing Narratives as Practices. *Qualitative Research,* 8(3): 379–387.

De Fina, A. and Georgakopoulou, A. (2012). *Analyzing Narratives: Discourse and Sociolinguistic Perspectives.* Cambridge: Cambridge University Press.

Gadinger, F., Jarzebski, S. and Yildiz, T. (2014). Politische Narrative. Konturen einer politikwissenschaftlichen Erzähltheorie. *In:* Gadinger, F., Jarzebski, S. and Yildiz, T. (eds.) *Politische Narrative. Konzepte – Analysen – Forschungspraxis*, 3–38. Wiesbaden: Springer VS.

Gholiagha, S. (2015). To prevent "future Kosovos and future Rwandas": A Critical Constructivist View on the Responsibility to Protect. *International Journal of Human Rights,* 19(8): 1074–1097.

Gifkins, J. (2016). R2P in the UN Security Council: Darfur, Libya, and Beyond. *Cooperation and Conflict,* 5(2): 148–165.

Hehir, A. (2018). *Hollow Norms and the Responsibility to Protect.* Cham, Switzerland: Palgrave Macmillan.

Hofius, M., Wilkens, J., Hansen-Magnusson, H. and Gholiagha, S. (2014). Den Schleier lichten? Kritische Normenforschung, Freiheit und Gleichberechtigung im Kontext des „Arabischen Frühlings". *Zeitschrift für Internationale Beziehungen,* 21(2): 85–105.

Holzgrefe, J.L. and Keohane, R.O. (eds.) (2003). *Humanitarian Intervention: Ethic, Legal and Political Dilemmas.* Cambridge: Cambridge University Press.

ICISS (2001). *The Responsibility to Protect. Report of the International Commission on Intervention and State Sovereignty.* Ottawa: International Development Research Centre.

Innes, A.J. and Steele, B.J. (2014). Memory, Trauma and Ontological Security. *In:* Resende, E. and Budryte, D. (eds.) *Memory and Trauma in International Relations: Theories, Cases, and Debates*, 15–29. London and New York: Routledge

Jahn, M. (2008). Freytag's Triangle. *In:* Herman, D. Jahn, M. and Ryan, M-L. (eds.) *Routledge Encyclopedia of Narrative Theory*, 189–190. London: Routledge.

Krebs, R.R. (2015). *Narrative and the Making of US National Security.* Cambridge: Cambridge University Press.

Labonte, M. (2016). R2P's Status as a Norm. *In:* Bellamy, A.J. and Dunne, T. (eds.) *The Oxford Handbook of The Responsibility to Protect*, 133–150. Oxford: Oxford University Press.

Levinger, M. and Roselle, L. (2017). Narrating Global Order and Disorder. *Politics and Governance,* 5(3): 94–98.

Loges, B. (2013). *Schutz als neue Norm in den internationalen Beziehungen. Der UN-Sicherheitsrat und die Etablierung der Responsibility to Protect.* Wiesbaden: Springer VS.

Mallavarapu, S. (2015). Colonialism and the Responsibility to Protect. *In:* Thakur, R. and Maley, W. (eds.) *Theorising the Responsibility to Protect*, 305–322. Cambridge: Cambridge University Press.

Miskimmon, A., O'Loughlin, B. and Roselle, L. (2013). *Strategic Narratives. Communication Power and the New World.* New York: Routledge.

Miskimmon, A., O'Loughlin, B. and Roselle, L. (2017). *Forging the World: Strategic Narratives and International Relations.* University of Michigan: Ann Arbor.

Morris, J. (2013). Libya and Syria: R2P and the Spectre of the Swinging Pendulum. *International Affairs,* 89(5): 1265–1283.

Organisation of Islamic Cooperation (2011). Final Communique Issued by the Emergency Meeting of the Committee of Permanent Representatives to The Organization of the Islamic Conference on the Alarming Developments in Libyan Jamahiriya. Available at: www.oic-oci.org/topic/?t_id=5022&ref=2110&lan=en

Patterson, M. and Renwick Monroe, K. (1998). Narrative in Political Science. *Annual Review of Political Science,* 1: 315–331.

Polletta, F., Chen, P.C.B., Gardner, B.G. and Motes, A. (2011). The Sociology of Storytelling. *Annual Review of Sociology,* 37(1): 109–130.

Puri, H.S. (2016). *Perilous Interventions. The Security Council and the Politics of Chaos.* Noida, London, Toronto, Scarborough, Sydney, New York: HarperCollins Publishers.

Rabinowitz, P.J. (2008). Audience. *In:* Herman, D., Jahn, M. and Ryan, M-L. (eds.) *Routledge Encyclopedia of Narrative Theory,* 29–31. London: Routledge.

Ralph, J. and Gifkins, J. (2017). The Purpose of United Nations Security Council Practice: Contesting Competence Claims in the Normative Context Created by the Responsibility to Protect. *European Journal of International Relations,* 23(3): 630–653.

Roselle, L. (2017). Strategic Narratives and Alliances: The Cases of Intervention in Libya (2011) and Economic Sanctions against Russia (2014). *Politics and Governance,* 5(3): 99–110.

Shenhav, S.R. (2015). *Analyzing Social Narratives.* New York: Routledge.

Somers, M.R. and Gibson, G.D. (1994). Reclaiming the Epistemological Other. Narrative and the Social Constitution of Identity. *In:* Calhoun, C.J. (ed.) *Social Theory and the Politics of Identity,* 35–99. Oxford: Blackwell Publishing.

Spencer, A. (2016). *Romantic Narratives in International Politics. Pirates, Rebels and Mercenaries.* Manchester: Manchester University Press.

Strauss, E. (2009). *The Emperor's New Clothes? The United Nations and the Implementation of the Responsibility to Protect.* Baden-Baden: Nomos Verlagsgesellschaft.

Subotic, J. (2016). Narrative, Ontological Security, and Foreign Policy Change. *Foreign Policy Analysis,* 12(4): 610–627.

UN (2005). Outcome Document of the 2005 World Summit. Available at: https://undocs.org/A/RES/60/1

UNSC (2011a). 6498th Meeting. Available at: www.un.org/en/ga/search/view_doc.asp?symbol=S/PV.6498

UNSC (2011b). Resolution 1970. Available at: www.un.org/en/ga/search/view_doc.asp?symbol=S/RES/1970%20%282011%29

Welsh, J.M. (2013). Norm Contestation and the Responsibility to Protect. *Global Responsibility to Protect,* 5(4): 365–396.

Wendt, A. (1987). The Agent-Structure Problem in International Relations Theory. *International Organization,* 41(3): 335–370.

Wheeler, N.J. and Egerton, F. (2009). The Responsibility to Protect: 'Precious Commitment' or a Promise Unfulfilled? *Global Responsibility to Protect,* 1(1): 70–89.

Wiener, A. (2018). *Contestation and Constitution of Norms in Global International Relations.* Cambridge: Cambridge University Press.

Wilkens, J. (2015). Contention and Constitutionalization in the Global Realm: Assessing the Uprisings in West Asia and North Africa and Their Impact on International Politics. *In:* Gerges, F. (ed.) *Contentious Politics in the Middle East: Popular Resistance and Marginalised Activism beyond the Arab Uprisings,* 25–50. London, New York: Palgrave Macmillan.

4 The Responsibility to Protect and the Protection of Civilians in UN peace operations

Interaction, feedback and co-evolution

Charles T. Hunt

Introduction

The Responsibility to Protect (R2P) and the Protection of Civilians (POC) have been heralded as critical elements of an emerging human protection normative landscape at the United Nations (UN) (Ban, 2011; Bellamy, 2016). The two frameworks share a number of common foundations and characteristics and therefore have a number of similarities. For instance, they: share important legal, normative and operational bases; enjoy high-level endorsement (WSOD and series of Council resolutions); have moral and procedural crossover; involve a myriad of actors with differing protection mandates; and share a focus on prevention as well as holding national authorities accountable for their responsibilities toward their own populations (Williams, 2016a: 526–528). However, while there are synergies, they also display important differences regarding their scope and applicability, responsible actors and modalities as well as positionality regarding state sovereignty (Lie and de Carvalho, 2012). The POC agenda is wider than R2P because it applies to protection of civilians from all violations of international humanitarian and human rights law in situations of armed conflict. However, not all mass atrocities occur in times of armed conflict and consequently aspects of R2P's prevention components extend beyond POC. Despite significant overlap between protecting civilians from mass atrocities and civilian protection in conditions of armed conflict,[1] the two objectives are distinct, have different prerequisites and, in many cases, different strategies are likely to be needed (Hunt and Bellamy, 2011: 5–7). In short, they are distinct but closely linked concepts (Popovski, 2011). In recent years there have been a number of attempts in the academic literature to grapple with the relationship between the R2P and the POC (e.g., Breakey and Francis, 2011; Francis et al., 2012; van Steenberghe, 2014). The majority of these focus, however, on the broad concept of POC as defined by international humanitarian, human rights and refugee law rather than how POC is operationalized in peace operations.

Since the beginning of this century, advocates of both R2P and POC have viewed the UN's peace operations as a potential vehicle for implementation and operationalizing these concepts. Indeed, POC has been taken up and has become a center of gravity for the majority of these missions. The relationship between

R2P and peace operations has been less clear – at times conceptually confused, institutionally contested and operationally undifferentiated. As van Steenberghe has noted, "UN institutions and States generally take care not to link R2P to the field of peacekeeping operations or at least remain particularly cautious in that regard" (2014: 97–98). Rare studies that focus on the relationship between the R2P and POC in peacekeeping have tended to focus more on the controversies and the issues they raise at political and operational levels – e.g., challenges to established principles of peacekeeping – than on the implications for contestation and consolidation of the norms and agendas involved (Williams, 2016a; Nasu, 2011; Hunt and Bellamy, 2011; Tardy, 2012; Hassler, 2010; Mégret, 2015). This is an important gap – particularly given that the two concepts emerged (1999/2001) and rose to prominence/gained traction institutionally (2009/2010) in a similar time frame. They have displayed periods of convergence (2010 and again after 2013) but have also diverged during periods of controversy (post-Libya). As a result, over the past 20 years the R2P and POC in peace operations have developed in parallel. As argued in the introduction (Hunt and Orchard, Introduction in this volume) at times they have interpenetrated in ways that provide interesting insights into how the R2P has shaped, but also been shaped by, other contiguous normative agendas, thematic areas and practices.

This chapter analyzes the R2P in conjunction with POC in peace operations. It examines how the R2P has intersected, influenced and been influenced by efforts to promote POC through peace operations. It proceeds in three main sections. The first clarifies the definitions of the R2P and POC in general and specifically in the context of peace operations for the purposes of this chapter. The second part examines where and how the two concepts have challenged, altered, led to reinterpretations and had feedback effects on each other. It does this through an examination of their: gradual institutionalization at the UN (i.e., articulations and expressions by the UN Secretariat and the pertinent Secretaries-General); deployment in the practices of the Security Council;[2] and influence over the actions of operations in the field. The third section discusses the implications of this relationship for understanding the normative trajectory and status of the R2P as it enters its third decade in popular lexicon.

The analysis shows that the R2P has been in a co-evolution with POC and particularly the implementation of POC through UN peace operations. The chapter argues that the emergence of the R2P and the trends in POC in peace operations have cross-fertilized in discourse and practice at the UNSC and influenced the UN system as a whole regarding the long-standing problem of preventing and responding in a timely and decisive manner to the most egregious of human rights abuses. It argues that this has influenced the respective trajectories of the two concepts but importantly that this has ramifications for the discrete nature of the R2P in normative terms. It further argues that in order to clarify the normative status of the R2P, a better comprehension of its implementation through instruments that are influenced by and draw on other normative agendas will be important. It also argues that harnessing this analysis can help: (i) better situate the R2P in relation to other normative agendas (mutually reinforcing as well as contradictory); and (ii) more accurately depict and describe the normative status of the R2P as a bundle of norms that intersect with, and sometimes rely on (e.g., for legal justification or practical operationalization), these other norms, regimes and agendas.

The R2P, POC in armed conflict and POC in peace operations

The emergence and content of the R2P has been covered in detail elsewhere in this volume (Hunt and Orchard, Introduction). It is nevertheless worthwhile reiterating a few key features. In sum, the R2P is a moral and political principle – an expression of political commitment and a guide for action to prevent and halt genocide, war crimes, ethnic cleansing and crimes against humanity. Having emerged from an independent commission in 2001, the R2P was unanimously adopted by Heads of State and Government at the 2005 World Summit as a framework for preventing and protecting civilians from the most egregious human rights abuses. The formulation in Articles 138–140 of the World Summit Outcome Document (WSOD) emphasized the responsibility of every state to protect its population from genocide, crimes against humanity, war crimes and ethnic cleansing; the onus on the international community to provide assistance to states in doing so; and, in event of 'manifest failure,' the duty to take collective, timely and decisive action in accordance with the means prescribed and circumscribed in the UN Charter.

The R2P has since been has been reaffirmed and referenced in a range of Security Council resolutions. It has also been subject to efforts to mainstream its implications throughout the UN system through a series of Secretary-General (SG) Reports and interactive dialogues relating to operationalizing the concept as well as the creation of the joint office for special advisors on the prevention of genocide and the R2P. Its added value lies in the political consensus that surrounds it, the responsibilities that member states have accepted for themselves and given to the UN and in its articulation of a holistic approach to preventing atrocities and protecting the targets which makes use of all the capacities available to the UN system.[3]

The POC is a framework concerned with mitigating harm to civilians resulting directly or indirectly from armed conflict. It is often referred to as a legal concept due to its firm roots in international humanitarian, human rights and refugee law. However, it can also be understood as a multifaceted normative framework for alleviating the effects of armed conflict on civilian populations as well as other non-combatants including humanitarians, health workers and journalists. POC writ large is therefore understood differently by different communities. Importantly, the foundations in International Humanitarian Law (IHL) mean there are strong ties to humanitarian actors who anchor this notion of POC in principles of impartiality and neutrality.

This broad notion of POC has also been internalized within the UN system – emerging as a thematic agenda of the Security Council after its Resolution 1265 stated a "willingness" to "respond to situations of armed conflict where civilians are being targeted or where humanitarian assistance to civilians is being deliberately obstructed," further pledging to consider "appropriate measures" for doing so (UN, 1999a). Subsequently, open debates of the Council on POC have been held periodically leading to 11 thematic resolutions[4] and 14 Reports of the SG as well as numerous Security Council Presidential Statements.[5] These developments have targeted progress on a range of measures for enhancing the protection of vulnerable civilian populations such as enhancing compliance by state and non-state actors with international humanitarian and human rights law (IH/HRL), ensuring humanitarian access, tackling the impunity of perpetrators through enhanced accountability and improving the capabilities of peace operations with protection mandates. In this chapter I will be focusing on this last element as a subset of this normative agenda.

Following a brief hiatus attributed to the catastrophes in Rwanda and Bosnia, there was a return to UN peacekeeping in 1999 when the UN created new missions in Kosovo, Sierra Leone and the Democratic Republic of Congo (DRC). Moreover, the latter two included, for the first time, an explicit mandate to protect civilians from harm. In 1999 for the first time the UN Security Council authorized a peace operation under Chapter VII to, inter alia, "protect civilians from imminent harm" (UN, 1999b: 3, para. 14). Resolution 1296 (2000) called for this POC mandate to become a common feature of the UN's peace operations. It has since become customary for the Security Council to act under Chapter VII of the UN Charter when mandating missions to use all necessary means to, inter alia, "protect civilians under imminent threat of physical violence" – albeit carefully circumscribed by a number of temporal and capabilities-based caveats (Holt and Taylor with Kelly, 2009).

Today over 95 percent of the UN's peacekeepers deployed across the world operate under such mandates. Importantly for this discussion of the R2P, this POC mandate is at the heart of UN efforts in the Central African Republic (CAR), the DRC, South Sudan, Mali and Darfur-Sudan where atrocity crimes have either been committed or where the risk of commission remains. Furthermore, recent years have witnessed examples where civilian protection rationales have been put

Table 4.1 R2P vis-à-vis POC in peace operations

	R2P	*POC in peace operations*
Nature	Overarching political commitment to prevent atrocity crimes	Tactical and operational guidance to respond to threats to civilian safety
Scope/Focus	Narrow but deep – Four mass atrocity crimes (genocide, war crimes, crimes against humanity, ethnic cleansing)	Broad – full range of threats to civilian rights
Relevance/ Applicability	Always and everywhere – in and out of armed conflict	In context of armed conflict – subject to certain temporal, capabilities and political authority-based caveats

forward to justify an escalation of the use of force in response to civilian vulnerability and targeting (e.g., Côte d'Ivoire, DRC, CAR). POC in peace operations has therefore emerged as its own distinct arena; a manifestation of one part of the broader POC normative agenda. In line with Wills' (2009) observations, the UN itself recognizes that its peacekeepers will be judged on their successes and failures in protecting vulnerable civilians. "This challenging mandate is often the yardstick by which the international community, and those whom we endeavour to protect, judge our worth as peacekeepers" (UN DPKO Webpage, 2019).

The relationship between the R2P and POC in peace operations is complex (GCR2P, 2009). Table 4.1 (above) distinguishes them based on their nature, scope/focus and relevance/applicability.

Paul Williams (2016a: 534) has depicted the relationship visually as follows:

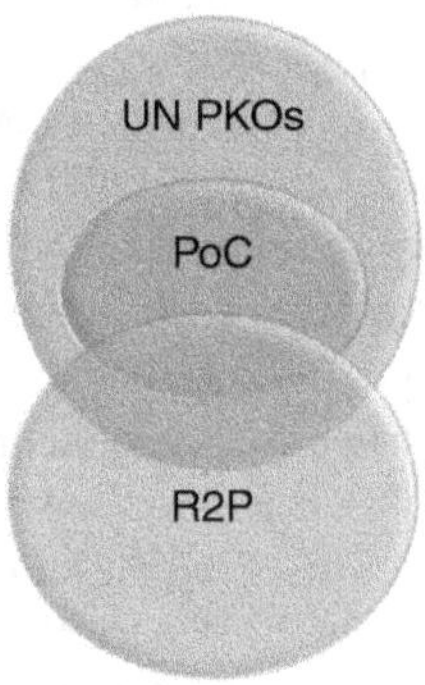

Figure 4.1 The relationship between R2P and POC in UN peacekeeping operations.
Source: Adapted from (Williams, 2016).

As argued by Hunt and Orchard in the Introduction to this volume, the normative status of the R2P is unsettled. However, it is clear that POC in peace operations is not 'equivalent' in normative terms to the R2P. The two have nevertheless shared a common terrain over the past 20 years. The following section examines the connections between these two elements of the human protection agenda and identifies areas where there may have been interweaving, influence and feedback between the two that has impacted on their respective trajectories.

Challenges, alteration, reinterpretations and feedback effects

The early years – 1999–2009

The first five years of the interplay was characterized by slow development and ad hoc action in the field. After its emergence in 1999, POC mandates were implemented in an ad hoc fashion in the field and remained under-developed in institutional frameworks. At the same time, the R2P was enunciated by the ICISS in 2001 but struggled to gain traction in the aftermath of the 9/11 attacks and pre-occupation with Afghanistan and Iraq. When the R2P was institutionalized in the 2005 WSOD, there was little in the way of formal advice or guidelines regarding how it was supposed to relate, if at all, to POC in peace operations. The same WSOD also contained sections on peace operations but they made no mention of the R2P or its implications for peacekeeping (UN, 2005). In the years that followed the World Summit, discussion, support and critique of the R2P was a feature of the Security Council's POC open debates and resolutions that flowed from them. For example, the landmark Security Council Resolution 1674 (2006) on POC constituted the first and one of the strongest linkages between those two agendas. However, this did not make any explicit reference to peace operations.

During this period, links began to be made by the Secretariat and the UNSC between POC in peace operations and the R2P. For instance, the resolution authorizing the UNAMID mission in Darfur-Sudan included a preambular paragraph: "recalling [resolution] 1674 (2006) on the protection of civilians in armed conflict, which reaffirms inter alia the provisions of paragraphs 138 and 139 of the 2005 United Nations world Summit outcome document" (i.e., those relating to the R2P). This was highly contentious at the time and the diplomatic fallout led to a silence on the R2P in future resolutions on Darfur, and indeed any other concurrent crises. However, only two years later, in a departure from earlier mandate language, UNSCR 1856 made POC a priority task for the UN Mission in the Democratic Republic of the Congo (MONUC) and further stated that it must "[e]nsure the protection of civilians, including humanitarian personnel, under imminent threat of physical violence, in particular *violence emanating from any of the parties engaged in the conflict*" (UN, 2008a [emphasis added]). At that time, some UNSC members declared that these alterations to MONUC's mandate "fully [integrated] the notion of the responsibility to protect" (UN, 2009a).[6]

Aside from the Darfur and DRC experience, between 2005 and 2009 a number of 'lessons learned' studies and non-papers were promulgated – for example, Capstone Doctrine (UN, 2008b); New Horizons, (UN, 2009b); Concept Note on Robust Peacekeeping (UN, 2009c). However, these also neglected to articulate how protection in peacekeeping was supposed to interact with protection under the R2P framework. This is indicative of the climate at the time that peacekeeping was not seen as the right tool to be involved in addressing mass atrocity crimes – partly due to the hesitation of member states and confusion about how the R2P and POC should sit together in peace operations (UN, 2009a: 34–35; UN, 2009d: 17–19. See also Hunt and Sharland, 2019). In effect, the presence of both frameworks in the normative arena was leading to separation and differentiation rather than convergence or influence on each other.

The institutionalizing years – 2009–2011

The year 2009 was a watershed year for the institutionalization of both R2P and POC in peace operations. In January that year, the SG released his first annual report on R2P. This outlined a three-pillar strategy for advancing the agenda and implementation (described above) (Ban, 2009). The report recommended that "goals relating to the responsibility to protect" should be "mainstreamed among [the] priorities" of UN peacekeepers and peacebuilders and identified roles for peacekeeping missions in Pillars Two[7] and Three (Ban, 2009: paras. 40, 55, 68). In March, the Special Committee on Peacekeeping Operations (C34) included explicit reference to POC for the first time in its 2009 report (UN, 2009e: paras. 125–128). This was followed by UNSC Resolution 1894 (2009f) which echoed the C34's call for strengthening POC (including in peacekeeping) and also reaffirmed R2P (UN, 2009f: preambular para. 1).[8] Along with the release of a DPKO-OCHA commissioned independent study on POC in peace operations reflecting on the first ten years of practice (Holt and Taylor with Kelly, 2009), these collectively triggered a series of efforts designed to institutionalize POC in peace operations. These developments were closely followed by a 2010 Operational Concept for POC in peace operations that articulated its substance in three "tiers" (UN, 2010a).

On the one hand, these developments can be seen as an effort to begin differentiating POC and R2P more clearly. This fits with accounts of humanitarians and the peace operations bureaucracy trying to distance the two concepts and drive a wedge between them – in particular based on the different place of host state strategic consent. However, on the other hand, these efforts reinforced the overlap and partial consonance. For instance, while they do not line up numerically, the content of some of these stages and elements of the two three-pronged frameworks find resonance (see also more detailed comparison of the three-pronged frameworks below). Furthermore, another document promulgated around the same time that provided guidance for drafting POC strategies points to further cross-fertilization, stating that:

> the protection of civilians is primarily the responsibility of the host government and that the mission is deployed to assist and build the capacity of the government in the fulfillment of this responsibility. However, in cases where the government is unable or unwilling to fulfill its responsibility, Security Council mandates give missions the authority to act independently to protect civilians. Bearing in mind that missions operate within the principles of peacekeeping and in accordance with the mandate, missions are authorized to use force against any party, including elements of government forces, where such elements are themselves engaged in physical violence against civilians.
>
> (UN, 2010b: 2–3, para. 5)

Notwithstanding the important caveat regarding the principles of peacekeeping, this acknowledged that peacekeepers should also be ready to respond to violations irrespective of the source (i.e., to include host state forces). Van Steenberghe has argued that this "evidences an evolution [in POC in peace operations] endorsing a logic close to the R2P one" (2014: 101–102). These developments (indicative of convergence) also appeared to manifest in the field in 2010 in the context of the UN peace operation in the DRC. A system-wide POC strategy for DRC – for both MONUC and its successor, the UN Stabilization Mission in the DRC (MONUSCO) – was developed and included a section labeled 'Rationale and the Responsibility to Protect' (UN, 2010c: 1, para. 2). These paragraphs referenced the R2P multiple times as it articulated the protection strategy for the peace operation in relation to each of the three pillars of the R2P. This is a clear indication of the issue linkage and cross-fertilization that was taking place at the time and could be seen to signify the influence of the R2P agenda on POC in peace operations.

Elsewhere in the Secretariat, the annual SG Reports on R2P continued to show a certain degree of linkage, if not convergence, with POC in peace operations. For instance, Ban Ki-moon's 2010 report on early warning and assessment mechanisms noted that peace operations in the field are a source of important information for prevention of mass atrocities (Ban, 2010: 4, para.10). The 2011 version on regional and sub-regional arrangements inter alia highlighted the need for better "Doctrine for the possible use of peacekeeping and military assets in the context of preventing, deterring or responding to atrocities" and advocated for the UNSC to undertake deeper consideration of mass atrocity prevention in their "growing attention to protection issues in a peacekeeping context" (Ban, 2011: para. 35: 11 and para. 32: 10). Even if the relationship was building through such cross-references and identification of mutually reinforcing elements at the UNSC and Secretariat, during this period POC in peace operations was seen as a way of implementing less controversial aspects of R2P, at most.

POC and R2P went through an intensive period of interaction in 2011. In particular, POC language was used in UNSC resolutions to address R2P considerations. First, in March, citing the threats to civilians and referring explicitly to the R2P, the Council determined the crisis unfolding in Libya as constituting a threat to international peace and security. Having already applied sanctions, imposed an arms embargo and referred the case to the ICC (UN, 2011a), the Council took the unprecedented step of authorizing the use of force against a recognized member state for human protection purposes (UN, 2011b: 3, para. 4). This was an important watershed, constituting the first time in its history that the UNSC authorized the use of force for the POC without the consent of the recognized government.[9] Furthermore, and of importance here, the Council utilized language synonymous with POC mandates for peace operations when justifying military intervention in the case of Libya (Williams, 2016a: 527).

It was only a few days after the unprecedented resolution on Libya that the Council unanimously adopted Resolution 1975 on the situation in Côte d'Ivoire. Contested election results and an escalating post-elections crisis led to the Council acting to reinforce the forces it had stationed in the country under UNOCI. Like 1973, the resolution similarly drew together R2P rationales with POC action – this time more directly through an *in situ* peace operation. While it is a matter of debate whether it was invocations of the R2P or POC that precipitated it (Lotze, 2011; Hunt, 2016), the Council stressed its full support "to use all necessary means to carry out its mandate to protect civilians under imminent threat of physical violence, … including to prevent the use of heavy weapons against the civilian population" (UN, 2011c: 3, para. 6).

Although Resolution 1975 was light on R2P language, Bellamy (2015: 182–184) has argued that "… something need not be labelled R2P in order to contribute to its goals" and this can therefore be understood as an example where the urgency and nature of the response can be attributed to the influence of R2P even if not explicitly badged as such (Hunt, 2016). As with the Libya case, POC language was used in UNSC resolutions to respond to a crisis that had been clearly described by Special Advisors to the SG in R2P terms. These can be seen as examples of SCR language not reflecting the 'work' that R2P may have been doing in mobilizing action. Specifically, the Côte d'Ivoire example illustrates how the R2P was influencing decisions by the Council about what should be pursued under the POC mandate of existing peace operations. Bellamy and Williams (2011) argued at the time that these cases pointed to a "new politics of protection" with the Security Council more willing than before to authorize the use of force under Chapter VII (Article 42) to protect vulnerable civilian populations. If so, this could be understood as the interplay between the R2P and POC in peace operations as generating normative change or at least achieving greater normative traction.

The period from 2009–2011 therefore represents a period of rapid institutionalization through reports, engagement and finally action. However, if this was the case then it did not last long or at least this normative shift in Council drafting and voting behavior did not filter through to the Secretariat and the guidance for POC in peace operations.

The blow-back years – 2012–2015

The fallout of the actions in Libya and Côte d'Ivoire put the *kibosh* on this new politics of protection. In Libya, a coalition of the willing led by NATO implemented the mandate to protect civilians under threat of attack. However, the eventual demise of President Gaddafi and the way in which outside intervention facilitated regime change in Libya led to consternation about how POC language in the relevant UNSC resolution could lead to regime change. In Côte d'Ivoire, UN peacekeepers alongside the parallel French forces of *Operation Licorne* intervened militarily to halt the violence and ultimately contributed to the deposing of President Gbagbo and the installation of his election contender, Alassane Ouattara. Prominent voices in Africa have argued that escalation of force by UNOCI was premature and questioned the legitimacy of such action by a peacekeeping mission pointing to the fact that it was largely a technicality (i.e., external recognition of Ouattara's election victory) that afforded host state consent to the use of force against Gbagbo – action that Thabo Mbeki, for example, believe exceeded the POC mandate (Mbeki, 2011). Such positions added to the controversy and push-back on the idea that UN peace operations and POC rationales should be involved – even if leading from behind with the French in front – in the ultimate removal of an incumbent President Gbagbo (albeit with a contested legitimacy at that point) (Mbeki, 2011; Hunt, 2016).

The discomfort and push-back on 'regime change' *ends* being pursued through protection of civilians *means* (or under POC rubrics) reverberated through the UN's peace and security architecture and subsequent efforts to develop policy and guidance were at pains to carefully distinguish between the two concepts and at times dissociate the civilian protection work of peace operations from the R2P.[10] Those seeking to advance the R2P also became more careful about where, when and how they have linked it to the work of peace operations. For instance, the SG's 2012 Report on R2P's third pillar downplayed the role of peace operations in timely and decisive responses. Mentioned in only one paragraph of the report, further delineating:

> United Nations peacekeeping missions are based on the principle of consent and generally deploy in support of and with the overall consent of the host State. As such, they fall under pillar two and are to be distinguished from pillar three tools.
>
> (Ban, 2012a: p. 5, para.16)[11]

Subsequent reports were discreet when drawing connections and emphasizing mutually reinforcing elements (Ban, 2013a, 2014). Similarly, in his 2012 and 2013 reports on POC, the SG reiterated that peace operations can be an important instrument for implementing R2P (Ban, 2012b: Section C., 2013b: Section C.). However, the 2012 report also cautioned against the "continuing and inaccurate conflation of the [R2P and POC] concepts" (Ban, 2012b: para. 21). This was echoed in the SG's 2012 Report on the R2P's Pillar Three stating: "While the work of peacekeepers may contribute to the achievement of R2P goals, the two concepts of the responsibility to protect and the protection of civilians have separate and distinct prerequisites and objectives" (Ban, 2012a: 5, para.16). This partial decoupling – or at least attempt to differentiate and distinguish between the two – can be seen as a response to the perceived risks of linking the two and the toxicity associated with the R2P, particularly in relation to the eventual regime change in Libya.[12]

Regarding POC in peace operations this precipitated a move to more subtle references to R2P and less framing POC in peace as an operationalization of R2P. For instance, Resolution 1996 (UN, 2011d) establishing the United Nations Mission in South Sudan (UNMISS), explicitly mandated peacekeepers to support national authorities in implementing their responsibility to protect (Giffen, 2016). This is indicative of R2P language appearing more customarily in the UNSC resolutions authorizing and renewing mission mandates. This usually takes the shape of one or more of three formulations: first, recalling the national government's 'primary responsibility to protect populations'; second, committing to supporting national authorities in preventing atrocity crimes and upholding their primary responsibility to protect (e.g., Mali, DRC); and, third, noting the commission of mass atrocity crimes – potentially by both government and opposition forces – and stressing the need to end impunity and hold perpetrators to account (e.g., Sudan). Interpreting the language in Security Council mandates is notoriously difficult as it is often – sometimes intentionally – vague. This has also led to some disagreement about what exactly qualifies as a 'reference' to the R2P (Gifkins, 2016; Hehir, 2016: 170).[13] Nevertheless, the insertion of clear references to the R2P within the resolutions' authorizing is unlikely to be accidental – not least given the controversies surrounding bringing together R2P and POC in peace operations.

However, as Bellamy has argued, sometimes a preoccupation with language in resolutions and reports is misleading and the Council can be "doing it though not always saying it" (Bellamy, 2015: 182). In practice, peace operations with POC mandates have become increasingly involved in addressing mass atrocity crimes whether explicitly invoking the R2P or not. It is not 'new' to deploy to places that have experienced these atrocities such as Timor-Leste, Sierra Leone, Liberia and Côte d'Ivoire. Indeed, Lisa Hultman (2013) has shown that this is quite likely and reflects a commitment to implement protection norms. However, new missions deployed in 2013 to Mali and CAR were indicative of an emerging trend deploying missions to places where there is little or no peace to keep such that the likelihood of being stationed in locations where mass atrocities crimes are occurring is higher (Bellamy and Hunt, 2015). While it has been found that UN peacekeepers inconsistently, selectively and rarely use force to execute their POC mandate (UN, 2014) the decisions of the Council to send them to places where atrocities crimes are occurring could be read as a shift in peace operations policy that responds to the R2P.

Around the same time, the Council reconfigured other missions – adapting them in response to the outbreak or increased risk of atrocities. The 2013 authorization of a *Force Intervention Brigade* (FIB) within MONUSCO in the DRC, for instance, developed a more robust and proactive modality – in part justified for protecting civilians. Following the outbreak of civil war in South Sudan in December 2013, UNMISS took the unprecedented step of opening the gates of their bases to those fleeing from government forces and seeking protection. A Regional Protection Force was also authorized though never really eventuated (Williams, 2016b). These new and reconfigured missions demonstrated the Council's willingness to authorize greater intent and enable more proactive military strategies, operational concepts and robust Rules of Engagement (ROE) for protection purposes. In line with Bellamy, irrespective of if and how these innovations were attributed to the R2P principle,[14] they are certainly consistent with pursuit of R2P goals and point to tangible areas where the cross-fertilization may be shaping the expectations of the UN regarding protection. Consequently, despite the controversies of Libya (and Côte d'Ivoire), the years 2013–2015 displayed signs that peace operations were being influenced by normative expectations around protection of populations from atrocity crimes, including where host states are complicit or responsible for abuses (see discussion section below). Indeed, it could be argued that the

Council began using POC for newer and robust forms of protection because they wanted to avoid the R2P.

The reflective/resurgent years – 2015 →

More recently, it seems like there is a greater willingness to acknowledge overlapping imperatives and identify potential synergies between the agendas at the conceptual, strategic and operational levels. Taking stock of ten years of efforts to advance and implement the R2P, the SG's 2015 Report on the R2P was explicit in identifying peace operations as: "a front-line resource for assisting States under stress to uphold their responsibility to protect" (Ban, 2015: 11, para. 33). In addition to this Pillar Two role, the report advocated for the "integration of an atrocity crime perspective into … peacekeeping" (ibid.: 9, para. 27) and, recognizing that "[i]ncreasingly, these operations confront situations characterized by widespread and systematic violence," it advocated for missions to be provided with the "military and civilian capabilities necessary to respond rapidly and flexibly to situations at risk of atrocity crimes, and develop training and guidance relevant to the implementation of the responsibility to protect" (ibid.: 20, para. 74). Importantly, it also noted a number of other conflict prevention/peacebuilding activities that often occur under the auspices of peace operations and are mutually beneficial to the R2P agenda. This represented a changing tone on connectivities between the two areas and explicitly acknowledged the "… need to overcome the prevailing tendency to see the responsibility to protect as disconnected from related activities on conflict prevention, peacebuilding, the protection of civilians, the protection and empowerment of women and girls, and international criminal justice" (ibid.: 16–17, para. 60).

This latter point reiterated in his final annual report on R2P (Ban, 2016: para. 14: 5, para. 47: 13 and para. 59: 15), also set the scene for what emerged in the articulations that followed in subsequent years. For example, this has been echoed in the reports and expressions of SG António Guterres – including how protection agendas, including POC and the R2P, fit into the sustaining peace agenda (UN, 2018), and his focus on prevention – reflected in his first and second annual reports on the R2P, subtitled 'Accountability for prevention' (2017) and 'From early warning to early action' (2018), respectively.

The practice of incorporating R2P references into the resolutions authorizing peace operations continued and by 2018 it is now commonplace to find the formulation: "government of X has the primary responsibility to protect civilians/populations … including protection from crimes against humanity and war crimes."[15] Indeed, efforts to streamline and bring greater focus to UN peace operations has seen the POC mandates elevated rather than diminished. For instance, significant pressure to do away with the overloading of 'Christmas tree' mission mandates saw POC become one of two priority goals in the MONUSCO mission and similarly remains a headline goal in the other four of the 'big 5' missions in Africa (i.e., Mali, CAR, Darfur and South Sudan).

One equivocation can be seen in the 2015 POC policy which elaborates on the 2010 operational concept articulating the POC into three tiers. While this further strengthens some correspondences between the three-pillar R2P framework and the 2010 POC CONOP (see discussion section below), the authors of the 2015 POC policy were still at pains to differentiate and separate the POC from the R2P. An annex on 'Terminology' discusses the relationship between POC and the R2P stating that:

> The responsibility to protect (R2P) also aims at addressing instances of physical violence, with a specific focus on mass atrocities (genocide, war crimes, crimes against humanity and ethnic cleansing). While the R2P framework shares some legal and conceptual foundations and employs some common terminology with POC, they are distinct. Most importantly, R2P may be invoked without the consent of the host state, specifically when the host state is failing to protect its population. R2P thus envisages a range of action that goes beyond the principles of peacekeeping, which require the consent of the host state.
>
> (UN, 2015a: 19)

While this is true according to a strict reading of peacekeeping lore, it implies more clarity around the actions of peace operations than actually exists. As discussed above, it was Alassane Ouattara's democratic legitimacy claim rather than presidential incumbency that technically provided UNOCI with the strategic consent of the host government to use of force in Côte d'Ivoire. Furthermore, the nuances of strategic consent for the mission's presence as opposed to tactical level consent for operational activities further complicates such a clear distinction. Indeed, the POC policy itself states that the principles of peacekeeping do not preclude the use of force:

> … in self-defense and as otherwise authorized by the Security Council, including for the protection of civilians. This includes, where necessary, the use of force against elements of government forces at the tactical level where such forces are themselves engaged in, or pose an imminent threat of, physical violence against civilians.
>
> (UN, 2015a: 7, para. 23)

The sensitivities around host state consent for peace operations put clear limitations on what can be formalized in policy. However, even this statement in the POC policy speaks to the changes that include provisions for the event that host governments are complicit in abuses – a concern at the core of the R2P. Therefore, this conspicuous caveat may say as much about internal politics (i.e., the trade-offs of a negotiated text requiring sign-off from disparate member states and parts of the UN system) as it does about the differences/similarities between the R2P and POC in peace operations.

It is also worth noting that in parallel, the UN community has mostly also emphasized the consensual aspects of R2P under Pillars One and Two but been the most resistant to the non-consensual elements under Pillar Three. This, too, has brought about further convergence between the way R2P and POC in peace operations are understood and enacted.

Discussion: feedback effects and implications

The historical co-evolution traced above points to four key areas that are critical to the co-evolution between the two concepts and are therefore worthy of further consideration covering issues of: operationalization; consent; state-centrism; and accountability.

Operationalization

It is arguably in the operationalization of the R2P and POC in peace operations where significant amounts of convergence and co-evolution may have taken place. Although both the R2P and the POC in peace operations have long and disparate histories, efforts discussed above to operationalize them have displayed some correspondences. Fundamentally, concerted effort to articulate a vision of the concept that is not reduced to just direct physical protection by military (and possibly police) but instead articulating preventive and reconstruction activities envisaged by a range of civilian and police and Non-Governmental Organization (NGO) actors. This has led to parallel efforts to make protection about assistance/capacity-building for prevention and avoiding recidivism rather than intervention, even less about military focus (i.e., holistic conceptualization). Furthermore, just like the R2P framework, the POC concept does not see these elements as being sequential, hierarchical or mutually exclusive. Both highlight strategies and activities from across the UN Charter's various chapters (i.e., not just Chapter VII) and identify roles for the whole gamut of civilian and uniformed personnel as well as broader family of UN agencies and funds. Moreover, both highlight that the emphasis should be on prevention rather than reaction.

The three-tiered POC operational concept offers a convenient framework for conceptualizing actions that are consonant with the obligations under the three-pillar framework of the R2P. Tier I of the POC operational concept includes elements

Table 4.2 Three-pronged frameworks

R2P (2009 SG Report)	*POC in peace operations (20 10>2015 DPKO/DFS Operational Concept/ POC Policy)*
Pillar One: Primary responsibility of the state to protect its populations	Tier I: Protection through dialogue and engagement
Pillar Two: International assistance to uphold Pillar One	Tier II: Provision of physical protection
Pillar Three: Timely and decisive response	Tier III: Establishment of a protective environment

of preventive action that resonate with R2P's Pillar One (prevention and host-state responsibility); POC's Tier III focus on capacity-building toward the creation of a protective environment provides an avenue for the international assistance envisaged under R2P's Pillar Two (international assistance); and POC's Tier II focus on provision of physical protection from threats provides the enabling platform for timely and decisive responses required under R2P's Pillar Three.[16]

Though it is difficult to say if the two influenced each other in the development of these frameworks, what is apparent is the similar conceptualization – combining the provision for rapid response to imminent harm with longer-term efforts to prevent and build resilience as part of a holistic framework – albeit within different political contexts.

Consent

Another area where convergence can be seen is in the blurring of lines when it comes to the established principles of peace operations. Consent from the main parties to a conflict is one of these cardinal principles (UN, 2008b: 31). In particular, *strategic* consent of the host government is a non-negotiable and necessary precondition for the initial deployment as well as continued existence. However, *tactical* level consent is slightly more contentious. As alluded to above, there have been a number of situations where the host state is perpetrating violence against its own populations and the Council has omitted the conventional caveat stating that protection would be undertaken 'without prejudice to the responsibilities of host state,' replacing it with 'irrespective of the source of the threat'. This is a significant shift in the scripts of POC in peace operations though it is important to note that it is still extremely rare in practice for peacekeepers to act against, or even without express permission, of host state authorities.

Nevertheless, the imperative to maintain the consent of host governments (at both strategic and tactical levels) means there has been a glass ceiling on progress for R2P through this avenue. Peace operations can only offer limited implementation potential and ultimately struggle to be the agent of timely and decisive response (including the use of force as last resort), even though often the best situated to do so (albeit not sufficiently resourced). In addition to inaction vis-à-vis host government abuses (e.g., South Sudan, DRC, Mali) this dynamic has contributed to convergence between POC and R2P on willingness to support host states to tackle non-state armed groups. The decision to authorize the FIB in DRC to neutralize irregular armed groups (M23, ADF, FDLR, various Mai-Mai groups, etc.), for example, is an example of where it was deemed unnecessary to obtain the consent of these non-state parties to conflict. While not surprising in the machinations of an intergovernmental organization of sovereign member states, this points to normative co-evolution between the R2P and POC in peace operations as they have become more comfortable and adventurous undertaking efforts to prevent and halt atrocities when it involves neutralizing non-state actors than when the state is the perpetrator (Mégret, 2015: 145; Kurtz and Rotmann, 2016). This points to a broader consideration about the coalescence of both the R2P and POC in peace operations around state-centric solutions.

State-centrism

In addition to the argument that non-state armed groups are easier to deal with than sovereign states perpetrating atrocities, both POC in peace operations and the R2P continue to put the emphasis on host state's primary responsibility for protection of populations. In a way, this is simply recalling international legal obligations and reflects that R2P is primarily about state responsibilities – individually and collectively – albeit with roles for non-state actors. However, this also speaks to a dominant state-centrism in R2P that is also found in UN peace operations (Bellamy, 2015: 93). For instance, the logics of stabilization missions that partner strongly with host governments – sometimes conducting joint military operations against spoilers – who are strengthened through the extension of their authority throughout the territory concerned and coroneted as the guardian of a future protective environment. It could be argued that Tier III of the POC operational concept is less state-centric than R2P Pillar Two, allowing for a range of peacebuilding efforts and engagements beyond the formal architecture of central government. However, in reality, both overwhelmingly see solutions to protection deficits emanating from the national authorities and the state's institutional machinery such as the rule of law institutions. This is a difficult scenario to avoid and may be a practical rather than ideological commitment to statism (ibid.: 106). For instance, it is not clear peace operations could work in ways that does not put a sovereign state at the center of its exit strategy. After all, the UN is an intergovernmental organization. However, while situating both concepts in the society of states may be integral to obtaining the consensus and authority required to act, the risk of empowering those at the helm of abusive states is real and these two frameworks for protection currently reinforce this possibility.

Accountability

To some extent, the R2P and POC are both about holding perpetrators to account for large-scale and systematic violence against civilians. However, they have also precipitated debates and practical responses regarding accountability for their own implementation. As already discussed, the arrival of the R2P appears to correlate with the drive to make peacekeepers more responsible for POC. Furthermore, since these POC mandates have become normalized, a drive toward greater accountability has been evident. In the first instance, despite concern for some time,[17] accountability for the conduct and discipline of the peacekeepers themselves has been elevated in importance – impelling a 'do no harm' ethos amid reports of complicity in crime and sexual exploitation of vulnerable populations. Second, and particularly since the high-profile failures to prevent attacks on the UN's POC sites in South Sudan in 2016, there has been an accountability drive aimed at holding UN personnel accountable for inaction and not doing everything possible to act on their POC mandate. In line with Wills' (2009) observations, the UN itself recognizes – more than ever before – that its peacekeepers will be judged on their successes and failures in protecting vulnerable civilians, noting that, "This challenging mandate is often the yardstick by which the international community, and those whom we endeavor to protect, judge our worth as peacekeepers."[18]

In parallel, questions of accountability have been posed to the R2P. For example, the fallout from NATO's execution of the Libya mandate led to calls for greater accountability regarding the implementation of UNSC resolutions by would-be interveners. The Brazilian 'Responsibility While Protecting' (RWP) proposal was one attempt to address this proposing new reporting and oversight mechanisms for those taking action – particularly military – on the Council's behalf. Of course, the perennial criticisms of inaction – usually framed in terms of selectivity and inconsistency in responses – by the Council in the face of R2P crimes adds another call for accountability of the UNSC. This was perhaps most conspicuous in the rebuke by the General Assembly for what the membership deemed to be inadequate action on Syria (UN, 2012).

Ultimately, both the R2P and POC in peace operations have in parallel been coming to terms with the impact of accountability – or lack of it – on credibility and legitimacy of the concepts and indeed by extension the UN. While this may seem somewhat detached from discussions about their normative co-evolution it is relevant to the ways in which the prescriptive norm(s) involved in these protection agendas are being adhered to and consolidated in the process.

Summary

It is important to note that the rhetorical and public record is somewhat schizophrenic and may mask as much as reveal the work of particular concepts. It is therefore difficult to draw strong causal conclusions about whether R2P was influencing the development of POC in peace operations, and vice versa. However, it appears that there is some convergence in the ways that the two frameworks have been articulated and pursued. It is not unjustified, therefore, to think that discourse and conceptualization about these ideas may have been shaping each other.

Piiparinen claims that in general " 'bottom-up' initiatives stemming from the virtue ethics of senior UN officials have played a much more decisive role in generating the interventionist turn than 'top-down' institutional guidelines and doctrines, such as the Responsibility to Protect (RtoP) principle" (Piiparinen, 2016: 98). Others concur and argue that the R2P has had little effect on the legal framework for POC in peace operations (Sloan, 2014). However, its normative effect is more contested. Bellamy, for example, has argued that the R2P has become critical to the way the international community perceives and responds to crises where mass atrocity crimes are alleged or apprehended (Bellamy, 2012). Others go further, like van Steenberghe who argues that it is "since the emergence of the R2P" that things have evolved and that "R2P specific logic has been exported to the POC field" (2014: 100, 111) While the R2P may not have changed things legally or compelled behavior that would otherwise be unimaginable, it may be that the normative arena has been 'conditioned' in ways that is affecting choices of the UNSC. As a number of scholars have noted, the biggest impact of the R2P may be in 'habit-shaping' (Doyle, 2011; Bellamy, 2013: 352).

It is possible, therefore, that the emergence of R2P altered – maybe even enabled – the way in which the Council views and uses Chapter VII peace ops and 'protection' rationales. If nothing else, it can be argued that the R2P has raised the expectations of POC in peace operations. As Mégret (2015) argues, the affinities between robust peace operations, R2P and anti-atrocity norms has ultimately raised expectations of what peace operations should and can do. If peacekeepers can never again be bystanders to mass atrocities, then the R2P may have helped to build political will (among the UNSC and T/PCCs) to give these operations the mandates they need to protect civilians. However, if these are not met with commensurate resources it may only have made their job more difficult.

If it is indeed the case that the emergence of the R2P has altered the international political realm in which peace operations are imagined, authorized and executed then it seems possible that the evolution in peace operations has influenced the trajectory of R2P's institutionalization and traction. As illustrated here, the practice of peace operations with POC mandates (as examples of implementation of R2P) may too have influenced – through iterative feedback loops – the development of the R2P.

Conclusion

The R2P is not a consolidated, fixed and unchanging norm, but is better understood as a political principle with evolving institutional and operational manifestations that has at times been influenced by other agendas and practices. This chapter has examined the interplay and influence regarding overlapping and related efforts to protect civilians in the context of UN peace operations. The empirical examples and the associated trends in UN Security Council practice since 2005 suggest that despite efforts by some member states and parts of the UN institutional architecture to drive a wedge between them there has been instances of cross-fertilization and even convergence in both discourse and practice.

The foregoing analysis suggests that the emergence of the R2P has challenged, shaped and begun to lead to UN's Security Council and member states to reinterpret the meaning and extent of their civilian protection obligations. In particular it has accompanied the ascendency of POC as a core priority of UN peace operations. The analysis also suggests, however, that the experiences and development of POC strategies and approaches in the field may have provided critical feedback to the content and shape of the R2P. While controversial and facing resistance at times, the evolution of the R2P has been intertwined with the exploits of peacekeepers to protect civilians in field missions. It is therefore more accurate to think of the R2P and POC in peace operations as having influenced each other. In other words, these two frameworks for addressing vulnerability of civilians to large scale and systematic violence have been in a co-evolutionary relationship. While the linkage of R2P and POC in peace operations has been controversial at the politico-strategic and operational levels, their normative co-evolution offers an interesting example of where the R2P has been influenced, and in turn influenced, another normative agenda which it coexists alongside and at times overlaps with. This has important ramifications for our understanding of the ongoing contestation and the nature of consolidation of the R2P.

Only time will reveal the full implications of the interpenetration of these concepts. On the one hand it may be that this relational development leads to a stronger mutually reinforcing symbiosis in the way these frameworks guide and induce effective Security Council action to protect civilians from atrocity crimes – i.e., Bellamy's 'habits of protection' (2013: 352). On the other hand, the worst fears of those such as Tardy (2012: 436) may come to pass and the R2P will be increasingly diluted as the POC strategies in peace operations are politicized and consequently derailed and undermined. Despite the risks associated with the latter, the empirical record points to a shift away from traditional principles and orthodox positions and a convergence on frameworks for operationalizing these concepts that suggest the co-evolution of these norms is a very real phenomenon. Understanding where, when, how and why this is occurring is a vital to understanding emergent human protection normative regimes in the international system.

Acknowledgment

This chapter was originally published as: Hunt, Charles T. "Analyzing the Co-Evolution of the Responsibility to Protect and the Protection of Civilians in UN Peace Operations." *International Peacekeeping* (2019). Reprinted by permission of the publisher (Taylor & Francis Ltd). The author is grateful for the feedback received in the original review process as well as for this book manuscript. He is also grateful to Dr Shannon Zimmerman for her excellent research assistance.

Notes

1 Particularly when the former are commissioned in the context of the latter.
2 This draws on formal Security Council outputs and more informal accounts of Security Council practice as well as contributions to UN Security Council and General Assembly debates by UN member states which can be understood as a form of state practice, or *opinio juris*, that can be part of interpreting existing regulatory rules of the international system as well as contribute to the formation of customary law.
3 This is the "narrow but deep" approach to implementation identified by Secretary-General Ban Ki-moon (Ban, 2008).

4 UN Security Council Resolutions: 1265 (1999a); 1296 (2000); 1502 (2003); 1674 (2006); 1738 (2006); 1894 (2009f); 2150 (2014); 2175 (2014); 2222 (2015); 2286 (2016); 2417 (2018).
5 Accurate as at August 15, 2018. Available from: www.securitycouncilreport.org/un-documents/protection-of-civilians/
6 For instance, Belgium commented that the adjustment to MONUC's mandate "fully [integrated] the notion of the responsibility to protect" (UN, 2009a: 6).
7 Specifically noting that the preventive deployment of peacekeepers under Chapter VI or of combat forces under Chapter VII, with the consent of the host government, to counter armed groups committing mass atrocity crimes, could be considered acts of assistance to the state under the second pillar.
8 "Reaffirming the relevant provisions of the 2005 WSOD regarding the protection of civilians in armed conflict, including Paragraphs 138 and 139 thereof regarding the responsibility to protect populations from genocide, war crimes, ethnic cleansing and crimes against humanity."
9 Though it is worth recalling that UNSC 1265 (1999a) did not qualify response to attacks on civilians with caveats about host state consent.
10 Author interviews with UN DPKO officials – New York, 2012, 2013 and 2015
11 Mentioned in only one paragraph of the report, further delineating:

> United Nations peacekeeping missions are based on the principle of consent and generally deploy in support of and with the overall consent of the host State. As such, they fall under pillar two and are to be distinguished from pillar three tools.
> (Ban, 2012a: para. 16: 5)

12 The apparent contradiction may also be a reflection of the respective institutional homes for these two reports. As Thakur (2013) has pointed out, neither SG Ban nor anyone else in his office picked up on this contradiction.
13 For instance, some infer from restating state's primary responsibility to protect civilians that R2P is 'invoked' – presumably because the words 'responsibility to protect' are included in these formulations. The Global Centre for R2P runs a tally of references to the R2P in formal Security Council outputs based on this criterion, noting 75 references in resolutions and a further 21 in Presidential Statements (GCR2P, 2018). For differing opinions on this, see: (Gifkins, 2016; Hehir, 2016: 170).
14 For instance, other accounts suggest that the decision to 'open the gates' in South Sudan was driven by the SG's emergent Human Rights up Front initiative – following the failures of the UN system in Sri Lanka.
15 Mali: "Reiterates that the Malian authorities have primary responsibility to protect civilians in Mali …" (UN S/RES/2423 [June 28, 2018]). CAR: "Recalling that the CAR bears the primary responsibility to protect all populations within its territory from genocide, war crimes, ethnic cleansing and crimes against humanity …" (UN S/RES/2399 [January 30, 2018]). DRC: "Recalling that the Government of the DRC bears the primary responsibility to protect civilians within its territory and subject to its jurisdiction, including protection from crimes against humanity and war crimes," (UN S/RES/2409 [March 27, 2018]). South Sudan: "Emphasizing that … South Sudan's Transitional Government of National Unity bears the primary responsibility to protect its population from genocide, war crimes, ethnic cleansing, and crimes against humanity …" (UN S/RES/2428 [July 13, 2018]). Darfur: "Emphasizing that … the Government of Sudan bears the primary responsibility to protect civilians, including women and children, within its territory and subject to its jurisdiction, including protection from crimes against humanity and war crimes…" (UN S/RES/2429 [July 13, 2018]). Somalia: "Recognizing that the Federal Government of Somalia (FGS) has the primary responsibility to protect its citizens…" (UN S/RES/2431 [July 30, 2018]).
16 In other words, Tier I in the POC concept is described to include: "persuading the government and other relevant actors to intervene to protect civilians" (UN, 2015a: para. E2: 30.)

This echoes the calls under Pillar One of the R2P to recall and encourage the primary obligations of the state concerned to protect its populations. Tier II of the POC concept can be seen to reflect part of the content of R2P's Pillar Three insofar as this is where timely and decisive response to civilians are under threat of physical violence is envisaged. As with Pillar Three, the use of force is entertained as a last resort as necessary. In addition, Tier III of the POC concept can be understood to include the whole range of programs intended to develop a society more conducive to protection. This is similar to Pillar Two of the R2P framework which envisages myriad programs and partnership between the international community and concerned state to realize Pillar One responsibilities.

17 For instance, efforts to draw attention to the abuses of UN blue helmets have a longer history (e.g., Amnesty International, 1994).

18 UN DPKO (2019) Webpage on Protection of Civilians: www.peacekeeping.un.org/en/protection-of-civilians-mandate

References

Amnesty International (1994). Peacekeeping and Human Rights. IOR 40/01/94, January 1994. London: Amnesty International.

Ban Ki-moon. (2008). On Responsible Sovereignty: International Cooperation for a Changed World. Speech in Berlin, SG/SM/11701, July 15, 2008.

Ban Ki-moon. (2009). Implementing the Responsibility to Protect. *In: Report of the Secretary-General*. New York: United Nations, A/63/677.

Ban Ki-moon. (2010). Early Warning, Assessment and the Responsibility to Protect. *Report of the Secretary-General*, A/64/864, July 14, 2010.

Ban Ki-moon (2011). The Role of Regional and Sub-regional Arrangements in Implementing the Responsibility to Protect. *Report of the Secretary-General*, S/2011/393.

Ban Ki-moon. (2012a). Responsibility to Protect: Timely and Decisive Response. *Report of the Secretary-General*, UN Doc. A/66/874–S/2012/578, July 25.

Ban Ki-moon. (2012b). *Report of the Secretary-General on the Protection of Civilians in Armed Conflict*, UN doc S/2012/376, May 22.

Ban Ki-moon. (2013a). Responsibility to Protect: State Responsibility and Prevention. *Report of the Secretary-General*, UN Doc S/2013/399, July 9.

Ban Ki-moon. (2013b). *Report of the Secretary-General on the Protection of Civilians in Armed Conflict*, UN Doc. S/2013/689, November 22.

Ban Ki-moon. (2014). International Assistance and the Responsibility to Protect. *Report of the Secretary-General*, UN Doc S/2014/449, July 11.

Ban Ki-moon. (2015). A Vital and Enduring Commitment: Implementing the Responsibility to Protect. *Report of the Secretary-General*, UN Doc S/2015/500, July 13.

Ban Ki-moon. (2016). Mobilizing Collective Action: The Next Decade of the Responsibility to Protect. *Report of the Secretary-General*, UN Doc S/2016/620, July 22.

Bellamy, A.J. (2012). R2P – Dead or Alive? *In: The Responsibility to Protect – From Evasive to Reluctant Action? The Role of Global Middle Powers*, 11–28. Hanns Seidel Foundation, Konrad-Adenauer-Siftung, Institute for Security Studies & South African Institute of International Affairs.

Bellamy, A.J. (2013). The Responsibility to Protect: Added Value or Hot Air? *Cooperation and Conflict*, 48(3): 333–357.

Bellamy, A.J. (2015). *Responsibility to Protect: A Defense*. Oxford: Oxford University Press.

Bellamy, A.J. (2016). The Humanisation of Security? Towards an International Human Protection Regime. *European Journal of International Security*, 1(1): 112–133. doi:10.1017/eis.2015.5

Bellamy, A.J. and Hunt, C.T. (2015). Twenty-first Century UN Peace Operations: Protection, Force and the Changing Security Environment. *International Affairs,* 91(6): 1277–1298.

Bellamy, A.J. and Williams, P.D. (2011). The New Politics of Protection? Côte d'Ivoire, Libya and the Responsibility to Protect. *International Affairs,* 87(4): 825–850.

Breakey, H. and Francis, A.J. (2011). Points of Convergence and Divergence: Normative, Institutional and Operational Relationships between R2P and POC. *Security Challenges,* 7(4): 39–50.

Doyle, M.W. (2011). International Ethics and the Responsibility to Protect. *International Studies Review,* 13(1): 72–84.

Francis, A., Popovski, V. and Sampford, C. (eds.) (2012). *Norms of Protection: Responsibility to Protect, Protection of Civilians and their Interaction.* Tokyo: United Nations University Press.

GCR2P (2009). The Relationship between the Responsibility to Protect and the Protection of Civilians in Armed Conflict. *Policy Brief.* New York: Global Centre for the Responsibility to Protect.

GCR2P (2018). R2P References in UN Security Council Resolutions and Presidential Statements. New York: Global Centre for the Responsibility to Protect.

Giffen, A. (2016). South Sudan. *In:* Bellamy, A. and Dunne, T. (eds.) *The Oxford Handbook of the Responsibility to Protect,* 857–875. Oxford: Oxford University Press.

Gifkins, J. (2016). R2P in the UN Security Council: Darfur, Libya and beyond. *Cooperation and Conflict,* 51(2): 148–165.

Guterres, A. (2017). Implementing the Responsibility to Protect: Accountability for Prevention. Report of the Secretary-General, UN Doc S/2017/556, August 10.

Guterres, A. (2018). Responsibility to Protect: From Early Warning to Early Action. Report of the Secretary-General, UN Doc S/2018/525 June 1.

Hassler, S. (2010). Peacekeeping and the Responsibility to Protect. *Journal of International Peacekeeping,* 14(1–2): 134–183.

Hehir, A. (2012). *The Responsibility to Protect: Rhetoric, Reality and the Future of Humanitarian Intervention.* London: Palgrave Macmillan.

Hehir, A. (2016). Assessing the Influence of the Responsibility to Protect on the UN Security Council During the Arab Spring. *Cooperation and Conflict,* 51: 166–183.

Holt, V.K., Taylor, G. and Kelly, M. (2009). Protecting Civilians in the Context of UN Peacekeeping Operations: Successes, Setbacks and Remaining Challenges. *In: Independent Study Jointly Commissioned by the DPKO and the Office for the Coordination of Humanitarian Affairs.* New York: United Nations Department of Peacekeeping Operations, United Nations Office for the Coordination of Humanitarian Affairs.

Hultman, L. (2013). UN Peace Operations and Protection of Civilians: Cheap Talk or Norm Implementation? *Journal of Peace Research,* 50(1): 59–73. doi:10.1177/0022343312461662

Hunt, C.T. (2016). Côte d'Ivoire. *In:* Bellamy, A. and Dunne, T. (eds.) *The Oxford Handbook of the Responsibility to Protect,* 693–716. Oxford: Oxford University Press.

Hunt, C.T. and Bellamy, A.J. (2011). Mainstreaming the Responsibility to Protect in Peace Operations. *Civil Wars,* 13(1): 1–20.

Hunt, C.T. and Sharland, L. (2019). Implementing the Responsibility to Protect through United Nations Peacekeeping Operations: Opportunities and Challenges. *In:* Jacob, C. and Mennecke, M. (eds.) *Implementing R2P: First Experiences and a Future Agenda,* 215–235. Abingdon: Routledge.

Kurtz, G. and Rotmann, P. (2016). The Evolution of Norms of Protection: Major Powers Debate the Responsibility to Protect. *Global Society,* 30(1): 3–20.

Lie, J.H.S. and de Carvalho, B. (2012). Conceptual Unclarity and Competition: The Protection of Civilians and the Responsibility to Protect. *In:* de Carvalho, B. and Sending, O.J. (eds.) *The Protection of Civilians in UN Peacekeeping: Concept, Implementation and Practice*, 47–61. Baden-Baden: Nomos.

Lotze, W. (2011). A Tale of Two Councils – The African Union, the United Nations and the Protection of Civilians in Côte d'Ivoire. *Global Responsibility to Protect,* 3(3): 365–375. doi:10.1163/187598411X589617

Mbeki, T. (2011). What the World Got Wrong in Côte d'Ivoire. *Foreign Policy*, 29 April.

Mégret, F. (2015). Between R2P and the ICC: "Robust Peacekeeping" and the Quest for Civilian Protection. *Criminal Law Forum*, 26: 101–151.

Nasu, H. (2011). Operationalizing the Responsibility to Protect in the Context of Civilian Protection by UN Peacekeepers. *International Peacekeeping,* 18(4): 117–133. doi:10.1080/13533312.2011.588384

Piiparinen, T. (2016). The Interventionist Turn of UN Peacekeeping: New Western Politics of Protection or Bureaucratic Mission Creep? *Journal of Human Rights*, 15(1): 98–125.

Popovski, V. (2011). The Concepts of Responsibility to Protect and Protection of Civilians: "Sisters but not Twins." *Security Challenges,* 7(4): 1–12.

Sloan, J. (2014). The Evolution of the Use of Force in UN Peacekeeping. *Journal of Strategic Studies*, 37(5): 674–702.

Tardy, T. (2012). The Dangerous Liaisons of the Responsibility to Protect and the Protection of Civilians in Peacekeeping Operations. *Global Responsibility to Protect,* 4(4): 424–448. doi:10.1163/1875984x-00404003

Thakur, R. (2013). Protection Gaps for Civilian Victims of Political Violence. *South African Journal of International Affairs,* 20(3): 321–338.

UN Security Council Resolutions: 1265 (1999a); 1270 (1999b); 1296 (2000); 1502 (2003); 1674 (2006); 1738 (2006); 1856 (2008a); 1894 (2009f); 1970 (2011a); 1973 (2011b); 1975 (2011c); 1996 (2011d); 2150 (2014); 2175 (2014); 2222 (2015); 2286 (2016); 2399 [January 30, 2018]; 2409 [March 27, 2018]; 2417 (2018); 2423 [June 28, 2018]; 2428 [July 13, 2018]; 2429 [July 13, 2018]; 2431 [July 30, 2018].

UN DPKO (2019). Webpage on Protection of Civilians. www.un.org/en/peacekeeping/issues/civilian.shtml

UN (2005). World Summit Outcome Document (WSOD).

UN (2008b). *United Nations Peacekeeping Operations: Principles and Guidelines.* Peacekeeping Best Practices Section. New York: United Nations.

UN (2009a). SC Verbatim Records: 6066th Meeting, UN Doc S/PV.6066 (Resumption 1), January 14, 2009.

UN (2009b). *A New Partnership Agenda: Charting a New Horizon for UN Peacekeeping.* New York: DPKO/DFS.

UN (2009c). Concept Note on Robust Peacekeeping. New York: UN Department of Peacekeeping Operations (DPKO) and Department of Field Support (DFS).

UN (2009d). SC Verbatim Records: 6151st Meeting, UN Doc S/PV.6151 (Resumption 1), June 26, 2009.

UN (2009e). Report of the Special Committee on Peacekeeping Operations and its Working Group, 2009 Substantive Session (February 23–March 20, 2009), A/63/19, March 24, 2009.

UN (2010a). Draft Operational Concept for POC in Peacekeeping Operations. New York: DPKO/DFS.

UN (2010b). Framework for Drafting Comprehensive Protection of Civilians (POC) Strategies in UN Peacekeeping Operations. New York: DPKO/DFS. www.globalprotectioncluster.org/_assets/files/tools_and_guidance/protection_of_civilians/Framework_Comprehensive_PoC_Strategies_EN.pdf

UN (2010c). UN System-Wide Strategy for the Protection of Civilians in the Democratic Republic of the Congo. United Nations Organization Mission in the Democratic Republic of Congo (MONUC) and UN Office of the High Commissioner for Human Rights. www.globalprotectioncluster.org/_assets/files/field_protection_clusters/Democratic_Republic_Congo/files/UN_Wide_Protection_Strategy_Final_150110_EN.pdf

UN (2012). General Assembly Adopts Text Condemning Violence in Syria, Demanding That All Sides End Hostilities. General Assembly, UN Doc GA/11372. www.un.org/press/en/2012/ga11266Rev1.doc.htm

UN (2014). Evaluation of the Implementation and Results of Protection of Civilians Mandates in United Nations Peacekeeping Operations. Report of the Office of Internal Oversight Services. New York: United Nations OIOS.

UN (2015a). *Protection of Civilians Policy*. New York: DPKO/DFS.

UN (2018). Peacebuilding and Sustaining Peace. *Report of the Secretary-General*, A/72/707–S/2018/43. New York: United Nations.

van Steenberghe, R. (2014). The Notions of the Responsibility to Protect and the Protection of Civilians in Armed Conflict: Detecting Their Association and Its Impact Upon International Law. *Goettingen Journal of International Law*, 6(1): 81–114.

Williams, P.D. (2016a). The R2P, Protection of Civilians, and UN Peacekeeping Operations. *In:* Bellamy, A. and Dunne, T. (eds.) *The Oxford Handbook of the Responsibility to Protect*, 524–544. Oxford: Oxford University Press.

Williams, P.D. (2016b). Key Questions for South Sudan's New Protection Force. *IPI Global Observatory*, September 12, 2016. https://theglobalobservatory.org/2016/09/south-sudan-regional-protection-force-kiir-unmiss/

Wills, S. (2009). *Protecting Civilians: The Obligations of Peacekeepers*. Oxford: Oxford University Press.

5 R2P and WPS

Operationalizing prevention from alignment

Sara E. Davies and Sarah Hewitt

Introduction

How can two distinct normative agendas, the Responsibility to Protect (R2P) and Women, Peace and Security (WPS), be mutually advanced to deliver tangible benefit to raise women's participation in conflict prevention at the state, regional and international level? Together with other protection and prevention orientated norm regimes, such as Protection of Civilians (POC) (Hunt, Chapter 4 in this volume), R2P and WPS developed in separation but parallel to each other as watershed norms for prevention, protection and reconstruction (Hunt and Orchard, the Introduction in this volume; Davies and True, 2019; Shepherd, 2011; True, 2016). This is not to say that R2P and WPS are not contested international norms by different actors (Orchard, Chapter 1 in this volume; Ghogliagha and Loges, Chapter 3 in this volume; Gibbings, 2011) but they are constructed normative frameworks for state's R2P their populations in the case of R2P, and for WPS, the recognition of women's unique experiences of conflict and importance of women's participation in peace and security decision-making. In previous analysis of this relationship we, (Davies and Teitt, 2012) and Hewitt (2016), have argued for R2P and WPS to 'talk' more to each other. We have identified how shared pillars, such as prevention especially, provide opportunities for R2P and WPS advocates to develop a shared meaning and approach. In both WPS and R2P literature, it has been increasingly pointed out that it is vital to advocate for prevention measures in other venues where R2P and WPS may align such as the Human Rights Council and the General Assembly (Davies, 2016; Harris Rimmer, 2014; Welsh, 2016; Ralph, 2018).

Kirsten Ainley has argued that "R2P advocates should expand their gaze to the full field of human rights protection to maximize the potential impact of the doctrine" (2017: 244). The 2017 United Nations (UN) Secretary-General's report on the R2P called for states, regional organizations and international organizations to individually and collectively pay more attention to commitments to core international human rights instruments by UN member states as a core preventative measure (UN Secretary-General, 2017a). This call is a continuation of a deliberate shift to promote R2P as 'more' than an intervention norm and to emphasize its prevention capacity (UN Secretary-General, 2009;

UN Secretary-General, 2013). This approach aligns with contemporary WPS advocacy, particularly in the recent UN Women commissioned Global Study on UN Security Council Resolution 1325 (UN Women, 2015), to pay more attention to prevention mechanisms as the best way to address protection and participation gaps concerning women's peace and security (due to UN Security Council inaction). In this chapter we progress previous arguments on the need to identify shared meaning and approach of R2P and WPS in the area of women's human rights protection. We consider how shared advocacy for a women's rights protection focus as an atrocity-prevention measure may be promoted, even normalized, in post-conflict peace processes. To illustrate this, we examine the single case study of the Nepal peace process and the early warning activities of women's civil society within that country to promote the normalization of conflict prevention. The Nepal case is an important but overlooked case for R2P and WPS advocates in observing how the promotion of gender equality with minority groups human rights dialogue can serve to prevent further human rights violations, even mass atrocities.

Two normative agendas with one prevention agenda: R2P and WPS

The WPS agenda was first introduced in 2000 under UN Security Council Resolution 1325. Since then, the UN Security Council has endorsed nine additional WPS resolutions: 1820 (2008), 1888 (2009), 1889 (2009), 1960 (2010), 2106 (2013), 2122 (2013), 2422 (2015), 2467 (2019) and 2493 (2019). Included among the provisions endorsed in these resolutions are: the importance of women's leadership and political participation in peace and security institutions; introduction of gender-specific measures to protect women during conflict and instability, including against sexual and gender-based violence; the need to address impunity for such sexual and gender-based violations; recognition of the vital role women civil society organizations play in conflict prevention and peacebuilding; and the need for more systematic plans of action at the national, regional and international level to advance gender equality and women's rights protection (Security Council Report, 2017; Davies and True, 2019).

Promoting greater awareness and inclusion of the WPS agenda in all R2P prevention and response activities has increasingly become a core focus for several R2P partners and institutions. After the adoption of the R2P principle in Paragraphs 138 and 139 in the 2005 World Summit Outcome Document (WSOD); the General Assembly passed a unanimous resolution in 2009 in which it pledged to continue its consideration of the implementation of R2P (see Hunt and Orchard, in the Introduction in this volume). Since then, the Secretary-General has issued a report on R2P each year and the General Assembly has debated it in an informal and interactive dialogue. The R2P principle increasingly became part of the diplomatic language used in the Security Council, albeit unevenly and with patchy results, to call for preventative diplomacy and the use of force to prevent and respond to atrocity crimes. In 2011, the Security

Council's responses to the crises in Libya and Côte d'Ivoire demonstrated a determination to act on the responsibility to protect populations from atrocity crimes, including through the use of force when necessary (Bellamy and Williams, 2011). But the responses proved highly controversial. Russia in particular argued that the Libyan experience colored its thinking on the subsequent crisis in Syria, pushing it to resist Western pressure on the al-Assad regime (Averre and Davies, 2015).

The UN Security Council has been deadlocked on Syria, Yemen, and Myanmar, but at the same time the Security Council has continued to employ R2P and WPS in other contexts. Resolution 1996, adopted in July 2011, established a UN peace operation for South Sudan and called upon the international community to provide assistance to help the new government there to fulfill its R2P. Resolution 2117 (2013) on small arms and light weapons recognized their capacity to result in the commission of R2P crimes; and Resolution 2121 (2013) on the Central African Republic (CAR) underscored the government's responsibility to protect its own population. Resolution 2106 (2013) on sexual and gender-based violence was explicit on calling out for states to take responsibility to prevent these crimes through adopting military and police protocols concerning the investigation and prosecution of sexual crimes; the introduction of legislation and judicial processes to document, investigate and prosecute sexual violence in conflict and post-conflict; and for states to cooperate with UN Commissions of Inquiry (Murphy and Burke, 2015; Trillò, 2015).

As Phil Orchard (Chapter 1 in this volume) argues, R2P must move beyond being treated as a stand-alone issue but situated within the broader legacies of other human rights normative frameworks as well as more contemporary developments such as WPS. The two agendas are different but complimentary. The WPS agenda frames a four-pillar agenda (prevention, protection, participation, relief and recovery) for including women in international peace and security. The R2P principle frames a three-pillar agenda (prevention, assistance, action to prevent) for how world governments and international organizations think about the prevention of genocide and mass atrocities and responses to them. Where the two pillars intersect is in a collective goal to direct Security Council focus preventative diplomacy over intervention. Increasingly, as we explore below, when efforts in the Security Council reach a deadlock, both the WPS and R2P agenda (and their advocates) are turning to alternative institutions to realize the prevention agenda.

R2P and WPS prevention intersections

R2P

In 2017, UN Secretary-General António Guterres foregrounded prevention as a cornerstone of his tenure as UN Secretary-General in both the R2P and WPS agendas. The responsibility to prevent as outlined by the 2005 WSOD recognized that "Each individual State has the responsibility to protect its populations from genocide, was crimes, ethnic cleansing and crimes against humanity. This responsibility entails the prevention of such crimes, including their incitement, through appropriate and necessary means" (UN, 2005, para. 138).

In the 2017 R2P report, Guterres defines prevention as "doing everything we can to help States to avert the outbreak of the crises that take such a high toll on humanity" (UN Secretary-General, 2017a: para. 2). He calls for closing the gap between commitment and reality by strengthening international and national, legal, moral and political accountability to assist in implementing and operationalizing the responsibility to prevent. Guterres draws connections between the occurrence of atrocity crimes and migration and refugee flows and how international responsibility extends beyond national borders. The UN Secretary-General outlines several existing UN and international prevention initiatives, including the Human Rights Up Front action plan which is intended to improve early warning systems, efficiency, support for national authorities and internal accountability.

The report calls for greater synergy between the three pillars of the UN system: human rights, peace and security, and development (and all agendas that fall under those pillars). The report calls for implementation through addressing who is responsible for the prevention of atrocity crimes and ensuring accountability of those responsible for prevention to translate into collective and individual action to prevent (ibid.: para. 9). The report outlines three mirroring elements of responsibility and accountability to ensure mass atrocities are prevented: moral, legal and political. Therefore, Guterres argues, the approach to accountability and responsibility must encompass this (ibid.: para. 10) "to ensure those with a responsibility for preventing atrocity crimes are held accountable for fulfilling that responsibility" (ibid.: para. 11).

Legal, moral and political accountability engage with different actors, institutions and mechanisms but are united in the common goal to prevent mass atrocities. Legal accountability is the most straightforward and relates to obligations under national and international law. Legal responsibility is the legal obligation of states through national constitutions and legal codes that guarantee fundamental rights of populations to address the root causes of atrocity crimes, including patterns of identity-based discrimination, economic deprivation and associated weaknesses in state structures and institutions. The responsibility of states to prevent atrocity crimes is a legal obligation based on creating functioning and legitimate state structures and institutions that respect human rights, rule of law, equitable service delivery, enforcement of laws that prohibit mass atrocities, and the ability to diffuse and de-escalate tensions (ibid.: paras. 12–14).

Moral accountability challenges 'us' (as in the international community and member states) to reflect on whether ethical standards, based on the broad range of universally shared values, are being met (ibid.: paras. 12, 15). Political accountability in national settings refers to the relationship between governments, parliaments and the populations they serve including the political responsibility to implement explicit commitments states have made to the prevention of atrocity crimes through the WSOD as well as related international treaties and conventions such as the Geneva Convention and Protocols, Convention on the Elimination of all Forms of Discrimination Against Women (CEDAW), and Arms Trade Treaty (ibid.: paras. 12, 15–16, 18). International political accountability refers to those who have authority and responsibility (Security Council), are answerable to their peers and contribute to the prevention of atrocity crimes based on our common humanity (ibid.: paras. 12, 16).

The report outlines three sites to implement this accountability – through state and national mechanisms, intergovernmental bodies and the UN system (ibid.: sections III–V). National and state mechanisms may present the biggest opportunity for women's engagement and participation. The report outlines several compliance measures to meet their obligations stemming from international law. This includes: (1) ratifying and implementing core instruments of the international human rights architecture; (2) national self-assessments to understand potential risks within a state's own communities, the mechanisms and policies to reduce and mitigate those risks, and the capacity to protect populations if the need arises; (3) holding state governmental institutions accountable through the participation of civil society, parliamentary processes and requesting and allowing international assistance in meeting their responsibility when necessary; (4) establishing and maintaining independent national human rights mechanisms; (5) guaranteeing accountability of the security forces; (6) ensuring accountability and redress for past atrocity crimes; and (7) encouraging open and inclusive dialogue and reflection on national experience and transparency by including the participation of civil society (e.g., shadow reports) and perspectives of women and youth, in developing risk assessments, designing prevention measures and maintaining transparency and accountability.

Intergovernmental bodies to ensure prevention accountability include regional and international institutions and processes and cooperation between the two. Regional organizations and associated regional human rights mechanisms are vital in the prevention of atrocity crimes, having contextual knowledge and understanding to implement prevention and protection measures as well as mobilize collective action and foster regional cooperation. The Security Council has the greatest authority to take timely and decisive action to protect populations from mass atrocities and implementing R2P. However due to the growing P5 and geopolitical tensions, the Security Council has experienced deadlocks in instances where states were failing to protect civilians, such as acts of (possible) crimes against humanity and war crimes in Syria, and (possible) crimes against humanity and ethnic cleansing in the Rakhine State in Myanmar.

As such, a new development for R2P in the 2017 report is that it underlines the importance of alternative mechanisms and institutions to deliver protection outside of the Security Council (for instance, see Hunt, Chapter 4 in this volume on the POC mandate). For example, the UN Economic and Social Council is mentioned in the context of the Sustainable Development Goals, with a particular focus on Goal 16 on the promotion of just, peaceful and inclusive societies. This should not be overlooked as this alignment is presenting a relationship between mass atrocities and the need to address socioeconomic inequality: which is a critical aspect for women's participation and protection. Another intergovernmental mechanism mentioned as well placed to support prevention efforts is the Human Rights Council, specifically the Universal Periodic Review to support states to meet their international and national legal and political obligations to prevent atrocity crimes and uphold their populations' human rights. Lastly, the report refers to the establishment of a global network of R2P focal points to foster interstate collaboration, dialogue and exchange to strengthen prevention efforts. The UNSG report also recommends the UN System, through its umbrella bodies and country offices, play a vital role in supporting international and states' capacities and prevention efforts, responding to risk of and/or occurrence of atrocity crimes, and maintaining momentum in implementing R2P.

This is a report that does not ignore the Security Council but is clearly frustrated with its inability to advance the protection of populations at great risk of harm and rights violations. The report articulates a legal, moral and political responsibility to prevent and identifies the fulfillment of human rights, including (crucial given the importance of these rights in the gender empowerment space) the fulfillment of socioeconomic rights as benchmarks that sovereign states need to be measured against to successfully prevent mass atrocities. This shift permits the engagement of new institutions as responsible actors for implementing the R2P agenda, including (again, significantly, given the location of the gender and human rights space) the Human Rights Council.

WPS

In the WPS space there has also been the acceleration of engagement with the agenda outside of the Security Council. Crucially, in 2013, CEDAW opened the door to WPS discussion in its meeting and reports with General Recommendation No. 30 on Women in Conflict Prevention, Conflict and Post-Conflict Situations. On the remit of the WPS agenda the Committee stated a right to engage in matters that promoted "*the prevention of armed conflict itself, and the prevention of gender-based harms that precede and result from political violence*" (CEDAW, 2013: para. 29).

Fast forward to 2015, we see High-level reviews of three major peace and security frameworks – UN peacebuilding architecture, peace operations, and women, peace and security – all convey the need for greater attention toward prevention. The High-level Independent Panel on United Nations Peace Operations found that prevention was "the poor relative of better resourced peace operations deployed during and after armed conflict". Likewise, the 2015 Review of the United Nations Peacebuilding Architecture noted that there is "little effective UN attention to prevention, great attention to crisis response (though still frequently less than is needed), and again relatively little in the recovery and reconstruction phase": an 'inverted U' with prevention and recovery at the bottom.

The 2015 Global Study on WPS, "Preventing Conflict, Securing Peace" (UN Women, 2015) notes that despite 15 years of civil society advocacy of the prevention of conflict as the strongest realization of the WPS agenda, states and the UN have consistently failed to prioritize prevention.

The Global Study found that conflict prevention had not been taken seriously, consistently, in diplomatic and high-level political engagements. And the few conflict-prevention efforts that existed had rarely considered the fragility and instability caused by the failure to address gender inequality. In an environment where political, ethnic and religious persecution is widespread, women's inequality on account of their sex compounds their risk of human rights violations. In these situations, women are more likely to be subject to sexual and gender-based violence, and all forms of violence in general. States and non-state actors are likely to permit, even condone, impunity for widespread violations, which perpetuates the cycle of violence.

Like R2P prevention efforts, the Global Study approaches to conflict prevention are grouped in two categories. The first is operational, short-term practical strategies, such as early warning and response, preventive diplomacy, peacekeeping, and community-level mediation, dispute and conflict mitigation mechanisms (ibid.: 195). The second is structural long-term prevention, that addresses the roots of war, conflict and militarism, and the underlying causes of violence and insecurity. This is aimed at addressing structural inequality, discrimination and violence, promote human rights and human security, and de-militarization, disarmament and reduction of arms spending (ibid.: 204).

Long-term structural prevention is multisectoral in that it brings together the three pillars of the UN – development, human rights, and peace and security – as well as connecting other insecurities and grievances such as economic inequalities and oppression, climate change and environmental degradation and associated crises, and historical and social exclusion, contribute to overall insecurity and conflict, and potential mass atrocities. It also links gender equality with security and long-term prevention and highlights the transformative potential of the WPS agenda to transform structures that maintain inequality and the continuum of violence (True, 2012). The Global Study outlines three gendered, structural contributions to the emergence of conflict: the continuum of gender-based violence, the proliferation of arms, including small arms; and climate change and natural resource scarcity as causes of conflict.

At the opening of the debate on the Global Study in the Security Council in October 2015, then UN Secretary-General, Ban Ki-moon said: the "one common theme" across the reviews of the UN Peace Operations, Peacebuilding Architecture, and WPS in 2015 is that "any reforms must include gender equality and women's leadership as central ingredients, and must be strongly grounded in human rights." The High-level debate was followed by the UN Security Council adoption of UNSCR 2422 (2015) which included the proposal to create the Informal Experts Group (IEG) on WPS, who meet on specific situations under the attention of the Security Council, to prioritize and normalize the inclusion of gender considerations as well as the rights situation of women in situations on the Council's agenda.

In 2017, the UNSG's Report on WPS continued the focus on conflict prevention as core to the realization of WPS, noting, "the direct relationship between gender equality on the one hand and resilience to and prevention of conflict on the other" (UN Secretary-General, 2017b: para. 1). The report emphasizes women's participation and inclusion in prevention efforts, as well as the need to move beyond imminence of crises toward addressing structural and root causes of crises, including inequality (ibid.: para. 5). Former Secretary-General Ban Ki-moon's tenure largely presided over the development of WPS commitments. Guterres is able to build on the past 15 years of WPS development and put women's meaningful participation at the heart of his signature platform of prevention, the 'surge in diplomacy for peace,' to hopefully actualize tangible results. For instance, Guterres has set up an Advisory Board on mediation that has 50 percent women and has set the goal of gender parity in senior UN leadership by 2021 (UN Secretary-General, 2017c: 4, 7). Guterres argues that gender equality is crucial in conflict prevention, implementing by guaranteeing women's meaningful leadership and participation, strengthening technical gender expertise in conflict analysis, and ensuring financing for gender equality and WPS. Similar to the 2017 Report on R2P, in his 2017 Report on WPS, Guterres refer to the shortfalls of the Security Council in upholding agendas such as gender equality and WPS especially in emerging or deteriorating crises (UN Secretary-General, 2017b: para. 90).

Prevention has always been important to both the R2P and WPS agendas, but there is no doubt there is an increased turn to prevention with the Security Council facing protracted crises and, in some cases, refusing to discuss some crises at all. This frustration has led to, we suggest, important operational synergies for R2P and WPS to align. The creation of the IEG on WPS to hear briefings and reports on country situations where there is the risk of atrocities or a history of atrocities, lifts both WPS and R2P out of their silos to be understood holistically with reference to countries that require the attention of the Security Council and, we suggest crucially, additional institutions (Security Council Report, 2017).

Human rights alignment

An important, emerging, operational alignment between R2P and WPS is in the UN Human Rights Council in Geneva and its Convention Committees – particularly CEDAW. The introduction of General Recommendation 30 means that even if countries are unwilling to align WPS with R2P, minority groups and those facing discrimination within a country can establish the link through shadow reporting procedures attached to CEDAW and Universal Periodic Reporting. The focus on WPS and R2P has been, to date, primarily on establishing a mutual agenda where there is consensus, namely the prevention of and protection from sexual and gender-based violence. This relationship should continue to invest in reporting mechanisms, evidence gathering and early warning mechanisms. However, for an R2P and WPS relationship to flourish and prevent such atrocities, it is particularly important to look for avenues in different areas and institutional contexts. For example, the 2013 Secretary-General report specifically referred to the need for the inclusion of gender indicators to support early warning and the recognition of women's groups as agents of protection

(UN Secretary-General, 2013: 9). The incorporation of gender equality into the security and justice sectors, for instance, is recognized as a core component of the prevention of atrocity crimes. However, as evidenced by the 2017 informal interactive dialogue on the UN Secretary-General's Report on R2P, local women's expertise on early warning efforts and women's contributions toward mobilizing local action for peace continue to be disregarded and even ignored by most of the international community (PeaceWomen, 2017).

The UN Secretary-General has, over the years, made a number of recommendations for establishing the protection of women and promotion of gender equality as part of a framework for implementing R2P (UN Secretary-General, 2013, 2017a). Incorporating gender discrimination and gender rights abuses indicators into the operationalization of the Office of the Special Representative for the Prevention of Genocide and the R2P, particularly when making country-specific recommendations and statements on high-risk situations, would be a valuable contribution to IEG on WPS, IASC and Human Rights Council processes, especially since the introduction of CEDAW Committee General Recommendation 30 (Harris Rimmer, 2014). Such recommendations have sparked and enabled practical work in regional human rights bodies. For example, in 2017, one of the principal sites of R2P advocacy, the Asia Pacific Centre for the Responsibility to Protect, teamed up with the ASEAN Commission on the Protection and Promotion of the Rights of Women and Children to explore the linkages between atrocity prevention, gender empowerment and the elimination of discrimination (ASEAN, 2017). This is but one example of how to support women's human rights organizations on the ground, often in fragile situations, to report behaviors of discrimination and brutality as both a violation of WPS and R2P agendas in their shadow reporting. In post-conflict country situations, we have not yet seen regular practice of linking atrocity prevention and gender empowerment. We suggest, in our final section, that there is a clear opportunity to begin 'normalizing' this process by observing (and commending) practices in the post-conflict stage.

Going forward, R2P advocates and office holders need to embrace the struggle against gender discrimination and inequality on its own terms and recognize the multiple roles that women and girls play in contexts of genocide and mass atrocities as victims, bystanders, perpetrators, protectors and peacemakers. The Secretary-General has essentially recognized that R2P can achieve its objectives only when the UN's goals in WPS, and in relation to ending gender discrimination more broadly, are achieved. At the same time, however, advocates of WPS must also recognize that they will not achieve the goals set by their own agenda while that of eliminating atrocity crimes remains unfulfilled.

Prevention of human rights violations as an R2P-WPS prevention measure: the Nepal case

Endemic poverty and group inequality and marginalization in the political, economic and social spheres were key structural causes for the onset of the decade-long 'People's War' in Nepal (1996–2006) stemming from exclusion based on caste, religion, ethnicity, geographic location, gender and language (von Einsiedel et al., 2012; Yadav, 2016). Neither the monarchical constitutional government nor the Communist Party of Nepal-Maoists (SPN-M) who launched the insurgency were exempt from perpetrating human right violations including, inter alia, extrajudicial killings, enforced disappearances, forced conscription of children into armed ranks and sexual and gender-based violence. According to Nepal's Ministry of Peace and Reconstruction (MOPR), 17,886 people were killed, 1,530 were disappeared, 3,142 persons were abducted, 8,935 persons were disabled, 79,571 persons were displaced, 9,000 women became widows, 620 children became orphans and the property of 17,484 people was damaged (Upreti and Shivakoti, 2018: 78). Conflict was largely fought in rural areas, where 87 percent of women live, and civilians lived in a climate of fear caught between Maoists demanding support, free food and shelter, and security forces that would target providers of that coerced support (HRW, 2014: 20; Karki and Upadhyay, 2011: 210). Security forces raped and sexually abused female combatants after arrest and targeted female relatives of Maoist suspects or supposed supporters. Human Rights Watch (2014) found that Maoist combatants also abducted and raped women, particularly those who refused to join their ranks. In the absence of men, who had either joined the conflict or migrated for employment, women were extremely vulnerable and bore extraordinary burdens during the war (Karki and Upadhyay, 2011: 210).

Yet, women were active participants in the conflict, with an estimated 20–30 percent of Maoist combatants being female, women's emancipation being a key feature of Maoist ideology, and women's leadership and dedicated women's wings prominent within the Maoist military and civilian structures (Kolås and Tryggestad, 2017: 3–4). Furthermore, women and the women's movement were significantly involved and present in the broad-based peaceful protests, the Second People's Movement (*Jana Andolan II*), which eventually led to the peace process and the signing of the Comprehensive Peace Agreement (CPA) in November 2006 that began the constitution-making process. Despite women's involvement in, and experiences during, the conflict and a strong women's movement throughout the Second People's Movement, women were totally excluded from peace negotiations and the original six-member interim constitution-drafting committee. Due to lobbying and pressure from women's civil society and women leaders, the committee was eventually expanded to include four women representing the four major political parties. Consequently, via women's direct participation and consistent lobbying by the women's movement, the Interim Constitution (2007) included gender and women's rights provisions addressing issues such as non-discrimination, violence against women, sexual and reproductive health, property rights and proportional inclusion. This led to the unprecedented and historic election of 197 women to the Constituent Assembly (33 percent) from a variety of backgrounds and identities, where previously women's political representation had never exceeded 6 percent (Yadav, 2016: 61; IDEA, 2011). Proportional inclusion also extended to local peace committees that were formed to promote inclusive peacemaking and peacebuilding at district, municipal and village levels (Baniya et al., 2017: 6).

Though political instability and corruption plagued this post-conflict government, after a decade of constitutional negotiations and relative peace the Final Constitution was passed in 2015 in the aftermath of the devastating April earthquake (Baniya et al., 2017). It consolidated some women's rights and gender equality gains including women's political representation in federal, municipal and local governments, though retained discriminatory citizenship rights where women are unable to confer citizenship to their children. Ethnic group grievances over federalism and state restructuring issues contained in the 2015 constitution has led to the re-emergence of local conflicts (Paswan, 2017; Strasheim, 2019). For instance, the *Madhesi* ethnic group in the Terai area neighboring India argue that the final constitution disadvantages their community, where violent protests and clashes with police led to 50 people dead (von Einsiedel and Salih, 2017: 5).

In Nepal, violence against women, including domestic violence, sexual and gender-based violence, child marriage and human trafficking continue to be major concerns coupled with witchcraft accusations and stigma attached to single women and widows. Furthermore, many transitional processes that are tasked with dealing with the root and structural causes that led to conflict, as well as violations that occurred during it such as conflict-related sexual violence and enforced disappearances, are politicized and heavily influenced by political parties. The failure to independently address conflict-related violence has resulted in little faith in transitional justice endeavors and hope for reparations and accountability (Baniya et al., 2017: 8). This is a critical disappointment of Nepal's transition, and vital to rectify in the prevention of conflict and violence.

Despite political power wrangling between the major political parties, women's political and civil society campaigning has seen the passing of legislation relating to domestic and sexual violence, inheritance rights, witchcraft, human trafficking, reproductive rights as well as national action plans on WPS Resolutions 1325 and 1820. There is no doubt that women's rights on paper have progressed enormously since the Maoist conflict and that Nepal's constitutions have had a transformative impact on women's participation (Yadav, 2016; IDEA, 2011). However, implementation of these gains confront many challenges, including: patriarchal attitudes and mindsets; major gaps between policy and practice, lip service and action, tokenism and women's substantive participation; women's burden of care; access to sexual and reproductive health; and intersectional inequalities between different groups based on caste, indigeneity, geographic location, class and so on. Despite women's increased descriptive representation, access to decision-making power and influence is limited due to these constraints.

This has been particularly evident in the aftermath of the 2017 local elections which were held for the first time in 20 years since the outbreak of conflict. The 2015 constitution mandates that political parties must nominate at least one woman to major or vice-major positions at village, municipal and district levels. Further, two out of four seats on every ward committee at the village level must be filled by a woman and a Dalit woman (most underprivileged and socioeconomically lowest group in the Hindu caste system). In 2017, 14,339 ethnically diverse women were elected to local government positions. However, data reveals the overwhelming bias privileging men in decision-making positions of power, where only 2 percent of 753 mayor and chair positions went to women versus 91 percent of deputy mayor/chairs (Paswan, 2017). Initial observations of women in local government positions reflect that these women, like female representatives at the federal level, continue to face patriarchal gendered attitudes and norms that question women's capacity and leadership and constrain women's participation and influence (Baruah and Reyes, 2017).

Since the end of conflict, Nepal has begun the arduous transition from conflict to 'peace,' autocracy to democracy, and from an exclusionary centralized state to a federal one (von Einsiedel and Salih, 2017: 2). This has not been an easy process with many outstanding issues remaining, especially around transitional justice, and the potential for conflict re-emerging. How and in what ways women's increased descriptive participation in political institutions has had a substantive conflict-prevention impact requires further and lengthier inquiry. However, despite huge challenges to the full enjoyment of women's rights, the opening of space for women's diverse voices since the People's War has had a transformative impact on individual women's lives and perceptions of their own personal capacities and capabilities (Yadav, 2016; IDEA, 2011). Furthermore, what is evident in this post-conflict phase, is the persistent efforts to maintain inclusionary discourse, policies and (some) action to provide access for otherwise marginalized groups, including women. This is an important case study on how women's empowerment engagements post-conflict, combined with civil society and state efforts to protect marginalized groups is coalescing.

There is an enormous amount of sustained work and activism, as well as potential and opportunity, for the women's movement to hold the government of Nepal accountable, to mitigate violence and to continue dialogue at both federal and grassroots levels with networks of widows, economic cooperatives, Dalit women and mother groups spanning the entire country. This was apparent during the 2017 local elections where different women's organizations and networks coordinated and divided up tasks to support women's political participation, either through campaigning for female candidates or providing civic and voter education. The interconnectedness of female representatives and women's civil society is a critical relationship to maintain to ensure advocacy on increasing women's participation and gender equality and, ultimately, to create a more equal, just and peaceful society.

A critical juncture to connect R2P and WPS efforts and to specifically advance women's participation and protection of women's human rights is ensuring and supporting sustained efforts in the implementation of progressive gender legislation and policies through the inclusion of female representatives at all levels of government. The local elections and women's participation in those local and village governments brought an unprecedented number of women into the public discourse and a critical opportunity to empower not just federal governments but local women and men to creatively prevent and respond to the threat and occurrence of violence. This is not to advance essentialist assumptions that women are inherently peaceful or will advocate women's rights agendas. But to promote more meaningful and diverse dialogue from different standpoints of issues that individuals and communities face of political, social and economic marginalization including poverty, employment, gender- and caste-based violence, and political exclusion, and how addressing these grievances contribute to the prevention of violence.

Reporting to the Universal Periodic Review (UPR) and CEDAW (of which Nepal underwent in 2018 for CEDAW) are important measures for keeping track of how Nepal is progressing in these spaces, but Nepal also illustrates the importance of looking at individual countries needs and capacity to synergize R2P and WPS in practice. For instance, a major part of the prevention agenda of both R2P and WPS is early warning systems (Ainley, 2017). The benefit of early warning systems should not be viewed as only applicable to situations before the Security Council. If we look at Nepal, the creation of a WPS and R2P early warning network – where reports are made on the safety and capacity to work of the 14,339 local government female representatives (some representing marginalized groups) across the country where access to rural areas is limited – could be an incredibly valuable opportunity to prevent violence and build capacity and knowledge on R2P and WPS of these new female representatives.

Another opportunity to connect WPS and R2P prevention agendas would be through Nepal's National Action Plan (NAP) on 1325 and 1820 and link it to Nepal's CEDAW and UPR reporting obligations. Although the development of Nepal's second NAP has stalled, the development of its first NAP on 1325 and 1820 (2011–2016) is well regarded globally with its broad participatory consultations in different districts and populations affected by the conflict (UN Women, 2015). The second pillar (of five) of Nepal's NAP is protection and prevention aimed at "protecting the rights of women and girls and preventing the violation of these rights during conflict and post-conflict period" (MOPR, 2011: ix–x). Understanding how this process has occurred, and how the Plan has reached diverse populations in remote locations to hear their positions on gender inequality, and human rights, are important stories of conflict prevention that should be told in the WPS-R2P story. Yet, because the Nepal situation is not presently under discussion on the Security Council, with a few exceptions (Karki and Upadhyay, 2011), Nepal is not often brought into contemporary R2P conversations. However, it provides us with an interesting case study that has been relatively successful in preventing the re-emergence of conflict. We argue that inclusion of women and other marginalized groups and formal recognition of their political significance has been a major factor in preventing the outbreak of conflict in Nepal.

Conclusion

Women participate in political, economic, security and justice sectors in a variety of roles and power hierarchies. The journey for WPS at the global level, in particular, has been to ensure that the four pillars – prevention, participation, protection, relief and recovery – are achieved with equal attention. As the 2015 Global Study on WPS noted however, this goal is difficult:

> the capacity to provide gender-sensitive conflict early warning, support women's engagement in conflict resolution, deliver adequate immediate and long-term recovery services to women and girls affected by conflict or crisis, or provide the Security Council with adequate intelligence about gender-specific threats, challenges and opportunities for women's engagement in different processes will continue to fall short of expectations and needs.
>
> (UN Women, 2015: 282)

The R2P trajectory has been similar in experience with the prioritization of diplomatic engagement in situations where immediate protection is required; and at this point whether the Security Council will engage and to what extend comes down to P5 politics.

We have identified in this chapter an opportunity for the two agendas to create normative consensus on the prioritization of preventing conflict, preventing atrocities and preventing gender discrimination as essential to achieve protection. Moreover, we have identified that this discussion needs to be taking place outside of the Security Council. We have identified the R2P turn to the Human Rights Council in Geneva, specifically the call for R2P reporting in the UPR processes; which coincides with the WPS arriving in the CEDAW process thanks to the CEDAW Committee General Recommendation 30.

Crucially, we also identify the need to see R2P and WPS as being practically realized in situations where conflict prevention is occurring. The violence and atrocities may not be on the same scale as Syria or South Sudan, but it is important to recognize the practical work and difficulties being overcome by engagement strategies such as those in Nepal where there is an attempt to navigate gender inequality, human rights violations and marginalized groups grievances in the peace process.

The practical difficulty in promoting a shared agenda is not a clash of egos or offices, but how to achieve a shared vision that doesn't suffer political rejection and a loss of engagement in *both* agendas.

Acknowledgements

This work was supported by the Australian Research Council Linkage Scheme and its partner organization, the Australian Department of Foreign Affairs and Trade (grant number LP160100085).

References

Ainley, K. (2017). From Atrocity Crimes to Human Rights: Expanding the Focus of The Responsibility to Protect. *Global Responsibility to Protect*, 9(3): 243–266.

ASEAN (2017). The ASEAN Commission on the Promotion and Protection of the Rights of Women and Children (ACWC) to Advance Gender, Peace and Security Agenda in the Region, March 31. http://asean.org/asean-to-advance-gender-peace-and-security-agenda-in-the-region/

Averre, D. and Davies, L. (2015). Russia, Humanitarian Intervention and the Responsibility to Protect: The Case of Syria. *International Affairs*, 91(4): 813–834.

Baniya, J., Kharel, S., Thapa, D. and Ramsbotham, A. (2017). *Gender and Nepal's Transition from War*. London: Conciliation Resources.

Baruah, N. and Reyes, J. (2017). Nepal Elections: More Women Have a Seat at the Table but Will They Have a Voice? *The Asia Foundation,* December 13. Available from: https://asiafoundation.org/2017/12/13/nepal-elections-women-seat-table-will-voice/

Bellamy, A.J. and Williams, P.D. (2011). The New Politics of Protection? Côte d'Ivoire, Libya and the Responsibility to Protect. *International Affairs*, 87(4): 825–850.

CEDAW (2013). General Recommendation 30. CEDAW/C/GC/30, October 18.

Davies, S.E. (2016). Addressing the Gender Gap in R2P. *In:* Bellamy, A. and Dunne, T. (eds.) *The Oxford Handbook of the Responsibility to Protect*, 489–508. New York: Oxford University Press.

Davies, S.E. and Teitt, S. (2012). Engendering the Responsibility to Protect. *Global Responsibility to Protect,* 4(2): 198–222.

Davies, S.E. and True, J. (2019). *Oxford Handbook on Women, Peace and Security.* New York: Oxford University Press.

Gibbings, S. (2011). No Angry Women at the United Nations: Political Dreams and the Cultural Politics of United Nations Security Council Resolution 1325. *International Feminist Journal of Politics,* 13(4): 522–538.

Harris Rimmer, S. (2014). *Feminist Ripostes to the Responsibility to Protect.* Gender Institute 2014 Public Lecture Series Feminist Theory Now, Australian National University. July 22. http://genderinstitute.anu.edu.au/feminist-ripostes-responsibility-protect-doctrine

Hewitt, S. (2016). Overcoming the Gender Gap: The Possibilities of Alignment between the Responsibility to Protect and the Women, Peace and Security Agenda. *Global Responsibility to Protect,* 8(1):3–28.

HRW (2014). *Silenced and Forgotten: Survivors of Nepal's Conflict-Era Sexual Violence.* United States of America: Human Rights Watch.

IDEA (2011). *Women Members of the Constituent Assembly: A Study on Contribution of Women in Constitution Making in Nepal.* Available from: www.idea.int/sites/default/files/publications/women-members-of-the-constituent-assembly.pdf

Karki, A. and Upadhyay, J. (2011). Atrocities Prevented in Nepal? The Impact of Civic and Cultural Institutions. *In:* Mani, R. and Weiss, T.G. (eds.) *Responsibility to Protect Cultural Perspectives in the Global South,* 195–223. Abingdon, Oxon; New York: Routledge.

Kolås, Å. and Tryggestad, T.L. (2017). Introduction: Women, Peace and Security in Review. *In:* Kolås, A. (ed.) *Women, Peace and Security in Nepal: From Civil-War to Post-Conflict Reconstruction,* 1–8. Oxon and New York: Routledge.

MOPR (2011). National Action Plan on Implementation of United Nations Security Council Resolutions 1325 & 1820 [2011/12–2015/6]. Kathmandu: Government of Nepal.

Murphy, R. and Burke, R. (2015). *Sexual and Gender-based Violence and the Responsibility to Protect: Where Does Gender Come in? Irish Studies in International Affairs,* 26: 227–255.

Paswan, B. (2017). Data Reveals Local Elections a Disaster for Gender Equality. *The Record,* October 24. Available from: www.recordnepal.com/wire/features/data-reveals-local-elections-a-disaster-for-gender-equality/

PeaceWomen (2017). The United Nations General Assembly Informal Interactive Dialogue on the Report of the Secretary-General on the Responsibility to Protect: The

Responsibility to Protect and Accountability for Prevention, September 11. Available from: www.peacewomen.org

Ralph, J. (2018). What Should be Done? Pragmatic Constructivist Ethics and the Responsibility to Protect. *International Organization*, 72(1): 239–275.

Security Council Report (2017). Women, Peace and Security: Closing the Security Council's Implementation Gap. Available from: www.securitycouncilreport.org/research-reports/women-peace-and-security-closing-the-security-councils-implementation-gap.php

Strasheim, J. (2019). No "End of the Peace Process": Federalism and Ethnic Violence in Nepal. *Cooperation and Conflict*, 54(1): 83–98.

Shepherd, L.J. (2011). Sex, Security and Superhero(in)es: From 1325 to 1820 and Beyond. *International Feminist Journal of Politics,* 13(4): 504–521.

Trillò, T. (2015). *Gender Identity, Gender Based Violence, and the Responsibility to Protect.* Budapest Centre for Mass Atrocities Prevention. www.genocideprevention.eu/wp-content/uploads/2015/07/Tommaso-Trillo-GBV-07-April-153.pdf

True, J. (2012). *The Political Economy of Violence Against Women.* New York: Oxford University Press.

True, J. (2016). Explaining the Global Diffusion of the Women, Peace and Security Agenda. *International Political Science Review*, 37(3), 307–323.

UN (2005). *2005 World Summit Outcome*, High-level Plenary Meeting of the General Assembly, A/60/L.1, September.

UN Secretary-General (2009). Implementing the Responsibility to Protect: Report of the Secretary-General, A/63/677, January 12.

UN Secretary-General (2013). Responsibility to Protect: State Responsibility and Prevention: Report of the Secretary-General, A/67/929, July 9.

UN Secretary-General (2014). Fulfilling our Collective Responsibility: International Assistance and the Responsibility to Protect: Report of the Secretary-General, A/68/947, July 11.

UN Secretary-General (2017a). Implementing the Responsibility to Protect: Accountability for Prevention: Report of the Secretary-General, A/71/1016, August 10.

UN Secretary-General (2017b). Report of the Secretary-General on Women and Peace and Security, S/2017/861, October 16.

UN Secretary-General (2017c). United Nations Activities in Support of Mediation: Report of the Secretary-General, UNGA/A/72/115, June 27.

UN Women (2015). Preventing Conflict, Transforming Justice, Securing Peace: A Global Study on the Implementation of United Nations Security Council Resolution 1325. New York: United Nations.

Upreti, B.R. and Shivakoti, S. (2018). The Struggle of Female Ex-Combatants in Nepal. *Peace Review*, 30(1), 78–86.

von Einsiedel, S. and Salih, C. (2017). *Conflict Prevention in Nepal: Background Paper for the United Nations – World Bank Flagship Study on the Prevention of Violence Conflict.* United Nations University. Available from: https://i.unu.edu/media/cpr.unu.edu/attachment/2530/ConflictPreventioninNepal-Apr-2017.pdf

von Einsiedel, S., Malone, A.M. and Pradhan, S. (eds.) (2012). *Nepal in Transition: From People's War to Fragile Peace.* New York: Cambridge University Press.

Welsh, J. (2016). The Responsibility to Prevent: Assessing the Gap Between Rhetoric and Reality. *Cooperation and Conflict*, 51(2): 216–232.

Yadav, P. (2016). *Social Transformation in Post-conflict Nepal: A Gender Perspective.* Oxon and New York: Routledge.

6 Strange bedfellows

Terrorism/counter-terrorism and the Responsibility to Protect

Shannon Zimmerman

Introduction

Counter-terrorism and the Responsibility to Protect (R2P) are not often thought of together. Though distinct, the simultaneous evolution of these two regimes has resulted in them sharing a conceptual basis strongly moored in sovereignty and international obligations. In this chapter, I argue that the norm regimes of counter-terrorism and R2P coincide in important ways which allow them to either cooperate or conflict. First, I highlight how these two norm regimes share grounding in international law and have developed complimentary understandings of the role and obligations of the sovereign state. I will then demonstrate through two case studies how these norm regimes can be interpreted in vastly different ways: Sri Lanka's use of counter-terrorism during the civil war against the Tamil Tigers and the application of R2P to the Islamic State in Iraq. In the first case the responsibility to protect was used by Sri Lanka to justify counter-terrorism efforts that amounted to one of the four R2P crimes. In the second case, a successful R2P argument was made against a terrorist group to justify an intervention to protect civilians. The former case illustrates how R2P and counter-terrorism may be used in opposition to each other but debates following the Sri Lanka crisis and the use of R2P to intervene in Iraq clearly show how the evolution of these two norm regimes has placed them on a trajectory to make them more cooperative and collaborative than ever before.

Norm regimes

Norms are products of their environments. They emerge from a sociopolitical context as vague concepts, particularly at the international level, where they must be ambiguous enough to be adopted by multiple key players (Sandholtz, 2008; Wiener, 2004: 198; Van Kersbergen and Verbeek, 2007: 218; Krook and True, 2012: 105). As a result, norms take on different meanings and manifestations in response to the context in which they are implemented (Wiener, 2004: 199, 2009; Autesserre, 2009; Acharya, 2004; Checkel, 1997; Cortell and Davis, 2000) and are "appropriated for a variety of different purposes" (Krook and True, 2012: 104). Particularly with prescriptive norms such as R2P and counter-terrorism, actors are able to "fill" a norm with content that aligns with their needs (Krook and True, 2012: 104). Contestation and appropriation are common in unstable or conflict environments where existing norms fluid and susceptible to "... co-option, drift, accretion and reversal ..." (Krook and True, 2012: 104; Wiener, 2009: 179) and vulnerable to influence by larger international responses to crises (Hunt, 2016).

However, norms do not exist separate from other norms (Searle, 1995: 24–25; Ruggie, 1998: 869–870). Often norms emerge as or become part of a norm regime, defined as "a system of norms connected to one another in relationships of mutual support" (O'Neill, 1999: 197). Norms in a regime interact in mutually constituting ways – constantly reifying and refining each other. Because of their entwined nature they also have less flexibility to change. When norm regimes experience tension with external norms, resolving those conflicts can be difficult. To address these tensions, norm interpreters may reinterpret or reprioritize existing rules (Robertson, 2011: 617; Olsen, 2014: 484). They may also engage in strategic framing by interpreting problems and their potential solutions in a particular way as to align with particular normative understandings (Barnett and Finnemore, 2004: 33). Framing of this kind can result in 'strange bedfellows' where seemingly conflicting norms are used together (Krook and True, 2012: 111).

The norm regimes of counter-terrorism and R2P are a pair of such 'strange bedfellows.'

Counter-terrorism is explicitly state focused while R2P emphasizes the security of the individual. However, both norm regimes share a strong basis in international law and the primacy of the state. Continued contestation of these norm regimes has begun to push them to align along their core normative threads: the sovereign role of the state and the obligations of the international community. Their parallel evolution has fostered an understanding of the sovereign state that can be simultaneously interpreted by the nation-state as supporting its authority and by the international society as reinforcing the state's obligations to protect human rights.

The need to prevent terrorism and protect civilians from atrocity crimes has a strong basis in international law and convention. Virtually all forms of terrorism were prohibited by existing international conventions, international customary law, the Geneva Convention or the Rome Statute of the International Criminal Court.[1] R2P is also firmly based on established principles of international law. States were previously obligated to prevent and punish genocide, war crimes and crimes against humanity (acts of ethnic cleansing is not a crime under international law but may fall under one of the other three crimes) (UN General Assembly, 2009: 5). This indicates that both civilian protection and countering terrorism have been global priorities for decades, if not longer.

In Chapter 1 of this volume, Phil Orchard argues that the R2P is a *norm regime* which pulls together the proscriptive normative strands against the four R2P atrocity crimes. These strands are then used to craft three subsequent prescriptive norms: 1) the state's responsibility to protect its own population from the crimes of genocide, war crimes, ethnic cleansing and crimes against humanity; 2) the role and responsibilities of the international community to assist the state in fulfilling its responsibilities; and 3) the role of the international community to act when protection by the state is manifestly failing. These three norms first emerged in the 2001 Report of the International Commissions on Intervention and State Sovereignty (ICISS), were further refined and agreed to by all participating states in the 2005 World Summit Outcome Document (WSOD) and codified in the 2009 Secretary-General's Report on the R2P in which Ban Ki-moon laid out his three-pillar formulation of R2P.

Similarly, the United Nations (UN) Global Counter-terrorism Strategy is the manifestation of a norm regime with a very similar genesis. Terrorism,[2] and the need to counter it, were thrust to the center of normative and political debate after almost 3,000 people died in terrorist attacks on New York and Washington DC on September 11, 2001. The UN General Assembly had long been aware of the security threat posed by terrorism but previously dealt with such issues on an ad hoc basis (Weiss, 2007: 96). Shaken by 9/11, state and non-state actors alike sought to formulate a universal understanding of terrorism and how to combat it. Debates around the content of counter-terrorism as a norm became highly political and were first sidelined, then avoided, to enable action. Only after some interpretations of counter-terrorism violated human rights were these debates renewed. As a result, normative understandings of counter-terrorism emerged in two waves; the first focused on combatting terrorism, the second focused on preventing it. Each wave has brought the norm of counter-terrorism closer to alignment with that of R2P.

The modern norm regime of counter-terrorism emerged in 2001 with UN Security Council Resolution 1373 (UN Security Council, 2001). This resolution identified any act of terrorism as a threat to international peace and security. Resolution 1373 was accompanied by the creation of a dense network of organs within the UN focused specifically on countering terrorism. This initiated the first international wave of counter-terrorism efforts, which focused on state and legislative responses to terrorism (Boutellis and Fink, 2016: 9).

The initial prism of the "war on terror" emphasized the importance of the state and facilitated the early dominance of the state-centric understanding of counter-terrorism. A desire to be free from the fear of terror empowered heavy-handed state responses. By 2003, human rights violations during counter-terrorism measures were grave enough that UN Special Rapporteurs and independent experts adopted a joint statement expressing:

> profound concern at the multiplication of policies, legislation and practices increasingly being adopted by many countries in the name of the fight against terrorism which negatively effects the enjoyment of virtually all human rights – civil, cultural, economic, political and social.
>
> (UN, 2003: 118)

The exposure of significant human rights abuses committed in Abu Ghraib Prison and overseas detention centers, acted as a turning point for counter-terrorism advocates (Mokhtari, 2009: Chapter 2). Public outcry and emerging understandings of the negative effects of heavy-handed responses to terrorism forced member states to reassess the utility of a counter-terrorism norm which focused on state security to the detriment of human rights.

The 2004 High-level Panel on Threats, Challenges and Change noted the severity of the terrorist threat but echoed the concerns that efforts to fight the "war on terror" were undermining the very principles terrorists hoped to target, such as human rights and the rule of law (UN, 2004: 48). The Panel recommended that the Secretary-General take a leading role in crafting a global strategy against terrorism and strengthening the ability of states to counter terrorism while promoting the rule of law. Shortly thereafter, the 2005 WSOD – the same one that codified R2P – requested the UN Secretary-General submit proposals on both a UN counter-terrorism strategy and building the UN's capacity to assist states in combatting terrorism. These requests placed the UN at the center of the fight against terrorism at the normative level if not the operational level (Weiss, 2007: 97). The result of the Secretary-General's efforts was the UN Global Counter-terrorism Strategy. This strategy was the first time all UN member states agreed on a unified approach to fighting terrorism. It also signaled the start of the second wave of counter-terrorism efforts, which attempted to craft a wider approach to addressing not just terrorism itself but the wider conditions which lead to terrorism.

The Global Counter-terrorism Strategy has four pillars (UN General Assembly, 2006b):[3]

1. Addressing the conditions conducive to the spread of terrorism;
2. Measures to prevent and combat terrorism;
3. Measures to build states' capacity to prevent and combat terrorism and to strengthen the role of the United Nations system in that regard;
4. Measures to ensure respect for human rights for all and the rule of law as the fundamental basis for the fight against terrorism.

Each of these pillars act as constitutive norm which seeks to articulate particular actors, interests, identities and categories of action (Gelpi, 1997: 340; Finnemore and Sikkink, 1998: 891). Through the subsequent decade these norms coalesced into a clear regime which has undergone an astonishing amount of evolution as the international community has struggled to understand and respond to the normative challenges posed by transnational terrorism.

Unlike the pillars of R2P, which were supposed to be implemented simultaneously, the order of implementation for the four pillars for the counter-terrorism strategy were unclear (UN General Assembly, 2006b). Initial emphasis on state-centric counter-terrorism resulted in Pillar Two (preventing and combatting terrorism) and Pillar Three (building states' capacity and strengthening the role of the UN) receiving the bulk of the international community's attention and resources. These two pillars were more actionable and more closely aligned with individual states' national interests. The exceptionalist rhetoric around the "war on terror" initially made it difficult for proponents of human rights to criticize the actions of states combatting terrorism. As a result, Pillars One and Four, addressing the conditions that lead to terrorism and ensuring human rights in the fight against terrorism, remained sidelined.

Normative congruencies between counter-terrorism and R2P

The initially state-centric nature of the counter-terrorism regime placed it at odds with the rights-centric R2P. However, counter-terrorism failures in Iraq and Afghanistan saw the regime shifting from a state-centric focus powered by national security interests to broader attempts to deal with the conditions leading to terrorism, including human rights violations by states. The UN Secretary-General argued, "[e] ffective counter-terrorism measures and the protection of human rights are not conflicting goals, but complementary and mutually reinforcing ones." In fact, "… the defense of human rights is essential to the fulfilment of all aspects of a counter-terrorism strategy" (UN General Assembly, 2005: para. 5). The UN recognized that efforts at counter-terrorism in the past decade had continued to ignore the root causes of terrorism and failed to ensure respect for human right and the rule of law. Such "short-sighted policies, failed leadership, heavy-handed approaches, a single-minded focus only on security measures and an utter disregard for human rights have often made things worse" (UN Secretary-General, 2016). To address this, the Secretary-General released a new *Plan of Action to Prevent Violent Extremism* (PVE Plan) in December 2015 (UN General Assembly, 2015). This plan reoriented counter-terrorism efforts to address root causes of terrorism and tied the effectiveness of such approaches to their observance of human rights and international law.

The counter-terrorism regime was now called upon to emphasize similar norms to R2P.[4] Lloyd Axworthy and Allan Rock note that, "…when R2P is 'unbundled' and its component principles examined, its foundational principles can be applied to other problems that engage humanity as a whole" (Axworthy and Rock, 2009: 64). They identify three principles as particularly important,

> … the continued recognition of the primacy of the sovereign state as "first responder"; the duty of the international community to support the state in meeting that responsibility; and the refusal of the international community in areas of global priority to accept the single state's failure or refusal to act as the last word.
>
> (Ibid.: 64–65)

Broken down this way it is possible to see the similar conceptual basis shared by R2P and counter-terrorism. Both regimes emphasis the primacy of the sovereign state as an actor and international obligations of the state to act.

The sovereign state as first responder

Both R2P and counter-terrorism focus on the primacy of the state as the first responder. They also share the assumption (which is not always correct) that the state will have control of its territory, a monopoly on the use of force and the best interests of its citizens in mind.

The importance of the state in R2P is clear. The ICISS Report's very first principle is "[s]tate sovereignty implies responsibility, and the primary responsibility for the protection of its people lies with the state itself" (ICISS, 2001: xi). The first pillar of R2P focuses on the *state's* obligation to protect civilians.[5] This emphasis on the state ensures that most states are willing to, in theory, accept the norms of R2P because they reinforce the norms that underline with state sovereignty such as 'sovereign equality,' 'national ownership' and 'consent' (Gallagher, 2015: 1264). The role of international assistance in Pillar Two is, as Ban Ki-moon puts it, "a reminder that R2P is intended to reinforce, not undermine sovereignty" (UN General Assembly, 2014: 4).

The state's primary role in counter-terrorism is equally clear. UN Security Council Resolution 1373 (2001), obligated all states to take responsibility for preventing acts of terrorism based from their territory and ratify existing treaties against terrorism (UN Security Council, 2001). Subsequent UN documents, including the UN's Global Counter-terrorism Strategy, placed the primary onus for action with the state rather than other actors (UN General Assembly, 2006a). Much like R2P, it also had a norm (Pillar Three) indicating the willingness of the international community to support those states in fulfilling their counter-terrorism responsibilities.

International obligations

The counter-terrorism and R2P norm regimes strongly support international assistance to individual states and their populations. Regarding R2P, the WSOD urged the international community, including the UN, to assist states in building national and regional capacities in order to fulfill their protection responsibilities (UN General Assembly, 2005: para. 138). The same document also advocated that the UN be strengthened to better render assistance to states specifically to combat terrorism (ibid.: para. 88). However, with certain acts of terrorism constituting crimes against humanity, the distinction between R2P and counter-terrorism is not always clear.

Keeping in mind the primacy of the state to protect its population, both norm regimes enshrined the supporting role of the international community into their later iterations. Pillar Three of the counter-terrorism strategy and Pillar Two of the R2P doctrine recognize the importance of building state capacity and rendering assistance when asked, in order to prevent either terrorism or atrocity crimes. These norm regimes differ not in their conceptualization of international obligations but in how they perceive these obligations should be filled. The norm of international obligations of states to protect was clear but the manifestation of that protection varied widely both within and between counter-terrorism and R2P efforts. For counter-terrorism, the WSOD encouraged regional and bilateral cooperation, particularly at the level of law enforcement and technical exchange to help states combat terrorist threats (ibid.: para. 87). The later counter-terrorism strategy focused on ambitious plans for coordinating UN and other international efforts to combat terrorism and encourages member states to contribute to technical assistance projects (UN General Assembly, 2006b: 7). For R2P the WSOD advocated for assistance through appropriate diplomatic, humanitarian and other means (UN General Assembly, 2005: paras. 138–139). R2P also added the creation of an impartial and disciplined security sector as vital to preventing widespread violence (UN, 2009: 21). The international obligation of states to protect was clear but the manifestation of that protection varied widely both within and between counter-terrorism and R2P efforts.

Case studies

Differing interpretations of counter-terrorism and R2P have led to a disconnect in their situational impact, despite their shared basis in the role of the state, international obligations of the state and existing international law. This is especially true in cases of counter-terrorism. Early on, counter-terrorism efforts became bifurcated between state-centric and rights-centric interpretations (Phillips, 2012). The state-centric paradigm followed a pluralist understanding of the world that prioritized the sanctity of state self-determination, state authority, monopoly on the use of force and non-intervention (ibid.: 79, 87). International acts of terrorism were seen as acts of war warranting extraordinary measures. The state-centric paradigm was used by several states including China, India, Russia, the United States and the United Kingdom to justify actions such as torture, arbitrary arrest and extraordinary rendition (HRW, 2003). State-centric interpretations also opened up the door for states to use the label of countering terrorism to crack down on legitimate political opposition, such as in Nepal or Zimbabwe (Falk, 2003; Darby, 2012).

More recently, the rights-centric perspective of counter-terrorism is focused more upon the solidarist values outlined in the UN Charter. This perspective promotes liberal international values such as democracy, capitalism and human rights. As such, it sees the protection of human rights as a core part of countering terrorism. Though the first Security Council resolution addressing terrorism after 9/11, UNSCR 1373 (2001) did not mention human rights, subsequent UN resolutions, such as Resolutions 1456 (2003) and 1624 (2005), began to emphasize the importance of human rights while countering terrorism (UN Security Council, 2003, 2005). The resolutions reaffirmed that terrorism constituted one of the greatest threats to international peace and security but clarified that the Security Council was determined to combat terrorism in accordance with the UN Charter and international law. In this vein, all measures taken to combat terrorism had to comply with international humanitarian, human rights and refugee laws. The Berlin Declaration went so far as to identify human rights and counter-terrorism as complementary, stating that "safeguarding persons from terrorist acts and respecting human rights both form part of a seamless web of protection incumbent upon the State" (International Commission of Jurists, August 28, 2004: 1). In January 2004 the Chair of the Counter-terrorism Committee

(CTC) at the UN clarified the importance that states "ensure that any measure taken to combat terrorism comply with all obligations under international law, in particular human rights, refugee, and humanitarian law" (UN Security Council, 2004, 2003). By 2006 and the drafting of the UN's Global Counter-terrorism Strategy there was a clear connection drawn between the promotion of human rights with effective counter-terrorism efforts (UN General Assembly, 2006b). This stance has been echoed in subsequent UN documents (UN General Assembly, 2015).

Both rights-centric and state-centric understandings for counter-terrorism are based on the recognition that terrorism poses a genuine threat to international peace and security. However, each normative understanding had a different referent upon which they based their security, with the rights-centric group focusing on the rights and physical security of the individual (and therefore aligning with the norms underpinning R2P) and the state-centric group privileging the security of the state (potentially conflicting with R2P). In this next section I will use two case studies to illustrate different interpretations of counter-terrorism alongside R2P and the results from debates around these cases.

Counter-terrorism as an atrocity crime – the state response of Sri Lanka

The Liberation Tigers of Tamil Eelam (LTTE), known as the Tamil Tigers, had been in conflict with the Sri Lankan government since the 1970s. Their explicit goal was to carve out a separate Tamil State in the north and east of Sri Lanka. This was in response to the marginalization and political disenfranchisement of the Tamil minority. Throughout decades of conflict both the LTTE and the Sri Lankan government committed widespread human rights violations. The conflict escalated in 2008 when the government officially withdrew from a negotiated cease fire agreement after extensive violations by the LTTE (HRW, 2009b). Renewed fighting resulted in human rights violations by both sides. By March of 2009, the Office of the High-Commission on Human Rights (OHCHR) stated that actions by the government and the LTTE "may constitute international crimes, entailing individual responsibility, including for war crimes and crimes against humanity" (OHCHR, 2009).

The Sri Lankan government's military assault against the LTTE reached its zenith in the spring of 2009. During this time somewhere where between 150,000 and 300,000 civilians were caught between the LTTE and advancing government forces on a small strip of land not much larger than New York City's Central Park (Weiss, 2012: 8). Civilians were exposed to direct attacks by the LTTE, and heavy shelling by the government and had limited access to food and water (HRW, 2009a). Advocates of R2P argued that these civilians were being subjected to atrocity crimes. The Global Centre for the Responsibility to Protect (GCR2P), supported by states who saw the crisis characterized in R2P terms, called for the Security Council to dispatch an envoy to Sri Lanka and consider sanctions (GCR2P, 2009b).

In response, Sri Lanka strongly reaffirmed the government's right to be the primary responder to this threat against their civilians. As such, the government claimed it needed to be given time and space to deal with threats before the international community intervened. Sri Lanka's discomfort with R2P was reflective of the apprehensiveness shared by many East-Asian countries to any norms which impinges against non-intervention and state sovereignty (Kassim, 2014: 62–63). In a UN Security Council open debate on May 11, 2011 the Sri Lankan representative called on the UN:

> to recognize the fundamental role of the State in civilian protection. In the first place, the role of Governments in civilian protection should be respected as it is their primary responsibility to protect their own citizens. The United Nations and humanitarian agencies must support and assist Governments, and in doing so be sensitive to ground realities, including by respecting the sovereignty of States.
>
> (Kahona, 2011)

The government's position was supported by one of the ICISS Commissioners, Ramesh Thakur (Welsh, 2013: 386). Thakur stated that "[g]iven the Tigers' nature and record it was not unreasonable for the government to acquire the capacity and demonstrate the determination to defeat the Tigers as part of its responsibility to protect" (Thakur, 2011: 66). He also chided the Western states for hypocrisy in light of their own intense focus on counter-terrorism post 9/11.

Sri Lanka's narrative was incredibly effective in the post 9/11 period. Before 9/11 the Sri Lankan government had engaged the LTTE in a peace processes and had recognized them as a political entity with a political agenda, after 9/11 the government referred to them simply as 'terrorists' (Richmond and Tellidis, 2012: 126). The Sri Lankan government was able to simultaneously claim that R2P reinforced its right to address the threat of the LTTE against its citizens while also arguing that actions taken by the state to combat a terrorist threat of this magnitude were justifiable, regardless of the civilian cost. Public and policy-makers were more willing to accept the killing of civilians in the context of defeating murderous terrorist insurrection (Evans, 2012: 2). This was evident in the UN's approach to censure of the LTTE and the Sri Lankan government for civilian deaths. After a visit to Sri Lanka in May of 2009, the UK Foreign Minister noted that there was "no question of loss of life at a large scale," resulting from the use of heavy artillery by the government (Secretary-General's Internal Review Panel on United Nations Action in Sri Lanka, 2012: 84, para. 141). However, when the Security Council issued a press statement on Sri Lanka just two days later, the majority of its censure was against the LTTE with only oblique reference to the role of the government in causing civilian deaths (UN Security Council, 2009).

United Nation's headquarters engagement in Sri Lanka was heavily influenced by "what it perceived Member States wanted to hear, rather than by what member States needed to know if they were to respond" (Secretary-General's

Internal Review Panel on United Nations Action in Sri Lanka, 2012: para. 77). "The result was a disappointing failure by the UN member states to act" (ibid.: para. 1). Some countries, such as the US, did little to address the humanitarian crises and instead focused solely on counter-terrorism efforts regardless of their civilian cost – in essence giving tacit support for Sri Lanka's actions (Committee on Foreign Relations, 2009: 12–13; Nackers, 2016: 880).

The lackluster response by the international community may have been in part due to the Sri Lankan government's successful use of the rhetoric of the 'war on terror.' The Sri Lankan government portrayed a victory against the LTTE as a victory in the global fight against terrorism. The President of Sri Lanka stated in a speech before parliament that "[e]nding terrorism in Sri Lanka means a victory for democracy in the world. Sri Lanka has now given a beginning to the ending of terrorism in the world" (Committee on Foreign Relations, 2009: 1). The government was then able to justify an increasingly aggressive conventional war against the LTTE as necessary to address not just a terrorist threat that had been menacing its citizens for decades but an existential battle to preserve the country's very existence. With so much at stake, the government argued, its actions were necessary and proportionate (Welsh, 2014: 134). When fighting concluded at least 10,000 and possibly up to 40,000 civilians had been killed by government artillery fire, rebel gunfire and lack of access to food and medical care (Secretary-General's Internal Review Panel on United Nations Action in Sri Lanka, 2012: 14, para. 34). Caught between the norm regimes of R2P and counter-terrorism, the UN Security Council did nothing.

Since 2009, the Sri Lankan government's use of the R2P and counter-terrorism regimes has been dissected by external experts (Secretary-General's Panel of Experts on Accountability in Sri Lanka, 2011), an internal review panel for the UN Secretary-General (Secretary-General's Internal Review Panel on United Nations Action in Sri Lanka, 2012), UN officials (Weiss, 2012) and journalists (Harrison, 2012). The UN Panel of Experts concluded that the narrative maintained by the government of Sri Lanka during the crisis of 2008–2009 was starkly different from reality on the ground. There were credible allegations of serious human rights violations by both the government and the LTTE which would amount to war crimes or crimes against humanity (Secretary-General's Panel of Experts on Accountability in Sri Lanka, 2011: ii). While the Panel reaffirmed the state's right to ensure its national security, including against insurgents who may engage in acts of terrorism, it also clearly stated that such ends do not justify all means to achieve them. Rather, such actions must comply with international law and an "elementary consideration of humanity" (Secretary-General's Panel of Experts on Accountability in Sri Lanka, 2011).[6] In conclusion, the Panel found both sides guilty of reckless disregard for international norms (ibid.: 71, 116). However, the Panel's findings are in opposition to the majority of developing countries who, during a debate in the Human Rights Council in Geneva, backed the Sri Lankan government's right to suppress the Tamil Tigers with force (Thakur, 2013: 68 #1598). The Sri Lanka conflict highlighted the dangers of state-centered applications of counter-terrorism and R2P. Importantly, the Panel cautioned that "[t]he victory of one side has emboldened some to believe that these rules may now be disregarded in the causes of fighting terrorism" (Secretary-General's Panel of Experts on Accountability in Sri Lanka, 2011: 71).

Terrorism as an atrocity crime by non-state armed groups – the case of the Islamic State

Long-standing legal precedents enshrined in International Humanitarian Law, such as the Geneva Conventions, indicate that non-state actors have a responsibility to protect people under their control. Such laws apply equally to all actors in a conflict, regardless of their state or non-state status (International Committee of the Red Cross, 1949). Therefore, both state and non-state actors must refrain from harming civilians during a conflict. However, these conventions only apply in the context of armed conflict.

For R2P, this norm regime was crafted to address mass atrocities committed by *states* against their populations. UN member states have rarely explicitly addressed the roles and responsibilities of non-state actors, nor have they debated the application of R2P to such actors (The Stanley Foundation, 2015: 2). However, UN member states have never disputed the application of R2P to non-state actors, particularly in cases where national authorities do not hold control (ibid.). In applying R2P, it appears that the act, rather than the actor, is what matters. Therefore, non-state actors who have the monopoly on violence in an area also have the responsibility to protect civilians in that area.

A more recent example highlighting the tension between R2P and counter-terrorism focus on the roles and responsibilities of non-state actors. This debate centers on two questions: first, do non-state actors have the same civilian protection responsibilities as states? Second, can terrorist acts be considered an atrocity crime under R2P? The various international legal instruments forbidding terrorist acts provide strong normative guidelines for state behavior. But they do not provide expectations for non-state armed actors, nor do they prescribe the consequences if these actors fail to meet expectations. As a result, the actions of these groups, and state responses to them, fall into a normative gray area – the exact area that Sri Lanka was able to leverage in their fight against the LTTE.

While the obligations of non-state actors in such contexts is unclear, precedent in the UN implies that non-state actors are as responsible for civilian protection as states. The language used in the WSOD indicates that the entire international community bears the burden of prevention and protection (UN General Assembly, 2005). This includes both state and non-state actors. Later UN Security Council reports of R2P reaffirmed this idea (Luck, 2015: 2). Additionally, the Rome Statutes define genocide, ethnic cleansing and crimes against humanity without reference to those crimes being in the context of armed conflict. This firmly places non-state groups under the umbrella of R2P obligations when they are the authority in a geographic area, regardless of whether or not they are engaged in 'active' conflict.

If it is the case the non-state actors are responsible for protection and can therefore be responsible for the commission of atrocity crimes, then it is also possible that acts of terrorism and mass atrocity crimes may overlap. The actions of the Islamic State (IS) are a good example of how non-state groups can fall under the purview of both terrorism and R2P.

The IS emerged from the chaos of the wars in Iraq and Syria as the IS in Iraq and al-Sham (ISIS) in 2013 (Griffin, 2015). By 2014, the group controlled territory from Aleppo in Syria to Diyala in Iraq. They declared an Islamic caliphate and renamed themselves the IS. During the height of their power roughly ten million people were under the control of IS (BBC, 2018). As the authority over that geographic area, IS could be considered responsible for protecting civilians, a duty that the groups manifestly failed to fulfill. Instead, Amnesty International argues that the group is guilty of ethnic cleansing for its systematic targeting of minorities in Northern Iraq when that region was under the groups control (Amnesty International, 2014). In August 2014, IS advanced through Iraq into the Kurdish controlled north, taking the town of Sinjar which is home to tens of thousands of Yazidis (Burns, 2016: 2). As an ethno-religious minority group the Yazidis are protected under Article II of the Genocide Convention (UN General Assembly, 1948: 260[III]). The crimes committed by IS against the Yazidi people fall under the auspices of crimes against humanity, as defined by Article 7(1)(g) of the Rome Statute (UN, 1998). For example, Yazidi men who refused to convert to Islam were summarily executed (Burns, 2016: 4). Women and girls were given or sold to IS fighters and forced into sexual slavery (Human Rights Council, 2016: 3). Such sexual violence, if undertaken with the intent to destroy, in whole or in part, a protected group, may even count as genocide (ICTR, 2001). IS is responsible for atrocity crimes both within the context of war and outside of this context as well as committing atrocity crimes inside and outside of areas under its control.

Since 2015, coordinated efforts against IS have been successful in recovering more the 95 percent of the territory captured by IS but the group continues to carry out and inspire terrorist attacks all over the world (Glenn, 2018). Both before and after its territorial heyday IS's persistent attacks on civilians clearly fell into the realm of crimes against humanity.[7] This was indicted by the UN Security Council as early as 2014 with Resolution 2170 which labeled the atrocities committed by IS as human rights violations and indicated that they may count as crimes against humanity (UN Security Council, 2014: para. 3 #1596). IS has carried out, or claimed responsibility for, countless attacks including bombing mosques, peace rallies, markets, and hospitals and conducting attacks on resorts (Tunisia) and nightclubs (Istanbul and Florida). Human Rights Watch noted that such acts "when carried out as part of a widespread or systematic 'attack against a civilian population' … as part of a policy of a state or organized group … can constitute a crime against humanity" regardless of contexts of war or peace (Human Rights Watch, 2017).

It is clear that in some instances the difference between R2P crimes and terrorism is indistinguishable. Alex Bellamy argues that situations caused by groups such as IS, Boko Haram and al-Shabaab are simply "…different ways of talking about the same problem: violent attacks on civilian populations." (Bellamy, 2015). Despite this, an artificial normative divide has been created which appears to exempt certain acts by non-state actors using terrorist tactics from falling under R2P, even when the crimes themselves amount to war crimes or crimes against humanity. Bellamy notes, attacks committed by these groups are almost always referred to as terrorist attacks. Some even argue that attacks committed by non-state groups like this fall beyond the remit of R2P and instead belong in the realm of counter-terrorism (ibid.). However, this is an artificial bifurcation between the two norm regimes which obfuscates both the nature and possible solutions to these issues.

Normative alignment

The application of counter-terrorism and R2P to the Sri Lanka crisis and the crimes committed by IS bring to light ambiguities in the counter-terrorism and R2P norm regimes. It also highlights their convoluted relationship with each other. Normative contestation between these two regimes has continued, spurred on by current events such as the 2011 intervention in Libya and the conflict in Syria. With each event, contestation has resulted in increasing congruences between the counter-terrorism and R2P norm regimes. Growing similarities stem from a renewed emphasis on human rights within counter-terrorism and the growing acknowledgment that leveraging the overlaps between counter-terrorism and R2P help both regimes to be more effective (UN Security Council, 2015a).[8]

International actors concerned with R2P have long focused their efforts to preventing rather than ameliorating the impacts of R2P crimes. The "value of prevention" is seen as "a key ingredient for a successful strategy for the responsibility to protect" (UN General Assembly, 2009: 2, 9). This view was supported by UN member states during the July 2009 General Assembly debate on the topic (GCR2P, 2009a). The 2013 Secretary-General's Report on R2P made prevention a key agenda item for the next five years (UN General Assembly, 2009: para. 4). At the Security Council's first high-level debate on security, development and the root causes of conflict in 2015, Ban Ki-moon boldly stated that prevention should be an integral part in all UN actions (UN Security Council, 2015b). When focused on prevention, significant overlaps in the actions needed to prevent atrocity crimes and terrorism arise. The UN Secretary-General directly connected extremist views with "those who commit genocide and atrocities" (UN, 2006: 5).

At the same time counter-terrorism made a promising turn toward prevention as well. For the previous two decades the international community had primarily used security-based counter-terrorism measures to address terrorist groups. There was a growing consensus within the UN that such counter-terrorism measures were not effective (UN General Assembly, 2015: para. 4). The same risk factors that promote participation in violent extremism such as dehumanization of victims of terrorism, state repression, discrimination, human rights violations, and economic and political exclusion (just to name a few) mirror the risk factors for atrocity crimes (UN, 2006: 5; The Stanley Foundation, 2015: 5; UN General Assembly, 2013). These overlaps are significant enough that the 2015 annual meeting of the Global Network of RtoP Focal Points explicitly focused on the impact and management of terrorist groups. In their eyes, countering violent extremism is an important first step in preventing atrocities (Matthews and Mulcair, 2015).

The Secretary-General's long anticipated 2015 PVE Plan was created, in part, to influence the international community's responses to terrorism by expanding their focus from terrorism to violent extremism which "… encompasses a wider category of manifestations …" (UN General Assembly, 2015: para. 4). The PVE Plan admitted that the past decade of counter-terrorism efforts "overlooked" the two pillars of the 2006 UN Global Counter-terrorism Strategy that dealt with the root causes of terrorism and ensured respect for human rights and the rule of law (UN General Assembly, 2015). As a result, "short-sighted policies, failed leadership, heavy-handed approaches, a single-minded focus only on security measures and an utter disregard for human rights have often made things worse" (UN Secretary-General, 2015). A primary purpose of the 2015 PVE Plan was to reinvigorate these neglected aspects.

With the PVE Plan the Secretary-General made it his priority to shift the UN's focus to prevention and place human rights up front in efforts to stop terrorism (UN General Assembly, 2015: para. 6; Ban, 2016). For the first time the UN Secretary-General made clear that the UN would no longer ignore the actions of states who implement policies in violation of human rights in efforts to combat terrorism, stating that, "*International partners that are complicit in such action by States further corrupt public faith in the legitimacy of the wider international system*" (UN General Assembly, 2015: para. 27). This position is being carried on by the newly installed UN Secretary-General António Guterres, who, during his first formal briefing to the Security Council, pushed the importance of preventing violence and crises before they arose, boldly stating that, "[p]revention is not merely a priority, but the priority" (Guterres, 2017). This indicates a serious reorientation of the counter-terrorism norm away from a security focus toward a human rights focus, bringing it closer in alignment with R2P.

Conclusion

At times cooperative or conflictual, R2P and counter-terrorism regimes have progressively grown more linked in nature. With an emphasis on human rights and prevention, the latest 'wave' of counter-terrorism norm evolution is bringing the norm regimes of counter-terrorism and R2P closer together than ever before. However, there are still significant contradictions between them particularly regarding short- and long-term outcomes. Counter-terrorism's short-term, often kinetic focus on securing the state and countering violent extremism, remains often in tension with R2P's longer-term focus on prevention, with the former usually taking precedence over the latter (The Stanley Foundation, 2015: 5). The positive congruences between the two regimes represent potentially more effective ways of addressing both R2P and terrorism crimes. What remains to be seen is how that relationship will play out and whether or not the POC is given the same effort and attention as initiatives to stop terrorism.

Notes

1 There are now 19 international legal instruments designed to prevent terrorist attacks. These are: the 1963 Convention on Offences and Certain Other Acts Committed On Board Aircraft; the 1970 Convention for the Suppression of Unlawful Seizure of Aircraft; the 1971 Convention for the Suppression of Unlawful Acts against the Safety of Civil Aviation; the 1973 Convention on the Prevention and Punishment of Crimes Against Internationally Protected Persons; the 1979 International Convention against the Taking of Hostages; the 1980 Convention on the Physical Protection of Nuclear Material; the 1988 Protocol for the Suppression of Unlawful Acts of Violence at Airports Serving International Civil Aviation, supplementary to the Convention for the Suppression of Unlawful Acts against the Safety of Civil Aviation; the 2005 Amendments to the Convention on the Physical Protection of Nuclear Material; the 1988 Convention for the Suppression of Unlawful Acts against the Safety of Maritime Navigation; the 1988 Protocol for the Suppression of Unlawful Acts Against the Safety of Fixed Platforms Located on the Continental Shelf; the 1991 Convention on the Marking of Plastic Explosives for the Purpose of Detection; the 1997 International Convention for the Suppression of Terrorist Bombings; the 1999 International Convention for the Suppression of the Financing of Terrorism; the 2005 Protocol to the Convention for the Suppression of Unlawful Acts against the Safety of Maritime Navigation; the 2005 Protocol to the Protocol for the Suppression of Unlawful Acts Against the Safety of Fixed Platforms located on the Continental Shelf; the 2005 International Convention for the Suppression of Acts of Nuclear Terrorism; the 2010 Convention on the Suppression of Unlawful Acts Relating to International Civil Aviation; the 2010 Protocol Supplementary to the Convention for the Suppression of Unlawful Seizure of Aircraft; and the 2014 Protocol to Amend the Convention on Offences and Certain Acts Committed on Board Aircraft.

2 Terrorism in the UN context can roughly be defined as

> … any action, in addition to actions already specified by the existing conventions on aspects of terrorism, the Geneva Conventions and Security Council Resolution 1566 (2004), that is intended to cause death or serious bodily harm to civilians or non-combatants, when the purpose of such an act, by its nature or context, is to intimidate a population, or to compel a Government or an international organization to do or to abstain from doing any act.

This definition is taken from the Report of the High-level Panel on Threats, Challenges and Change, "*A More Secure World: Our Shared Responsibility*" (2004, para. 164). There is, however, no official definition of terrorism for the UN and there remains a high level of ambiguity surrounding definitions of terrorism and insurgency.

3 The UN Global Counter-terrorism Strategy is a living document. It is reviewed every two years and evolves to meet UN member states' counter-terrorism priorities. Each review incorporates an understanding of the evolving terrorism landscape and current

responses being undertaken by member states and UN entities. For more information see: www.un.org/counterterrorism/ctitf/en/un-global-counter-terrorism-strategy
4 In Chapter 5 of this volume, Davies and Hewitt illustrate a similar possible approach to identifying shared meaning and approaches between R2P and the Women, Peace and Security agenda.
5 For a detailed look at R2P and civilian protection see Charles T. Hunt's Chapter 4 in this volume on the protection of civilians in UN Peace Operations.
6 *Military and Paramilitary Activities in and against Nicaragua (*Nicaragua *v.* United States of America*), Merits, Judgment. I.C.J. Reports, 1986*: 14, para. 218.
7 According to Article 7 of the Rome Statute of the International Criminal Court defines Crimes Against Humanity as any of the following acts when committed as part of a widespread or systematic attack directed against any civilian population, with knowledge of the attack: murder; extermination; enslavement; deportation or forcible transfer of population; imprisonment or other severe deprivation of physical liberty in violation of fundamental rules of international law; torture; rape, sexual slavery, enforced prostitution, forced pregnancy, enforced sterilization or any other form of sexual violence of comparable gravity; persecution against any identifiable group or collective on political, racial, national, ethnic, cultural, religious, gender as defined in Paragraph 3, or other grounds that are universally recognized as impermissible under international law, in connection with any act referred to in this paragraph or any crime within the jurisdiction of the Court; enforced disappearances of persons; the crime of apartheid; other inhumane acts of a similar character intentionally causing great suffering, or serious injury to body or to mental or physical health.
8 One participant of the fifth meeting of the Global Network of R2P Focal Points noted that, in order for the R2P norm to avoid being seen as a mechanism for addressing only past threats, it needed to adapt to new challenges.

References

Acharya, A. (2004). How Ideas Spread: Whose Norms Matter? Norm Localization and Institutional Change in Asian Regionalism. *International Organization,* 58, 239–275.

Amnesty International (2014). Iraq: Yezedi Women and Girls Face Harrowing Sexual Violence. Amnesty International. Available from: www.amnesty.org/en/latest/news/2014/12/iraq-yezidi-women-and-girls-face-harrowing-sexual-violence/

Autesserre, S. (2009). Hobbes and the Congo: Frames, Local Violence, and International Intervention. *International Organization,* 63, 249–280.

Axworthy, L. and Rock, A. (2009). R2P: A New and Unfinished Agenda. *Global Responsibility to Protect,* 1, 54–69.

Ban, Ki-Moon. (2016). Uniting to Preventing Violent Extremism, Op-Ed by the United Nations Secretary-General. *Huffington Post*, January 15, 2016.

Barnett, M.N. and Finnemore, M. (2004). *Rules for the World: International Organizations in Global Politics.* Ithaca, NY: Cornell University Press.

BBC (2018). *Islamic State and the Crisis in Iraq and Syria in Maps* [Online]. British Broadcasting Corporation. Available from: www.bbc.com/news/world-middle-east-27838034

Bellamy, A.J. (2015). The Islamic State and the Case for Responsibility to Protect. Available from: www.opencanada.org/features/the-islamic-state-and-the-case-for-responsibility-to-protect/

Boutellis, A. and Fink, N.C. (2016). *Waging Peace: UN Peace Operations Confronting Terrorism and Violent Extremism*. New York: International Peace Institute.

Burns, R. (2016). Battle for Sinjar, Iraq. *Threat Action Report*. Fort Leavenworth: US Army TRADOC.

Checkel, J.T. (1997). International Norms and Domestic Politics: Bridging the Rationalist-Constructivist Divide. *European Journal of International Relations,* 3, 473–495.

Committee on Foreign Relations (2009). Sri Lanka: Re-charting U.S. Strategy after the War. United States Senate, December 7. Available from: www.foreign.senate.gov/imo/media/doc/SRI.pdf

Cortell, A.P. and Davis, J.W. (2000). Understanding the Domestic Impact of International Norms: A Research Agenda. *International Studies Review,* 2, 65–87.

Darby, J. (2012). The Meaning of War. *In:* O'Connell, M.E. (ed.) *What is War?: An Investigation in the Wake of 9/11*, 251–260. Netherlands: Martinus Nijhoff Publishers.

Evans, G.J. (2012). Remembering Sri Lanka's Killing Fields. *Project Syndicate*, October 26, 2012.

Falk, R.A. (2003). *The Great Terror War*. New York: Olive Branch Press.

Finnemore, M. and Sikkink, K. (1998). International Norm Dynamics and Political Change. *International Organization,* 52, 887–917.

Gallagher, A. (2015). The Promise of Pillar II: Analysing International Assistance under the Responsibility to Protect. *International Affairs,* 91, 1259–1275.

Gelpi, C. (1997). Crime and Punishment: The Role of Norms in Crisis Bargaining. *American Political Science Review,* 91, 339–360.

Glenn, C. (2018). *Timeline: The Rise, Spread and Fall of the Islamic State* [Online]. The Wilson Center. Available from: www.wilsoncenter.org/article/timeline-the-rise-spread-and-fall-the-islamic-state

GCR2P (2009a). The 2009 General Assembly Debate: An Assessment. New York: Global Centre for the Responsibility to Protect.

GCR2P (2009b). Open Letter to the Security Council on the Situation in Sri Lanka. New York: Global Centre for the Responsibility to Protect.

Griffin, M. (2015). *Islamic State: Rewriting History*. London: Pluto Press.

Guterres, A. (2017). Secretary-General's Remarks to the Security Council Open Debate on Maintenance of International Peace and Security: Conflict Prevention and Sustaining Peace. New York: United Nations.

Harrison, F. (2012). *Still Counting the Dead: Survivors of Sri Lanka's Hidden War*. London: Portobello Books.

Human Rights Council (2016). "They Came to Destroy": ISIS Crimes Against the Yazidis. Independent International Commission of Inquiry on the Syrian Arab Republic. New York: United Nations. Available from: www.foreign.senate.gov/imo/media/doc/SRI.pdf

HRW (2003). In the Name of Counter-terrorism: Human Rights Abuses Worldwide, March 25. New York: Human Rights Watch. Available from: www.hrw.org/legacy/un/chr59/counter-terrorism-bck.pdf

HRW (2009a). War on the Displaced: Sri Lankan Army and LTTE Abuses against Civilians in the Vanni. New York: Human Rights Watch. Available from: www.hrw.org/report/2009/02/19/war-displaced/sri-lankan-army-and-ltte-abuses-against-civilians-vanni

HRW (2009b). World Report 2009: Sri Lanka, Events of 2008. New York: Human Rights Watch.

HRW (2017). Iraq: ISIS Bombings are Crimes Against Humanity: Compensate Civilian Victims. New York: Human Rights Watch. Available from: www.hrw.org/news/2017/01/15/iraq-isis-bombings-are-crimes-against-humanity

Hunt, C.T. 2016. Emerging Powers and the Responsibility to Protect: Non-linear Norm Dynamics in Complex International Society. *Cambridge Review of International Affairs,* 29, 761–781.

ICISS (2001). *The Responsibility to Protect: Report of the International Commission on Intervention and State Sovereignty.* Ottawa, ON, Canada: International Development Research Centre.

ICTR (2001). The Prosecutor v. Jean-Paul Akayesu (ICTR-96–4-A). *In:* Judgement, A.C. (ed.) Arusha: International Criminal Tribunal for Rwanda.

International Commission of Jurists (2004). The Berlin Declaration: The ICJ Declaration on Upholding Human Rights and the Rule of Law in Combating Terrorism, August 28. Available from: www.icj.org/wp-content/uploads/2004/08/Berlin-Declaration-human-rights-in-fight-terrorism-analysis-brief-2004-eng.pdf

International Committee of the Red Cross (1949). Geneva Convention Relative to the Protection of Civilian Persons in Time of War (Fourth Geneva Convention), August 12, 75 UNTS 287. Available from: www.refworld.org/docid/3ae6b36d2.html

Kahona, P. (2011). Protection of Civilians in Armed Conflict. *United Nations Security Council Open Debate, May 10, 2011.* New York: United Nations.

Kassim, Y.R. (2014). *The Geopolitics of Intervention: Asia and the Responsibility to Protect.* Singapore: Springer.

Krook, M.L. and True, J. (2012). Rethinking the Life Cycles of International Norms: The United Nations and the Global Promotion of Gender Equality. *European Journal of International Relations,* 18, 103–127.

Luck, E. (2015). The Responsibility to Protect at Ten: The Challenges Ahead. *Policy Analysis Brief.* The Stanley Foundation. Available from: https://stanleycenter.org/publications/pab/LuckPAB515.pdf

Matthews, K. and Mulcair, C. (2015). *#R2P10: The Responsibility to Protect and Counter-terrorism* [Online]. ICR2P Blog: International Coalition of the Responsibility to Protect. Available from: https://icrtopblog.org/2015/07/22/r2p10-the-responsibility-to-protect-and-counter-terrorism/

Mokhtari, S. (2009). *After Abu Ghraib: Exploring Human Rights in America and the Middle East.* Cambridge UK, New York: Cambridge University Press.

Nackers, K. (2016). Sri Lanka. *In:* Bellamy, A.J. and Dunne, T. (eds.) *The Oxford Handbook of the Responsibility to Protect.* Oxford: Oxford University Press.

O'Neill, B. (1999). *Honor, Symbols, and War.* University of Michigan: Ann Arbor.

OHCHR (2009). Navi Pillay: Serious Violations of International Law Committed in Sri Lanka Conflict. Report of the UN High-Commissioner for Human Rights. Available from: https://reliefweb.int/report/sri-lanka/serious-violations-international-law-committed-sri-lanka-conflict-un-human-rights

Olsen, G.R. (2014). Fighting Terrorism in Africa by Proxy: The USA and the European Union in Somalia and Mali. *European Security,* 23, 290–306.

Phillips, A. (2012). The Wars on Terror, Duelling Internationalisms and the Clash of Purposes in a Post-unipolar World. *International Politics,* 50, 77.

Richmond, O.P. and Tellidis, I. (2012). The Complex Relationship Between Peacebuilding and Terrorism Approaches: Towards Post-Terrorism and a Post-Liberal Peace? *Terrorism and Political Violence,* 24, 120–143.

Robertson, C.B. (2011). Organizational Management of Conflicting Professional Identities. *Case Western Reserve Journal of International Law,* 43, 603.

Ruggie, J.G. (1998). What Makes the World Hang Together? Neo-utilitarianism and the Social Constructivist Challenge. *International Organization,* 52, 855–885.

Sandholtz, W. (2008). Dynamics of International Norm Change: Rules against Wartime Plunder. *European Journal of International Relations,* 14, 101–131.

Searle, J.R. (1995). *The Construction of Social Reality.* New York: Free Press.

Secretary-General's Internal Review Panel on United Nations Action in Sri Lanka (2012). Report of the Secretary-General's Internal Review Panel on United Nations Action in Sri Lanka. New York: United Nations.

Secretary-General's Panel of Experts on Accountability in Sri Lanka (2011). Report of the Secretary-General's Panel of Experts of Accountability in Sri Lanka. New York: United Nations.

Thakur, R. (2011). *The People vs. the State: Reflections on UN Authority, US Power and the Responsibility to Protect.* Tokyo: United Nations University Press.

Thakur, R. (2013). R2P after Libya and Syria: Engaging Emerging Powers. *The Washington Quarterly,* 36, 61–76.

The Stanley Foundation (2015). Violent Nonstate Actors as Perpetrators and Enablers of Atrocity Crimes. Policy Dialogue Brief. 56th Annual Strategy for Peace Conference 14–16, October 2015. Warrington, VA: The Stanley Foundation.

UN (1998). *Rome Statute of the International Criminal Court.* Treaty, UN Diplomatic Conference on the Establishment of an International Criminal Court, Rome, July 17. New York: United Nations.

UN (2003). Report of the United Nations High Commissioner for Human Rights and Follow-up to the World Conference on Human Rights. E/CN.4/2004/4. August 5, Economic and Social Council. New York: United Nations.

UN (2004). Report of the Secretary-General's High-level Panel on Threats, Challenges and Change: A More Secure World: Our Shared Responsibility. A/59/565. New York: United Nations.

UN (2006). Uniting Against Terrorism: Recommendations for a Global Counter-terrorism Strategy. *Report of the Secretary-General.* A/60/825, April 27. New York: United Nations.

UN General Assembly (1948). *Convention on the Prevention and Punishment of the Crime of Genocide,* December 9. New York: United Nations.

UN General Assembly (2005). 2005 World Summit Outcome Document. A/RES/60/1, October 24. New York: United Nations.

UN General Assembly (2006a). General Assembly Resolution 60/288 (2006). A/RES/60/288, September 8. New York: United Nations.

UN General Assembly (2006b). The United Nations Global Counter-Terrorism Strategy. A/RES/60/288, September 20. New York: United Nations.

UN General Assembly (2009). Implementing the Responsibility to Protect. *Report of the Secretary-General.* A/63/677, January 12. New York: United Nations.

UN General Assembly (2013). Responsibility to Protect: State Responsibility and Prevention. *Report of the Secretary-General.* A/67/929-S/2013/399. July 9, 2013. New York: United Nations.

UN General Assembly (2014). Fulfilling our Collective Responsibility: International Assistance and the Responsibility to Protect. *Report of the Secretary-General.* A/68/947-S/2014/449, July 11. New York: United Nations.

UN General Assembly (2015). Plan of Action to Prevent Violent Extremism. *Report of the Secretary-General.* A/70/674, December 24. New York: United Nations.

UN Secretary-General (2015). Remarks at General Assembly Presentation of the Plan of Action to Prevent Violent Extremism. January 16, 2016. New York: United Nations.

UN Secretary-General (2016). UN Secretary-General's Remarks at General Assembly Presentation of the Plan of Action to Prevent Violent Extremism [As Delivered]. New York: United Nations.

UN Security Council (2001). Security Council Resolution 1373 (2001). S/RES/1373, September 28. New York: United Nations.

UN Security Council (2003). Security Council Resolution 1456 (2003). S/RES/1456, January 20. New York: United Nations.

UN Security Council (2004). Report by the Chair of the Counter-Terrorism Committee on the Problems Encountered in the Implementation of Security Council Resolution 1373 (2001). S/2004/70, January 26. New York: United Nations.

UN Security Council (2005). Security Council Resolution 1624 (2005). *Threats to International Peace and Security.* S/RES/1624, September 14. New York: United Nations.

UN Security Council (2009). Security Council Press Statement on Sri Lanka. SC/9659. New York: United Nations.

UN Security Council (2014). Security Council Resolution 2170 (2014). S/RES/2170, August 15. New York: United Nations.

UN Security Council (2015a). Letter dated October 22, 2015 from the Permanent Representatives of Chile and Spain to the United Nations addressed to the President of the Security Council. S/2015/815, October 26. New York: United Nations.

UN Security Council (2015b). Prevention Should Be Integral to All United Nations Efforts, Secretary-General Tells Security Council in First Open Debate on Root Causes of Conflict. *Meetings Coverage.* 7561st meeting. SC/12124, November 17. New York: United Nations.

Van Kersbergen, K. and Verbeek, B. (2007). The Politics of International Norms: Subsidiarity and the Imperfect Competence Regime of the European Union. *European Journal of International Relations,* 13, 217–238.

Weiss, G. (2012). *The Cage: The Fight for Sri Lanka and the Last Days of the Tamil Tigers.* New York: Bellevue Literary Press.

Weiss, T.G. (2007). *The United Nations and Changing World Politics.* Boulder, CO: Westview Press.

Welsh, J.M. (2013). Norm Contestation and the Responsibility to Protect. *Global Responsibility to Protect*, 5(4): 365–396. doi.org/10.1163/1875984X-00504002

Welsh, J.M. (2014). *Implementing the "Responsibility to Protect": Catalyzing Debate and Building Capacity. In:* Orchard, P. and Betts, A. (eds.) *Implementation and World Politics*, 124–143. Oxford: Oxford University Press.

Wiener, A. (2004). Contested Compliance: Interventions on the Normative Structure of World Politics. *European Journal of International Relations,* 10, 189–234.

Wiener, A. (2009). Enacting Meaning-in-use: Qualitative Research on Norms and International Relations. *Review of International Studies,* 35, 175–193.

7 Resistance and accommodation in China's approach toward R2P

Sarah Teitt

Introduction

There is a central contradiction in China's approach toward the Responsibility to Protect (R2P). On the one hand, China has repeatedly affirmed its support for the R2P principle and has declared that it "stands ready to work together with the international community to fully implement the objective laid out in the 2005 World Summit Outcome Document" (WSOD) (PRC, 2015). On the other hand, China insists that R2P should be implemented with respect to sovereignty and national ownership, and resists efforts to hold state leaders accountable for perpetrating atrocity crimes. In other words, China declaratively endorses R2P, yet also appears to routinely block R2P implementation and persistently contest a key premise of the norm that conditions sovereignty on the protection of populations from mass atrocities.

This chapter explores this apparent contradiction in China's position and what it reveals about the resilience and normative consolidation of R2P. Others have explored this paradox in China's R2P policy before. Existing studies have assessed China's simultaneous acceptance of and resistance to R2P as a strategic effort to contain or shape R2P to make its prescriptions cohere better with China's defense of a pluralist world order, and to render R2P-guided interventions more compatible with China's state-centered foreign and security policies (Prantl and Nakano, 2011; Foot, 2011; Job and Shesterinina, 2014; Foot and Walter, 2011; Job, 2016; Foot, 2016). By these accounts, Beijing has adeptly maneuvered to weaken or dilute the R2P norm of sovereign accountability by prioritizing national responsibility, state-driven capacity building and consent-based prevention measures.

China's apparent support for *and* resistance to R2P is therefore interpreted not as a paradox per se, but rather as a norm-shaping strategy. By fulsomely endorsing relatively anodyne prescriptions under what the United Nations (UN) Secretary-General refers to as Pillars One and Two, while at the same time resisting decisive international action to confront atrocity crimes under Pillar Three, existing studies argue that China has actively sought to recalibrate the meaning and scope of R2P to fit a statist implementation agenda that reifies rather than conditions sovereign authority. These observations have led some studies to conclude that China's professed support for R2P belies that China is, in practice, an R2P rejectionist state (Claes, 2012: 71–72), whose sophisticatedly piecemeal acceptance of R2P "has served to fortify, rather than erode, the sovereignty protectionist agenda" (Job, 2016: 898).

While accepting these general observations about Chinese goals and strategies to contest and contain R2P, this chapter offers a nuanced challenge to the conclusion that China is an R2P rejectionist state that advances a narrow sovereignty protectionist agenda through its engagement with the norm. The chapter advances this argument in three sections. The first section provides an overview of how China has reconciled R2P with its own normative positions on sovereignty, intervention and human rights, which has resulted in a distinctly minimalist interpretation of R2P as a norm of 'non-indifference' toward large-scale humanitarian crises. The second section explores the arguments that China's foreign policy elites moved forward to critique R2P and contest its implementation, demonstrating that China's most vehement arguments are largely based in pragmatic and prudential concerns rather than a strident principled defense of sovereignty. That is, China generally agrees that R2P implies that the international community should take action to prevent and halt atrocities, but China has its own set of prescriptions for the most appropriate and effective means to this end (see the discussion of applicatory contestation in the Introduction of this volume). China's preferred strategies are largely based in mediation, stabilization and conflict resolution strategies, and depart from the liberal accountability and liberal interventionist measures that are understood as the orthodox 'toolbox' for implementing R2P. As the third section of the chapter demonstrates, at the same time as China has resisted certain R2P response measures at the UN, in recent years Beijing has taken proactive and unprecedented steps to address human protection crises overseas. The chapter concludes by arguing that China's engagement with R2P is not simply a story of a sovereignty-obsessed state intent on containing post-sovereignty norms. Rather than shrewdly subverting R2P or jealously safeguarding sovereignty, China appears to be leveraging the ambiguity of R2P (see Chapter 2 by Glanville and Widmaier) to promote an alternative pathway to achieving R2P's aim of ending atrocity crimes that nevertheless veers from the liberal forms of justice, human rights accountability and intervention often associated with R2P. In this sense, China approaches R2P as a coherent norm complex, but one that is less situated in existing norms of robust human rights and individual accountability for atrocity crimes than Orchard's discussion of R2P as an international regime suggests (see Introduction and Chapter 1).

China's R2P 'minimalism'

Though China is often viewed as one of the most vocal defenders of sovereignty in world affairs, Beijing did not mount much of a resistance to UN endorsement of R2P in 2005 and has repeatedly reaffirmed the WSOD agreement (Teitt, 2017). China's initial support for R2P was made possible by an assurance that R2P represented a different paradigm than humanitarian intervention that could both protect people and protect sovereignty and would uphold the authority of the UN Security Council (UNSC) (Teitt, 2009; Liu, 2012). These qualifications eased some of China's resistance to arguments that condition sovereignty on human rights – resistance which has roots in China's pluralist worldview and sovereignty-centered foreign policy principles. Chinese foreign policy is guided by the Five Principles of Peaceful Co-existence (FPPC), which enshrine the defense of sovereignty and non-interference the centerpiece of Chinese foreign relations. Originally enumerated in 1954, these principles include: mutual respect for each other's territorial integrity and sovereignty; mutual non-aggression; non-interference in each other's internal affairs; equality and mutual benefit; and peaceful co-existence (China Daily, 2005).

While Chinese actors voice concern over the potential for R2P to amplify external scrutiny of China's own human rights record in Tibet, Xinjiang and even Taiwan (Liu, 2012), there is an arguably deeper set of pluralist norms and perspectives that shape Chinese skepticism toward R2P. Chinese foreign policy discourses offer a strong moral defense of sovereignty as the equal right of each state to independently choose its own social and political systems free from the encroachment of external actors. To justify China's commitment to non-interference, China's ruling elite have routinely invoked China's experiences during the 'century of humiliation' – the period that began with the First Opium War of 1839, continued through China's invasion and occupation by Western and Japanese forces, and lasted until external powers officially renounced extraterritorial rights in China in the 1940s – to portray the defense of sovereignty as the basis for restoring the Chinese people's dignity, ensuring their well-being and protecting basic human rights (Hays Gries, 2005). This victimhood narrative, which gained traction after the Tiananmen crackdown in 1989, has helped Chinese leaders to cultivate China's national identity as an aggrieved post-colonial developing country and (re)emerging major power whose defense of sovereignty is part of an international mission to offer an alternative to US hegemony and Western imperialism (Wang, 2012). President Xi Jinping's speech at the high-level debate at the UN in 2015 is an exemplar of this narrative and worldview. After recalling China's heroic efforts to "save its people from subjugation" and noting that "history is a mirror," Xi called for "a new type of international relations" based on renewed commitment to the principles of the UN Charter. The bedrock of the Charter, Xi continued, is sovereign equality:

> All countries are equals. The big, strong and rich should not bully the small, weak and poor. The principle of sovereignty not only means that the sovereignty and territorial integrity of all countries are inviolable and that their internal affairs are not subjected to interference. It also means that all countries' right to independently choose social systems and development paths should be upheld.... Big countries should treat small countries as equals and take a right approach to justice and interests by putting justice before interests.
>
> (Xi, 2015)

Critics of China's stance on sovereignty tend to portray China's position as narrowly self-interested and antithetical to protecting individual human rights. China inverts this argument, and in line with the realpolitik lens that dominates Chinese foreign policy analysis (Shambaugh, 2013), contends that in a world of self-interested states and extreme power imbalances, China's defense of sovereignty is, in Xi Jinping's words, "putting justice before interest" (Xi, 2015).

China's pluralist defense of sovereignty is also an extension of its human rights culture that prioritizes state-centered collective socioeconomic rights over individual rights. In a departure from Western liberal traditions which view the human subject as an abstract moral entity bearing inalienable rights to be protected from incursions of the state, both China's traditional and Maoist articulation of rights view citizen rights as granted by the state, and define people's rights as the benefits enjoyed by fulfilling obligations to contribute to the good of the Chinese nation (Kent, 1999: 29). As Elizabeth Perry points out, the Chinese word for citizen (*gongmin*) literally translates to 'public person,' which "connotes collective membership in the polity, rather than a claim to individual or inalienable rights vis-à-vis the state" (Perry, 2008: 46). In this thinking, the core duty born by the government to its citizens is to ensure their decent and secure livelihoods. China's collective rights tradition privileges the supremacy of state rights over individual rights and defines the legitimacy of the state based on its ability to maintain stability and foster conditions conducive to people's socioeconomic well-being. The consequence of this thinking is a strong bias in China on the primacy of the state, and – particularly since Deng Xiaoping's Reform and Opening Policy of 1978 – a conviction that state-led economic development is the key means for upholding people's rights and for ensuring peaceful state–society relations. More recently, this thinking has manifested in China's pressing for greater priority to be placed on the "right to development" as the basis for realizing other rights (Yao, 2019).

Narratives of historical victimhood and China's collectivist human rights tradition serve as powerful rhetorical touchpoints for Chinese actors to forward a moral defense of sovereign equality and contest R2P on pluralist grounds. These arguments are born out in Jennifer Welsh's assessment that concerns over the possibility for states "to impose their conception of justice" are the motivation behind "some of the deepest contestation surrounding R2P." Welsh continues,

> The effort to preserve legal egalitarianism – even if an empirical fiction – flows from a deeper desire to maintain diversity and pluralism within the international system. This has resulted in efforts to downplay the remedial responsibility of the international community, and the conditionality inherent in R2P's understanding of sovereignty, and instead to emphasize the continued salience of principles and process that emphasize domestic jurisdiction, consent, and multilateral cooperation.
>
> (Welsh, 2013: 394)

It is this normative position that shapes China's 'minimalist' endorsement of R2P. Although China agrees that the international community has a responsibility to address large-scale humanitarian crises, China is reluctant to characterize this responsibility as a normative shift in the meaning of sovereignty – preferring instead to emphasize the international community's remedial role as an emergency exception to the non-interference rule. Chinese analysts explain China's emphasis on Pillars One and Two not as a disavowal that action should be taken to halt genocidal violence, but as a way to reinforce that responses on behalf of the international community should be understood as "temporary and supplementary with the final aim being the restoration of the state's sovereignty" and that "the aim of R2P is to establish a responsible sovereignty but not weaken sovereignty" (Liu and Zhang, 2014: 413). As an official in China's Ministry of Foreign Affairs reflected, China's shares the common aspiration and end goal espoused in the Secretary-General's R2P implementation strategy:

> The hope should be to transplant R2P in [the government's] own system [and] to get a situation where each government has to fulfill its own responsibility to protect rather than fear external intervention or ask for military force to protect … this is the goal.[1]

Understood in this light, China's simultaneous endorsement of R2P and insistence on respect for state sovereignty could be seen as an attempt to find a way to fit the goals of R2P (which China has repeatedly professed to support) within China's principled commitment to defend sovereign equality (which remains a normative cornerstone of China's foreign policy and Chinese identity). That is, rather than merely limit Pillar Three action, China's paradoxical rhetoric on R2P carves out space for China to endorse certain remedial international action to protect populations under attack, while also remaining true to what President Xi Jinping portrays as China's "endeavor to uphold international fairness and justice" and ensure respect for the "diversity of civilizations" (Xi, 2017). This is unsatisfactory for some critics who would like to see China embrace a less qualified stance on R2P, but it is also a sign of China's willingness to yield some ground on sovereignty in atrocity situations (Chen, 2016).

China's R2P contestation

The preceding analysis helps explain how China's normative position on sovereignty and non-interference inform China's paradoxical stance on R2P. Yet, as the following section demonstrates, some of the most common explanations Chinese officials and analysts offer for China's cautious stance on R2P are less concerned with the normative contestation than objections to the ways in which R2P is implemented. In other words, China's underlying skepticism toward R2P is rooted in deep principled critiques, but the most prominent and vehement arguments against R2P made by China's foreign policy elite are often based in pragmatic and prudential concerns. This distinction between China's principled and prudential contestation is important, as it adds another layer of analysis that helps explain why, even as China's accepts that the international community should take action to halt atrocities in extreme emergencies, China often resists R2P implementation in practice.

There are five key arguments that most commonly feature in Chinese critiques of R2P: (1) intervention does more harm than good; (2) interveners fail to take adequate responsibility for post-intervention peacebuilding; (3) R2P is inconsistently invoked and is susceptible to double standards and ulterior motives; (4) the pressure R2P raises to act against states results in imprudent response measures; and (5) despite assurances that R2P rests in three equally important pillars, R2P advocates pay mere lip service to the preventive role of state capacity building and development assistance. While the first three issues pertain mostly to China's apprehensions regarding the utility of coercive military intervention, the latter points relate to a broader set of prudential concerns regarding 'confrontational' approaches to managing crises, and to the priority China places on socioeconomic development as key to conflict prevention and societal peace.

On the first point, Chinese analysts and media commentators argue that large-scale military intervention is not a suitable policy response for improving security outcomes for local populations, but rather further inflames conflicts and exacerbates civilian vulnerabilities. As evidence, analysts draw attention to the continued turmoil and civilian death toll associated with Western intervention in Iraq and Afghanistan, as well as the security vacuum and ongoing abuses in Libya. This position is aptly reflected in the remarks of Assistant Foreign Minister Le Yucheng on the Libya intervention:

> We must not forget the lessons from Libya. On the first day of the NATO-led multinational forces' 'protection' mission in Libya last year, 64 civilians were killed and 150 were injured. The entire 'protection' mission resulted in the deaths of over 20,000 civilians and the displacement of 900,000 people without bringing the country together or ending the violence there – some regions in Libya even declared autonomy. Such 'protection' has been likened to a 'successful surgery that kills the patient'. Obviously, it has failed completely. It is irresponsible 'protection' and in truth, intervention under the name of 'protection'. Being responsible means saying 'no' to such things.
>
> (Le, 2012)

It is worth noting that this harsh critique does not question whether civilians ought to be protected, but rather objects to large-scale intervention as the means to that end. Even in extreme cases, China tends to call for what can be viewed as traditional conflict resolution and stabilization measures, such as mediation, negotiated ceasefires and consent-based peacekeeping deployments.

This relates to a second common point of critique of R2P in Chinese discourse, namely that Western leaders are plagued by short-term vision, and the initial enthusiasm or capacity for military intervention is not matched by the willpower, resources or strategic planning to guarantee security and build peace post-intervention. As Ruan Zongze, a Vice President of the China Institute of International Studies (the think tank of China's Ministry of Foreign Affairs) pithily summarized, "the West has a very short attention span to start a war, feel tired, and leave in exhaustion."[2] Chinese experts also call for greater critical reflection by Western policymakers on the association of R2P and regime change, and critique the underlying assumption that building peace and improving human security in the aftermath of regime change (whether by military force or rapid power transition) is even possible. In the words of one prominent Middle East analyst, "China thinks the US is so naïve to think they can overthrow a dictator in the Middle East and then lead to democracy and economic growth. We tell them to look at history. So naïve!"[3]

A third explanation for China's caution on R2P lies in the apparent lack of genuine humanitarian motives on the part of states who claim to be concerned with preventing mass atrocities. Chinese analysts point to the US' unwillingness to hold Israel to account for attacks in Gaza, and the overwhelming concern over the repressive tactics of the regimes in Syria and Libya as opposed to Bahrain in 2011, as evidence that geopolitics rather than the nature of state violence determines the targets of Western criticism and intervention (Ruan, 2012). Perceptions that NATO overreached its civilian protection mandate to pursue a policy of regime change in Libya was fuel added to the fire of this grievance. The Libya intervention sparked heated Chinese criticism that in theory R2P constrains the use of force and makes it more accountable by affirming the authority of the UNSC, but in reality R2P is a 'Trojan Horse' that is easily manipulated to carry out military intervention to depose leaders according to Western self-interests. One senior diplomat noted,

> NATO's overreach of its mission in Libya turned NATO air force into the opposition force. This was a sure case to say the West humanitarian intentions cannot be trusted.... Of course, democracy and human rights are the most beautiful concepts for all people, but governments are not motivated by this. These beautiful concepts are lost in a jungle of geopolitics.[4]

A recurrent theme in Chinese discourse on the Libya intervention is that China was "tricked" by the assurances that R2P represented a significant departure from humanitarian intervention, and that Chinese suspicions that R2P was just " 'old wine' of humanitarian intervention in a 'new bottle' " were justified (Liu and Zhang, 2014: 409).

A fourth point regularly raised by Chinese commentators is that the impetus to hold state authorities accountable for atrocity crimes can lead to ill-advised or imprudent response measures that enact liberal values but defy well-reasoned conflict analysis. For example, a leading *Global Times* article published at the outset of the intervention in Libya questioned Western support for the Benghazi-based rebel movement, as it was not primarily a democratic force but a composite of "heterogeneous political forces" that share the "same temporary objectives to subvert [the] Gaddafi regime but no long-term plan to build a true democracy."

Ascribing the rebel forces with a sense of "deep tribalism," the article warned that external intervention that led to the swift collapse of the Gaddafi regime would augur "endless civil wars over the leadership of the country" (Global Times, 2011).

Similar words of caution circulated in Chinese media regarding the P3's "politics of confrontation" in Syria (People's Daily, 2012). According to a *People's Daily* article published in March 2012, by pressing for sanctions and power transition in Syria, leaders in the West were "indulging provocation and nurturing the armed struggle," as they gave Syrian President Bashar al-Assad no face-saving exit from power and encouraged the opposition to make unrelenting demands (ibid.). The article forewarned that the "American version" of a "Syrian Solution" would further militarize the conflict until "Syria sinks into the quagmire of civil war," which would lead to the destabilization of the Middle East, and allow for the infiltration and expansion of al-Qaeda and other violent extremist groups amid the resulting chaos (ibid.). Consistent with this analysis, a dominant interpretation circulating among Chinese analysts was that the 2016 refugee problem and terrorist attacks in Europe were a consequence of Western diplomacy in Syria and US intervention in the Middle East. In the words of Wu Sike, China's former Special Envoy to the Middle East,

> The war in Iraq sowed the seeds of instability and the US-led military intervention in the 'Arab Spring' spread turbulence across the region, turning it into the hotbed for terrorism. Though the refugee crisis broke out recently, its root cause can easily be traced to America's self-righteous actions and foreign policy mistake.
>
> (Wu, 2015)

While Wu's statement reflects the propensity among Chinese officials to downplay the Assad regime's atrocities and place the blame for the Syria crisis on external actors, it also embodies a deeply held conviction in China that Western, primarily US, efforts to spread democracy and liberal values in the Middle East have resulted in misguided policy choices that have destabilized the region, given rise to violent extremism and resulted in new global security challenges. There is a perception that the turmoil caused in the effort to uphold liberal values is vindicating China's position that "freedom and democracy are less appealing than political stability and economic growth."[5]

In addition to these concerns, China's contestation of R2P centers on differences in Chinese versus Western interpretations of the root causes of and appropriate remedies for large-scale humanitarian crises, which renders China generally resistant to 'confrontational' approaches to civilian protection. Policymakers in the West tend to view the lack of human rights accountability and state repression as core causal factors leading to civil conflict and atrocity crimes and call for coercive measures as necessary tools for compelling states to abide by international human rights and humanitarian law. Chinese foreign policy actors, by contrast, tend not to distinguish state-sponsored killing from other forms of large-scale humanitarian emergencies, which they primarily attribute to problems associated with poverty, underdevelopment and deep-seated identity-based conflict. This perspective overwhelmingly privileges persuasive forms of crisis diplomacy and response rather than coercive protection measures. For example, as Liu Tiewa and Zhang Haibin (2014: 417) have noted, China's Special Envoy to Darfur, Liu Guijin, portrayed the crisis in Darfur as a result of ethnic/clan conflict and resource scarcity, and "repeatedly emphasized that the key problem in Darfur is development and poverty as opposed to genocide." When it came to addressing the crisis, China rejected Western policies of "blaming, threatening, criticizing and sanctions" not merely on principled grounds, but also based on the pragmatic argument that any UN intervention in the crisis ultimately relied on working with authorities in Khartoum, which in turn required a "certain degree of basic trust" and a "sound atmosphere" to garner Omar al-Bashir's compliance (PRC, undated, 2008).

A 'better the devil we know' approach also informed China's resistance to applying overwhelming pressure on the Assad regime. China's leading Middle East experts argued that the Syrian opposition was incapable of containing the splintering factions and extremist forces, and there was no guarantee that the administration that would take Assad's place would promise better protection or security or be able to maintain the territorial integrity of Syria.[6] This analysis reflects the deep sense of risk aversion among Chinese diplomats, who place great purchase in gradual, long-term reform and are quite wary of pushing for swifter or more forceful action. It also aligns with what Chinese academics refer to as the "Chinese culture" approach to preventive diplomacy, which exhibits a strong preference for more subtle efforts to induce state authorities to exercise restraint and embark on reforms, as opposed to outwardly coercing them to comply with external demands (Li, 2012).

Finally, Chinese foreign policy actors express concern that R2P "capacity building and assistance" tends to focus narrowly on civil and political rights and the "freedom from fear" human security agenda, while insufficient attention is paid to state-led poverty alleviation and economic development as sources of domestic resilience and conflict prevention (Teitt, 2016). This point of contention relates to China's home-grown 'developmental peace thesis' that derives from the Chinese Communist Party's own experience in recovering from the Chinese civil war, and is grounded in the idea that state-led economic development with minimal external political interference and strong state control over society is the path to long-term peace and stability (Wang, 2018). Ambassador Liu Jieyi, China's former Permanent Representative to the UN, offered a cogent summary of this position in 2014:

> In post-conflict peacebuilding, the international community has long emphasized human rights, the rule of law and security sector reform without paying adequate attention to the economic and social development of the countries concerned and with limited input in that regard. We call on the international community to focus more on the economic and social development of the

> countries concerned. Only through rapid economic recovery and reconstruction will the affected populations be able to enjoy the dividends of peace and will a solid foundation for political reconciliation, the stabilization of security and the establishment of a political basis for the peace process be laid.
>
> (Liu, 2014)

While Chinese officials and analysts are apt to portray state-led economic development as panacea for all grievances leading to conflict (and in turn leverage these arguments to contest the liberal good governance and human rights accountability agenda), this position also reflects deeply ingrained thinking among Chinese leaders that economic development is key to maintaining peace and achieving civilian protection. It also indirectly links to a repeated critique in Chinese academic discourse of liberal approaches to 'solving' crises. Chinese analysts argue that Western countries are animated to solve only those problems that they diagnose as a fault of brutal state leadership and bad governance, but are ultimately unwilling to address the underlying economic and social conditions that create a fundamentally unfair and unjust international order and contribute to conflict in the developing world (Qiu and Zhou, 2012).

What do these critiques reveal about China's seemingly contradictory endorsement of and resistance to R2P? For the most part, China's foreign policy elite agree that the international community should not be indifferent to genocidal violence. However, Chinese actors have their own understandings about the appropriate and most effective means for actioning this norm. Chinese analysts tend to view atrocity prevention through a 'negative' peace lens: the key goal is to halt violence and return stability, not to confront wicked acts and uphold individual human rights. Many of the objections Chinese actors raise regarding R2P center on the conclusion that Western approaches to responding to atrocity situations are imprudent and short-sighted because they associate R2P with too 'thick' liberal principles. In an effort to uphold principles of good governance, justice and accountability, liberal ideals become the enemy of what China views as the most effective means to prevent and halt violence. To this end, Chinese actors call for a much narrower, less coercive, and more 'pragmatic' R2P response agenda that recognizes that protection cannot be demanded or even driven by external actors but entails working with state authorities, however bad or brutal these leaders may be. While this perspective has its own shortcomings, the key point here is not to defend but rather to understand Chinese positions on R2P. It is China's agreement on R2P goals but deep divergence on means and strategy that helps to explain why China simultaneously endorses R2P and also persistently contests its implementation (for comparison on how this comports with US and Russian policies, see, respectively, Chapters 2 and 8 by Glanville and Widmaier and Orchard and Rae).

China's proactive response to atrocity situations

Despite the concerns raised by Chinese officials and analysts regarding R2P, China at times demonstrates greater openness to a wider range of R2P response measures than its official rhetoric or expert analysis suggests. Though China's official policy requires the consent of the host state, China abstained on Resolution 1973, which authorized coercive intervention to protect Libyan populations from Gaddafi's onslaught in March 2011. That same month, China also voted in favor of Resolution 1975, which strengthened the mandate of the UN operation in Côte d'Ivoire to protect civilians from the heavy artillery of state security forces. China's flexibility in these situations relate to China's desire to protect its international image as a responsible power, and China's reluctance to override the requests of regional leaders (Teitt, 2009, 2017; Fung, 2015).

Since the late 1990s, Chinese leaders have attempted to burnish China's image as a responsible power that is constructively part of the solution to global problems. China's reputational concerns emerged in part from Beijing's interests in dispelling fear that China's rise and expanding global footprint would destabilize the liberal world order and posed a threat to Western values and interests. Chinese officials and commentators have routinely pointed to China's contribution to UN peacekeeping and its unprecedented role in managing humanitarian crises as evidence that China is a status quo power that complies with existing international norms and regimes and upholds common standards of responsible behavior (Li, 2012). For audiences outside the West, China has leveraged its contribution to conflict management in Africa in particular to demonstrate that China is not singularly motivated by self-regarding economic interests but is also committed to advancing peace and stability to benefit local populations (PRC, 2003). Whether a means to assuage Western anxieties that China's rise threatens liberal norms and institutions or to demonstrate China's South–South solidarity, China's desire to be recognized as a responsible power has compelled it to assume more active roles in addressing human protection crises (Chen, 2016).

Most notably, China has expanded its contributions to UN peacekeeping, at a time when missions are deployed in complex conflict environments that exhibit ongoing risk of atrocity crimes (Teitt, 2017). The UN Secretary-General noted this trend in 2015:

> United Nations peace operations are often a front-line resource for assisting States under stress to uphold their responsibility to protect.... Increasingly, these operations confront situations characterized by widespread and systematic violence, the specific targeting of groups based on identity and the indiscriminate use of force. Peacekeepers are also being deployed with greater frequency into complex and hostile environments where there is no peace to keep.
>
> (UNSG, 2015: para. 33)

Although UN peacekeeping missions deploy with the ostensible consent and cooperation of the host government, there is pressure for UN peacekeepers to protect local populations that are targeted by state security forces. For example, the 2015 UN Department of Peacekeeping Operations and Department of Field Support (DPKO/DFS) guidelines state that,

> UN peacekeepers are authorized and are duty bound to undertake actions to protect civilians. Within the mission's area of operations, peacekeepers may act independently to protect civilians, irrespective of the source of the threat, in the absence of an effective host government effort or willingness to carry out its responsibilities to protect its civilians.
>
> (UN DPKO/DFS, 2015: 3)

These guidelines set expectations for UN peacekeepers to deter attacks by *any* armed group that targets civilians, including government forces, which blurs the line between consent-based peacekeeping and peace enforcement measures endorsed under Pillar Three of R2P (for a deeper discussion of POC in relation to R2P, see Hunt, Chapter 4 in this volume).

Despite its discomfort with peace enforcement and robust civilian protection mandates, China currently provides more financial support for UN peacekeeping than any other country barring the US, and it currently contributes more peacekeeping personnel than any other permanent member of the UNSC. China has also at times endorsed robust civilian protection mandates – such as in Côte d'Ivoire, Democratic Republic of Congo (DRC) and Central African Republic – in consideration of the requests of regional organizations and out of concern that attacks could spiral into wider cycles of violence that threatened regional stability. Moreover, Chinese peacekeepers are deployed to UN peacekeeping missions operating under robust Chapter VII mandates where a mission priority is civilian protection, such as in South Sudan and the DRC. China has also made high profile and ambitious commitments to strengthen peacekeeping capabilities. In September 2015, President Xi Jinping's announced that China would set up a permanent peacekeeping force of 8,000 police personnel; provide $100 million to the African Union to create a standby force to respond to emergencies; contribute $1 billion to set up a UN–China 'peace and development fund'; commit a helicopter squad for peacekeeping operations in Africa; and train 5,000 peacekeepers from other countries over the next five years. This followed China's dispatching an infantry battalion of 700 soldiers in April 2015 to South Sudan under the UN mandate to protect civilians, UN personnel and humanitarian workers.

While China's role in international peacekeeping has been the subject of plenty of policy and academic analysis, relatively less attention has been paid to how China's reputational concerns have also nudged China into a more proactive role in crisis diplomacy in R2P situations. China's foray into special envoy diplomacy initially emerged in response to widespread international condemnation of China's defense of the government of Sudan despite Khartoum's complicity in crimes against humanity in Darfur from 2004. International criticism is widely seen as the impetus behind China applying subtle pressure on the Sudanese government to help alleviate the crisis in Darfur, including through taking the unprecedented step in May 2007 of appointing a senior diplomat to address an 'internal' crisis – naming Ambassador Liu Guijin as Special Envoy to Darfur (Holsag, 2008). As Chengqiu Wu notes, Beijing "deliberately played a visible role in pressuring the

Sudanese government, in order to improve its national image that [was] undermined by the Darfur issue" (Wu, 2009: 83). A number of prominent foreign policy analysts in China connected the criticism China faced over its diplomacy toward Sudan to normative shifts associated with R2P. The collective expectation for the UNSC to take action to halt mass atrocities led to a greater conviction among Chinese officials and analysts that "resistance to … interventions by invoking the principles of absolute sovereignty and non-intervention, either in legal terms or on moral grounds, cannot be justified, nor will such resistance be widely recognized, sympathized with or supported" (Zhu, 2010: 45).

To be sure, the conviction among China's foreign policy elite that China cannot simply invoke sovereignty to excuse inaction has *not* prevented China from blocking R2P protection measures in the UNSC. At the critical early phases of the crisis in Syria from 2011–2014, China joined Russia in weakening then jointly vetoing four draft resolutions, which would have signaled to the Assad regime that Syrian authorities were accountable for their attacks against populations in Syria, and applied measures to compel warring factions to address the severe vulnerability of civilians. Yet, even as it blocked measures in the UNSC, China went to significant lengths to communicate that its policy represented responsible action in Syria, and considered the protection needs of local populations. A *People's Daily* article published under the byline *Zhong Sheng* ('voice of China') after China cast its second veto on Syria in February 2012, clarified that China's vote "does not mean that China will sit by and watch the sad situation going on," but that China was "responsible for the fundamental interests of the Syrian people" (Zhong Sheng, 2012). In four separate paragraphs, the article outlined how China's UNSC vote qualified as responsible action toward Syrian people and regional stability, suggesting that China was compelled to justify its position with reference to norms of sovereign responsibility, and acknowledged a special responsibility of the UNSC to respond to the protection needs of Syrian populations (ibid.).

China also adopted proactive measures to signal that its acknowledgment of the international responsibility to address the suffering of Syrian civilians was not just a rhetorical device to deflect international criticism. From early 2012, China repeatedly dispatched special envoys to the Syrian conflict, which represented unusually vigorous Chinese diplomacy that had only been witnessed in China's proactive approach to conflicts in Darfur and South Sudan. Wu Sike and Gong Xiaosheng, China's special envoys to the Middle East, engaged in shuttle diplomacy between Syrian factions, regional leaders and Western powers to coordinate and promote a political solution. Wu Sike characterized China's efforts to promote a peace process as an extension of China's "principled stance" on Syria, and manifestation of "China's sense of responsibility as a permanent member" (Wu, 2012).

China also offered to host high-level delegations from the Syrian government as well as the opposition following the UNSC's unanimous endorsement of Resolution 2254 in December 2015, which called for talks between the government and opposition that would lead to negotiations for a nationwide ceasefire.

In advance of talks scheduled between warring factions in Geneva, China hosted a visit by Syrian Deputy Prime Minister/Foreign Minister Walid al-Moallem in late December 2015, then hosted the president of the National Coalition for Syrian Revolutionary Opposition Forces Khaled Khoja during the first week of January 2016 (Rudolf, 2016). Following these meetings held in Beijing, in March 2016 China made a rare decision to appoint a special envoy to the crisis, naming seasoned diplomat Xie Xiaoyan as China's Special Envoy to Syria. As trailed in China's proactive diplomacy in Sudan and South Sudan, China appeared intent on demonstrating that it was not merely blocking measures aimed at halting atrocities but was offering alternative strategies for advancing peace and fostering conditions for civilian protection. As Joel Wuthnow (2013) argued, China's active diplomacy signaled that China wanted to "show the world that it can play a constructive role in any solution to the conflict" in Syria.

It is worth noting as well, that China endorsed UNSC Resolution 2139 (February 22, 2014), which demanded unfettered humanitarian access in Syria, and later supported Resolution 2165 (July 14, 2014), which strengthened this mandate to deliver aid across four border crossings into rebel-held areas without the consent of the Syrian government. With regard to the latter, though China joined Russia in rejecting the resolution falling under a Chapter VII mandate, China was seen to be more "supportive and constructive" in negotiations for the UNSC to authorize humanitarian aid delivery into besieged areas without Assad's prior approval (What's in Blue, 2014). As in many of the Council's debates on Syria from early 2012, Chinese diplomats "appeared cautious rather than obstructive or adversarial," and appeared to be acting on China's own convictions on how best to ease the situation rather than simply defending Damascus (Adams, 2015: 14). According to a prominent Chinese international relations academic, although China was more assertive in rejecting Western-led UNSC action on Syria, China's support for good offices and humanitarian assistance were aimed at "sending a signal to the world that China was enacting its R2P in Syria."[7]

Just as China's posture toward Syria defies overly simplistic labels of R2P rejectionism, attempts within China to engage with the R2P agenda amid intense criticism of the Libya intervention speak to China's commitment to the principle while also attempting to shape R2P in a manner that responds to China's concerns. Ruan Zongze's "responsible protection" (RP) proposal is perhaps the most prominent example of what Chinese analysts deem "constructive engagement" with the R2P agenda (Ruan, 2012). Ruan presented RP as a proposal to help "make humanitarian interventions more acceptable" by providing criteria to guide UNSC decision-making on military intervention, and to ensure that the UNSC retains oversight and accountability on any future coercive action it authorizes.

The core elements of RP largely mirrored Brazil's 'Responsibility While Protecting' (RWP) concept introduced in November 2011, which proposed tighter regulations and criteria for military intervention and called for enhanced procedures to monitor and assess the implementation of UNSC mandates (UNSC, 2011).

Although RWP initially provoked concerns that Brazil might, intentionally or not, erode the normative standards R2P sets for the UNSC to authorize decisive military action in extreme cases, it was later badged as a timely initiative to address political fallout from the Libya intervention. As Oliver Stuenkel argued, Brazil's initiative should be understood as "an important framework for emerging powers who seek to strike a balance between protecting threatened populations while reducing the negative implications of military intervention" and an initiative to "bridge the gap between an overly trigger-happy NATO and excessively resistant China and Russia" (Stuenkel, 2012; Stuenkel and Tourinho, 2014: 397). The guidelines for military intervention that Ruan proposed recognized that military action under Pillar Three of the R2P framework may be necessary to protect civilians "albeit under a more restrictive set of conditions than Western powers tend to follow" (Garwood-Gowers, 2016: 92). While Beijing has made no formal efforts to promote the RP concept, RP has since featured in Chinese academic discourse as evidence of China's attempt to promote "a more holistic, pragmatic and balanced notion of R2P" (Chen, 2016).

Analyzed alongside China's continued resistance to decisive UNSC responses to some of the most egregious situations of state-sponsored violence, China's purported attempt to promote a more "balanced notion of R2P" could easily be interpreted as another plot point in a sophisticated strategy of norm containment. Yet, as the preceding analysis has shown, China has demonstrated both more flexibility on sovereignty and greater concern for affected populations than its posture on the UNSC sometimes suggests. Chinese elites appear to have internalized the conviction that China must share the burden of finding solutions to the world's most pernicious human protection crises and are intent on signaling that China is normatively committed to preventing mass atrocities. The key point of difference is that, for China, the pathway to realizing protection is not through confronting abusive regimes, but encouraging restraint, stabilizing the security situation, and facilitating conditions for parties to negotiate reforms that could address the most acute grievances that lead to mass violence.

Conclusion: China and the future of R2P

What insight does this analysis of China's position on R2P offer for answering the key questions posed in the introduction of this volume regarding the normative status of R2P and its potential for consolidation? Unlike other studies that suggest that China endorses Pillars One and Two but contests Pillar Three, this chapter has demonstrated that China endorses R2P as a singular or coherent norm complex, which entails national responsibilities, duties of assistance and multilateral responses to emergency situations. That is, China's contestation of R2P should be understood as something more than a sophisticated form of Pillar Three rejectionism or a cynical attempt to defend unconditional sovereignty.

China's contestation of R2P extends from an attempt to fit R2P within the normative defense of sovereignty that constitutes China's foreign policy identity, as well as deep reservations China has about Western approaches to implementing

R2P. China endorses a minimalist interpretation of R2P as a basic agreement that the international community ought to prevent and halt mass atrocities, but does not interpret R2P as an endorsement of coercive measures to achieve this end. China instead promotes what Chinese foreign policy elite portray as a more pragmatic, results-driven and non-confrontational approach that purports to balance human protection with upholding sovereignty. The R2P emergency response measures Chinese foreign policy endorses are largely centered on international actors playing an active but neutral mediating role, endeavoring to facilitate compromised solutions that can end the most extreme forms of violence.

While China's approach fails to uphold and is less embedded in standards of liberal justice and accountability, it is not a broadside defense of sovereignty. China is promoting an alternative pathway to achieving R2P's aim of ending atrocity crimes that is largely confined to the 'negative peace' goals of halting violence and restoring a semblance of stability but is ambivalent about holding states accountable for widespread human rights violations. In other words, China has carved out space to embrace R2P on its own terms, and has taken unprecedented measures to proactively respond to atrocity situations all the while contesting the liberal interventionist underpinnings of R2P. China's simultaneous contestation and accommodation of R2P suggests that R2P may be more resilient than some of the more pessimistic assessments of the norm predict, but it is equally likely to remain imprecise, subject to compromise, and open to critique from its most adamant proponents and skeptics alike.

Notes

1 Interview with official from China's Ministry of Foreign Affairs, Beijing, December 2011.
2 Author interview with Ruan Zongze, Beijing, June 2014.
3 Author interview with a Chinese Middle East expert, Beijing, April 2016.
4 Author interview with a senior Chinese diplomat, Beijing, April 2016.
5 Author interview with a Chinese Middle East expert, Beijing, April 2016.
6 This perspective was repeated in a number of interviews the author conducted with senior Chinese foreign policy experts and senior diplomats in Shanghai and Beijing, March–April 2016.
7 Author notes, Workshop on R2P, Beijing Foreign Studies University, June 2014.

References

Adams, S. (2015). Failure to Protect: Syria and the UN Security Council. *In: Occasional Paper No. 5*. Global Centre for the Responsibility to Protect, March.

Chen, Z. (2016). China and the Responsibility to Protect. *Journal of Contemporary China*, 25(101): 686–700.

China Daily (2005). Five Principles of Peaceful Coexistence, April 20. www.chinadaily.com.cn/world/2015xivisitpse/2015-04/22/content_20509374.htm

Claes, J. (2012). Protecting Civilians from Mass Atrocities: Meeting the Challenge of R2P Rejectionism. *Global Responsibility to Protect*, 4: 67–97.

Foot, R. (2011). The Responsibility to Protect and its Evolution: Beijing's Influence on Norm Creation in Humanitarian Areas. *St Antony's International Review*, 6(2): 47–66.

Foot, R. (2016). The State, Development, and Humanitarianism: China's Shaping of the Trajectory of R2P. *In*: Bellamy, A.J. and Dunne, T. (eds.) *The Oxford Handbook on the Responsibility to Protect*, 932–947. Oxford: Oxford University Press.

Foot, R. and Walter, A. (2011). *China, the United States and Global Order.* Cambridge: Cambridge University Press.

Fung, C.J. (2015). Global South Solidarity? China, Regional Organisations and Intervention in the Libyan and Syrian Civil Wars. *Third World Quarterly,* 37(1): 33–50.

Garwood-Gowers, A. (2016). China's 'Responsible Protection' Concept: Re-Interpreting the Responsibility to Protect (R2P) and Military Intervention for Humanitarian Purposes. *Asian Journal of International Law,* 6(1): 89–118.

Global Times (2011). Full-Blown War in Libya Could be a Disaster. March 23.

Hays Gries, P. (2005). *China's New Nationalism: Pride, Politics, and Diplomacy.* Berkeley, CA: University of California Press.

Holslag, J. (2008). China's Diplomatic Maneuvering on the Question of Darfur. *Journal of Contemporary China,* 17(54): 71–84.

Job, B.L. (2016). Evolution, Retreat or Rejection: Brazil's, India's and China's Normative Stances on R2P. *Cambridge Review of International Affairs*, 29(3): 891–910.

Job, B.L. and Shesterinina, A. (2014). China as a Global Norm-shaper. *In:* Betts, A. and Orchard, P. (eds.) *Implementation and World Politics: How International Norms Change Practice*, 144–159. Oxford: Oxford University Press.

Kent, A. 1999. *China, the United Nations, and Human Rights: The Limits of Compliance.* Philadelphia, PA: University of Pennsylvania Press.

Kuo, Steven C.Y. 2015. Chinese Peace? An Emergent Norm in African Peace Operations. *China Quarterly of International and Strategic Studies,* 1(1): 155–181.

Le, Y. (2012). China's Relations with the World at a New Starting Point. Speech by Assistant Foreign Minister Le Yucheng at the CIIS Forum, Beijing, April 10. www.fmprc.gov.cn/mfa_eng/wjdt_665385/zyjh_665391/t925181.shtml

Li, D. (2012). China's Participation in UN Peacekeeping and Peacebuilding: Prospects and Ways Forward. *Foreign Affairs Review,* 29: 5–18.

Liu, J. (2014). Statement by Ambassador Liu Jieyi at the Security Council Briefing on Post-Conflict Peacebuilding. Permanent Mission of the People's Republic of China to the UN, March 19. www.china-un.org/eng/chinaandun/securitycouncil/thematicissues/peacekeeping/t1144076.htm

Liu, T. and Zhang, H. (2014). Debates in China about the Responsibility to Protect as a Developing International Norm: A General Assessment. *Conflict, Security & Development*, 14(4): 403–427.

People's Daily (2012). US Solution to Syria Issue Doomed to Failure. Originally Published in *Liberation (Jiefang) Daily*, March 02.

Perry, E.J. (2008). Chinese Conceptions of "Rights": From Mencius to Mao – and Now. *Perspectives on Politics*, 6(1): 37–50.

Prantl, J. and Nakano, R. (2011). Global Norm Diffusion and East Asia: How China and Japan Implement the Responsibility to Protect. *International Relations,* 25(2): 204–223.

PRC (Undated). Darfur: China is doing right things. Embassy of the People's Republic of China in the Republic of Kenya. http://ke.china-embassy.org/eng/zt/MediaComment/t425636.htm

PRC (2003). "China's Stand on South-South Cooperation," Permanent Mission of the People's Republic of China to the UN, August 18, 2003. www.china-un.org/eng/gyzg/wjzc/t24884.htm

PRC (2008). China's SR on Darfur Holds a Briefing in Beijing. Permanent Mission of the People's Republic of China to the UN, March 7. www.china-un.org/eng/chinaandun/securitycouncil/regionalhotspots/africa/darfur/t468259.htm

PRC (2015). Statement of the People's Republic of China at the General Assembly Informal Interactive Dialogue. A Vital and Enduring Commitment: Implementing the Responsibility to Protect, September 8. www.globalr2p.org/media/files/china-1.pdf

Qiu, M. and Zhou, Q. (2012). Responsibility to Protect: A Theoretical Study of Western Humanitarian Intervention after the Cold War. *Chinese Journal of European Studies*, 2: 122–138.

Ruan, Z. (2012). Responsible Protection: Building a Safer World. *China Institute of International Studies*, June 2012.

Rudolf, M. (2016). China's New Era of Diplomacy: Engaging in Syria. *The Diplomat,* Januray 25. https://thediplomat.com/2016/01/chinas-new-era-of-diplomacy-engaging-in-syria/

Shambaugh, D. (2013). *China Goes Global: The Partial Superpower.* Oxford: Oxford University Press.

Stuenkel, O. (2012). BRICS and the "Responsibility While Protecting" Concept. *The Hindu,* March 12.

Stuenkel, O. and Tourinho, M. (2014). Regulating Intervention: Brazil and the Responsibility to Protect. *Conflict, Security & Development,* 14(4): 379–402.

Teitt, S. (2009). Assessing Polemics, Principles and Practices: China and the Responsibility to Protect. *Global Responsibility to Protect,* 1(2): 208–236.

Teitt, S. (2016). Is Human Security a Solution? *In:* Carr, A. and Wallis, J. (eds.) *Asia-Pacific Security*, 241–258. Washington, DC: Georgetown University Press.

Teitt, S. (2017). The Responsibility to Protect and China's U.N. Peacekeeping Policy: Integrating Atrocity Prevention. *The Journal of International Studies*, 4: 68–84.

UNSC (2011). Letter Dated November 9 from the Permanent Representative of Brazil to the United Nations Addressed to the Secretary-General: Responsibility While Protecting: Elements for the Development and Promotion of a Concept. United Nations Security Council Document A/66/551-S/2011/701, November 11.

UNSC (2015). Security Council Resolution 2254 S/Res/2245, December 18.

UNSG (2015). A Vital and Enduring Commitment: Implementing the Responsibility to Protect. Report of the UN Secretary-General UN Document A/69/981, July 13.

Wang, X. (2018). Developmental Peace: Understanding China's Africa Policy in Peace and Security. *In:* Alden, C. et al. (eds.) *China and Africa: Building Peace and Security Cooperation on the Continent*, 67–82. London: Palgrave.

Wang, Z. (2012). *Never Forget National Humiliation: History Memory in Chinese Politics and Foreign Relations.* New York: Columbia University Press.

Welsh, J. (2013). Norm Contestation and the Responsibility to Protect. *Global Responsibility to Protect*, 5: 365–396.

What's in Blue (2014). Syria: Monday Vote on Draft Resolution on Cross-Border and Cross-Line Humanitarian Access. July 13.

Wu, C. (2009). Sovereignty, Human Rights and Responsibility: Changes in China's Response to International Humanitarian Crises. *Journal of Chinese Political Science,* 15(1):71–97.

Wu, S. (2012). Building a Political Consensus on Syria. *China–US Focus*, November 9.

Wu, S. (2015). European Refugee Crisis: More than Just a Refugee Problem. *China–US Focus*, September 22. www.chinausfocus.com/peace-security/european-refugee-crisis-more-than-just-a-refugee-problem

Wuthnow, J. (2013). China as a Swing State on Syria. *China–US Focus*, October 8.

Xi, J. (2015). Working Together to Forge a New Partnership of Win-Win Cooperation and Create a Community of Shared Future for Mankind. Statement by H.E. Xi Jinping President of the People's Republic of China at the General Debate of the 70th Session of the UN General Assembly, New York, September 28. www.fmprc.gov.cn/mfa_eng/topics_665678/xjpdmgjxgsfwbcxlhgcl70znxlfh/t1305051.shtml

Xi, J. (2017). Secure a Decisive Victory in Building a Moderately Prosperous Society in All Respects and Strive for the Great Success of Socialism with Chinese Characteristics for a New Era. Speech delivered at the 19th National Congress of the Communist Party of China, October 18. www.xinhuanet.com/english/download/Xi_Jinping_report_at_19th_CPC_National_Congress.pdf

Yao, K. (2019). Positively Lead Sustainable Development and Effectively Implement the Right to Development: A Chinese Perspective. China Society for Human Rights Studies, January 10. www.chinahumanrights.org/html/2019/MAGAZINES_0110/12532.html

Zhu, L. (2010). *China's Foreign Policy Debates*. European Union Institute for Security Studies: September 2010.

Zhong S. (2012). Why China Vetoes UN Draft Resolution for Syria Issue. *People's Daily,* February 8.

8 Russia and the R2P

Norm entrepreneur, anti-preneur, or violator?

Phil Orchard and Heather Rae

Introduction[1]

In 2005 Russia, along with every other state, endorsed the World Summit Outcome Document (WSOD) which first provided international recognition to the Responsibility to Protect (R2P) doctrine.[2] Despite this, Russia has a bifurcated understanding of what the R2P is. The Russian government is hostile toward those aspects of R2P that may be taken to impinge on traditional conceptions of sovereignty; at the same time Russia is willing to violate that conception of sovereignty in support of its citizens and states it identifies as historic allies. Russia has generally refrained from blocking United Nations (UN) Security Council resolutions that fall under Pillar One (states' own responsibility toward their populations) and Pillar Two (the international community's responsibility to assist states), as introduced in the Secretary-General's 2009 report, through the use of their Security Council veto.[3]

Russia's practice with respect to Pillar Three, which establishes that the Security Council should, on a case-by-case basis, take timely and decisive action in situations where a state has manifestly failed to protect its population, is more complicated. While in 2011 Russia abstained from Security Council Resolution 1973, which authorized collective action on Libya, it quickly became an outspoken critic of the US and its allies once it became clear they were intent on regime change.[4] Russia has also vetoed resolutions with respect to the conflict in Syria which could have led to the use of force, though it has abstained on other resolutions that have either focused on aid delivery, on purely political responses to the crisis or on chemical weapons (Gifkins, 2012).[5] It has directly supported Syrian President Bashar al-Assad through arms sales and, since September 2015 with direct military support and air strikes directed against both the Islamic State and other rebel groups (Averre and Davies, 2015: 820).

Because of these actions, Russia has been accused of taking an approach to R2P that is both instrumental and at odds with widespread international understandings of the doctrine (Averre and Davies, 2015). This was the case with the 2008 Georgian War, which the Russian government defended in part as reflecting its responsibility to protect Russian citizens outside of Russia, but also with its 2014 annexing of Crimea, which used a similar, if more tempered, language of "responsibility" (Evans, 2008; Stafford and Dzelyte, 2014). Bloomfield has gone even further, suggesting that Russia is a norm 'anti-preneur' with respect to the R2P, particular Pillar Three, and is focused on defending the prior status quo (Bloomfield, 2016: 328).

Thus, the question can be asked: How can Russia have 'signed on' to R2P yet be so contradictory in its approach? To understand this, it is important to discuss the normative dimensions of the R2P doctrine, and how normative contestations can lead to differing interpretations of what R2P means. In particular, we argue that that this has had two effects on Russian understandings of R2P, which sets the country at odds with the understandings of the wider international community. The first effect is that today they deeply resist the potential interventionary nature of R2P, but this resistance has grown over time, rather than reflecting a fixed position. While this difference may be driven by instrumental reasons, these are underpinned by deeper questions relating to Russian national identity, including how the Russian government conceives of sovereignty and, related to this, its role as a great power and what responsibilities and rights are therefore due to it. The second effect is that Russia sees itself as having privileged interests within its region and in relations with its close historical allies. This difference sees Russia not necessarily contesting the R2P itself, but rather employing a hierarchical ordering of norms: it sees these privileged interests as trumping requirements under the R2P, and therefore permits Russia – in their view – to engage in norm violation.

Theoretical contentions of the R2P doctrine

Norm anti-preneurs have been defined by Bloomfield as those who seek to resist efforts to change global norms and "defend the entrenched normative status quo against challenges" (Bloomfield, 2016: 321). Bloomfield suggests they can do this through two forms of strategic blocking. The first is by refuting claims made by new norm entrepreneurs that the existing, entrenched, norm "produced morally problematic outcomes." The second is by undermining the new norm prior to it building up credibility and socio-institutional support (ibid.: 324). They "implacably resist to prevent the accumulation of precedents which would otherwise strengthen a new norm" (ibid.).

Bloomfield specifically identifies Russia, along with China, as anti-preneurs with respect to R2P, particularly Pillar Three (Bloomfield, 2016: 328).[6] However, following on from Orchard's discussion of R2P as a regime in his earlier chapter, Chapter 1, this raises the question of whether – if Russia is indeed an anti-preneur – it is one with respect to R2P as whole, or only with respect to the specific Pillar Three responsibilities. Pillar Three does not, in itself, reflect a specific normative understanding within the R2P doctrine. Instead, following Glanville's phrasing, it is an element of the normative commitment "that the international community has the responsibility to do what it can to ensure that populations are protected from atrocity crimes" (Glanville, 2016: 186) which, as Orchard argues in Chapter 1, has been linked to a separate norm requiring actions to go through the UN Security Council.

In addition, however, the anti-preneur definition assumes that the actors involved seek to resist any changes to the established norm which are being put forward by norm entrepreneurs. But this pattern is unclear with respect to Russia's behavior toward R2P. Claes, for example, while arguing that Russia is an R2P rejectionist, notes it "generally refrains from openly rejecting R2P" but that their positions in thematic debates appears to confirm "their opposition to the principle" (Claes, 2012: 71–72). Further, if both China and Russia hold such a position (which Teitt also argues against in Chapter 7), they have access to a great deal more direct and institutional power than more typical anti-preneurs given their role within the Security Council. And the record in terms of key moments of the development of the R2P regime – that accumulation of precedents – does not demonstrate Russia playing such a definitive role in blocking the R2P regime as a whole or even the use of Pillar Three.

To begin with the 2005 World Summit negotiations, Bloomfield notes rightly that Russia along with other states including India sought to resist the introduction of the R2P. This resistance, he suggests, led to the requirement that Pillar Three measures would only be authorized by the Security Council – "this outcome is probably the single most significant achievement by the anti-preneurs" (Bloomfield, 2016). Yet, Bellamy tells a different story, one in which Russia's opposition was significantly less developed. He notes that during the initial negotiations, the Russian delegation's legal advisor had raised a series of issues with the R2P paragraphs. However, Canada's then ambassador, Allan Rock, approached the Russian permanent representative directly who "indicated that Russia had no objections of principle and would cease its obstructionism" (Bellamy, 2009a: 87).

With respect to the subsequent UN Security Council resolution which endorsed R2P, Russia initially indicated that they wanted to have "a detailed discussion in the General Assembly of the issue of the responsibility to protect before we can discuss its implementation,"[7] a position supported by China, Algeria, the Philippines and Brazil. As Bellamy notes, however, the UK privately negotiated with China on a new text "in order to isolate Russia" (Bellamy, 2009b: 114). While Russia could have chosen to take action to block this agreement, either by vetoing or abstaining from the resolution, it voted in favor which saw the resolution pass unanimously.[8]

Further, while Baranovsky and Mateiko (2016: 50) are right in referring to a "lack of enthusiasm" on the part of the Russian government for R2P during this period, the government did allow a number R2P actions to proceed beyond Libya. The government noted its concern around the political crisis in Kenya following the 2007–2008 elections, and welcomed Kofi Annan's mediation efforts.[9] Similarly, when the Security Council chose to expand the mandate of the UN peacekeeping mission in Côte d'Ivoire due to concerns that attacks against the civilian population could amount to crimes against humanity, the Russian government again allowed the resolution to pass unanimously.[10] In this case, they did subsequently raise concerns over its implementation, with Foreign Minister Sergei Lavrov noting that "We are now looking into the legality of this situation, because the peacekeepers were authorized to remain neutral, nothing more. We've requested an emergency briefing in the UN Security Council."[11]

Therefore, this early record does not accord with Russia as full norm antipreneur. The Russian government did not use its considerable institutional power within the Security Council to block the R2P doctrine. In the precedential cases over its first six years, Russia either supported the Security Council's use, or was willing to allow it to proceed. And, with the Russo-Georgian War, they were willing to instrumentally seek to use the R2P doctrine for their own purposes.

Instead, we suggest that Russia's behavior toward the R2P doctrine represents a mix of contestation and violation toward the norm. Contestation reflects the critical questioning of norms and rules (Wiener, 2014: 2–3) and it is not inherently problematic. It can actually have significant positive effects by helping to clarify and refine how actors understand the application of a norm in a given context. Violation, by contrast, reflects a deliberate effort to circumvent the norm. Norms have a degree of oughtness, and therefore should not be subject to routine violation. But violation does occur – for Shannon, this can be due to self-interest, but it can also be "permitted by the nature of the norm and the situation, which conditions one's ability to define a situation in a way that allows socially accepted violation" (Shannon, 2000: 301). And violations can have two forms of effects on norms. If actors are not prepared to sanction the violating behavior, non-compliance will increase and potentially lead to disappearance of the norm or its replacement by another norm. By contrast, sanctions by other states or international actors can positively remedy the norm violation and restore compliance (Panke and Petersohn, 2012: 722).

While the 2005 WSOD can be seen as an important moment in the institutionalization process of R2P, this process has continued over the past 14 years. The multiple dimensions in which R2P is meant to operate, coupled with the socially constructed nature of norms generally, means that there is always ambiguity and scope for interpretation and contestation over what a norm requires. Public endorsement of a norm can, as Welsh argues, "lead to renewed arguments about both the norm's desirability and the norm's scope, thereby affecting the willingness of norm followers to embrace implementation. In some cases, these arguments can lead to backsliding or differential interpretations of the norm's meaning" (Welsh, 2013: 380). Thus, as Bellamy suggests, in the years immediately after the WSOD there was a 'revolt against R2P,' albeit one which eventually subsided, over what obligations the R2P doctrine created (Bellamy, 2011: 263). Debates over subsequent actions, including in Libya and Syria have, however, highlighted renewed contestations over how R2P should be understood and applied (Morris, 2013).

Such contestation over new or developing norms is not unusual. These issues appear not only in a norm's institutionalization process, but also in its parallel implementation process, which "draws attention to the steps necessary to introduce the new international norm's precepts into formal legal and policy mechanisms within a state or organization in order to routinize compliance" (Betts and Orchard, 2014: 22). During the implementation process, basic understandings of state identity can be used in two ways. The first is as a resource by actors to mobilize action to adopt a particularly understanding of the norm (Acharya, 2004; Busby, 2010: 51; Wiener, 2007, 2009). But core ideas related to a state's identity, such as its constitutional framework and legal system, can also channel new norms in certain ways that will vary from state to state (Simmons, 2009). In addition, Acharya notes that as new norms are adapted or reconstructed, it may be grafted into an "existing norm hierarchy" (Acharya, 2004: 251). This hierarchy may be displaced over the long term through the norm localization process, but it would also be possible for a new external norm to simply be integrated into an existing hierarchy.

We can identify clear markers around the implementation process. It starts when new norms emerge in domestic discourses and, subsequently, in domestic institutions through either replacement or formal alteration of existing practices and is likely to vary across states (Cortell and Davis, 2005: 9; Orchard, 2014). But the result is that, as Welsh notes, an agreed upon norm may not signify "the same thing to all actors, post-institutionalization." As she puts it, "contestation over the meaning of a new norm can persist into the implementation phase, particularly as new circumstances and crises, different from those surrounding the norm's genesis, arise" (Welsh, 2013: 380).

Thus, Russian identity and self-perception significantly affects how it understands the R2P doctrine. This leads it first to support a view that remains anchored to sovereignty and sovereign equality and, increasingly, that specifically opposed, and views as illegitimate, any forms of regime change. Here, Russia is seeking to engage in an ongoing contestation or attempt to reinterpret how the R2P doctrine is understood. Second, and in contradiction to this, Russia also views its privileged interests and relationships as sitting hierarchically above the R2P doctrine. It – importantly – understands that there is no international support for this position, and so is generally not engaging in an international contestation process. But this does lead it to engage in a distinct process of norm violation when these two understandings come into conflict. However, since Russia has received little support for these violations and has come under significant pressure because of them, they are unlikely in themselves to undermine the R2P.

Russian identity and international order

The R2P reflects the wider set of norms that help to constitute a liberal world order, including democratic accountability to citizens and human rights (Ikenberry, 2013; Kurowska, 2014). For much of the twentieth century Soviet communist ideology proclaimed an alternative to this order, but with the collapse of the Soviet Union, Russia was faced with the seeming triumph of Western values and the 'end of history' proclaimed in the West (Fukuyama, 2006). Since the breakup of the Soviet Union, Russia has sought to position itself relative to this order, first in unsuccessful efforts to 'come on board' and receive continued recognition as a great power in the 1990s, and then in increasingly critical terms. This has meant that Russia's interpretations of the R2P are fused with aspects of contemporary Russian identity which has led it to make two, separate, normative arguments. The first accepts the bulk of R2P but seeks to challenge the capacity of the international community to engage in intervention. Thus, this argument is a specific contestation of R2P, specifically the requirements of the third pillar. The second normative argument, by contrast, fuses Russia's perception as a great power with the idea that it has privileged interests; a role that requires it to both assist its historic allies as well as protect its own citizens whether inside or outside its territory and a wider category of ethnic Russians or Russian-speaking minorities. This argument is at odds with the first argument, and as it has been applied in the cases of Crimea and southeastern Ukraine and with respect to Russian support of the Syrian government, it is also in violation of other, more established, normative principles.

Russia as a great power

There is a long history of Russia feeling aggrieved by lack of recognition on the part of European powers, articulated in what Neumann and Pouliot, echoing Ayse Zarakol and numerous other authors, see as a long-standing "clash between Russian and Western diplomatic dispositions" (Neumann and Pouliot, 2011: 108; Zarakol, 2010). While they suggest Russia has been on a quest for recognition of equal status for a millennium, Western Europeans from the nineteenth century onward have treated it as part of an uncivilized or barbarian "other." Indeed, Putin and Vladislav Surkov, described by Charles E. Ziegler as the "Kremlin's ideologist," both describe Russia as part of European civilization, but with its own "unique characteristics" (Surkov, 2008). Despite this self-presentation Russia has not been seen as part of the West and Western rebuffs have played a role in developments over the last few decades. This is the continuation of a long history of seeking status in an international society that is socially stratified between insiders and outsiders (Zarakol, 2010: 202) and in which Russia has generally been on the outside.

Following the end of the Cold War, the new Russian leadership, driven in part by late Soviet programs including Gorbachev's 'New Thinking,' sought to integrate the country into both the global economy and into the wider liberal normative order. Yet it faced Western skepticism. There were questions of whether Russia remained a genuine great power (its nuclear arsenal aside), and widely shared views that Russia could be ignored (Zarakol, 2010: 228; Kanet, 2015: 506). Further, Western countries not only did not respond to Russian overtures toward collective security, but NATO embarked upon expansion into Eastern Europe. This was regarded with great suspicion by the Russian government, and yet their concerns were consistently brushed aside. As Roger E. Kanet notes, "this Western downplaying of Russia's place in the international system directly challenged the sense of honour and status that … lies at the heart of Russian foreign policy" (Kanet, 2015: 506).

The lack of international recognition meant that reformists within Russia consistently lost influence to more conservative and nationalist voices. As early as the mid-1990s, there were widespread domestic arguments that the West was humiliating Russia and "taking advantage of Russia's weakness" (Kanet, 2015: 505).[12] NATO interventions in the former Yugoslavia and in Kosovo only added to these fears and fed into a growing domestic narrative that Russia needed to reassert itself as a great power (Tsygankov, 2014: 25). The appointment of Vladimir Putin as prime minister in 1999 and his election as president in 2000 reinforced these trends.

Sovereignty and sovereign equality

Today, the Russian government frames Russia as an important pole in a multipolar, global system and advocates the principle of sovereign equality. As Richard Sakwa notes, Russia under Putin is presented as neo-revisionist, not wanting to "change the fundamentals of international order," so much as seeking to "ensure that Russia and other 'rising' powers [are] treated as equals within the international system" (Sakwa, 2015: 557).

Thus, in asserting the value of the status quo, "Russia does not repudiate the existing normative framework, but seeks to ensure its universal application" (Sakwa, 2012). It should be noted, however, that this "normative framework" is the "equalitarian regime" instituted post-World War II and *not* the US dominated liberal world order of which Russia is increasingly critical and in which there is a hierarchy of status in which non-liberal powers inevitably rank lower (Reus-Smit, 2005: 71). In so doing, Russia's discourse "explicitly and systematically references the Western one" while doing so "in relation to norms that constitute grey areas of international law, where the relevant standards of behaviour are profoundly contested" (Burai, 2016: 68).

Russia's 2013 Foreign Policy Concept notes that Russia "follows a policy aimed at creating a stable and sustainable system of international relations based on international law and principles of equality, mutual respect and non-interference in internal affairs of states" and that "the United Nations should remain the centre for regulation of international relations…"[13] This is supported by Russia's championing of the BRICS, one of only a number of regional groupings that Russia has sought to build. Russia's most recent Foreign Policy Concept, released in 2016, contains similar language, stating that one of its main objectives is to "further promote the efforts to strengthen international peace and ensure global security and stability with a view to establishing a fair and democratic international system."[14]

Hence the Russian government has generally (and with notable exceptions, as will be discussed below) asserted a traditional conception of sovereignty as equated with non-interference in the domestic affairs of a recognized state. Based on this it supports the existing structure of the UN in general and the UN Security Council in particular (including the veto power) as reflecting such an understanding. The Russian government also frequently frames itself as a defender of the principle of sovereign independence and a critic of actions that violate this principle, such as the US-led 2003 invasion of Iraq, or which may shift the exclusive right to authorize the use of international force away from the

UN Security Council, such as the expansion of NATO. As Putin stated at the 2007 Munich Security Conference:

> I think it is obvious that NATO expansion does not have any relation with the modernisation of the Alliance itself or with ensuring security in Europe. On the contrary, it represents a serious provocation that reduces the level of mutual trust. And we have the right to ask: against whom is this expansion intended? And what happened to the assurances our Western partners made after the dissolution of the Warsaw Pact? Where are those declarations today?[15]

Similarly, Russia's 2013 Foreign Policy Concept notes that "some concepts that are being implemented are aimed at overthrowing legitimate authorities in sovereign states under the pretext of protecting civilian population." These measures, it suggests "only lead to the expansion of the conflict area, provoke tensions and arms race, aggravates interstate controversies and incite ethnic and religious strife."[16] And in the 2016 Foreign Policy Concept, Russia notes not only that it intends "to prevent military interventions or other forms of outside interference contrary to international law, specifically the principle of sovereign equality of States, under the pretext of implementing the 'responsibility to protect' concept" but also that particularly with respect to the Middle East and North Africa it "consistently promotes political and diplomatic settlement of conflicts in regional States while respecting their sovereignty and territorial integrity and the right to self-determination without outside interference."[17]

It is clear that Russia's view of sovereignty remains based on a pluralist reading of the international system. It is focused on the prerogatives of states. It is equally critical of the dominance of the US and other Western powers and of what Russia sees as a drive to impose liberal norms and institutions and a wider solidarist view of sovereign authority. It sees the norms on which EU expansion is predicated, most notably of democratic institutions as universally desirable – "transdemocracy" (Sakwa, 2015: 564) – as a threat, particularly as seen in the so-called color revolutions of the 2000s and also in the 2014 overthrow of the Kremlin-backed Yanukovych regime in Ukraine.

At the domestic level, this interpretation of sovereignty is tied into Russia's increasingly authoritarian politics, with arguments put forward for their own concept of "sovereign democracy," which is distinctly illiberal in tenor and is "characterized by freedom from external standards or influences" (Kanet, 2015: 514). As Ziegler (2012: 401) notes, this approach:

> reflects a close linkage between Vladimir Putin's recentralizing project domestically, and his reassertion of Russia's position as a great power on the international scene. The enthusiastic reception that Mr Putin's project has received from the Russian elite, and from the general population, suggests that concerns with both domestic and international variants of sovereignty predate him, but have received new impetus under Putin's authoritarian, aggressive leadership.

In his defense of 'sovereignty democracy' Vladislav Surkov uses a romanticized view of Russian culture as a base to suggest that, though it is part of European civilization, Russia has its own unique political culture and arising out of this it has its own particular view of sovereignty. His arguments, however, amount to a justification of authoritarian rule and an interpretation of sovereignty as control. As Ziegler (ibid.: 406) notes, according to Surkov:

> Russian political culture is more holistic, centralized and emotional than Western cultures, and more personalized. Individuals, according to this convoluted reasoning, may serve as institutions ... or the leaders of Russia's personalistic parties. Russia also has a tendency toward chaos and fragmentation if not held together by a strong executive, and such fragmentation undermines Russian internal sovereignty.

This understanding of sovereignty motivates the Russian government to subject independent civil society groups seeking to build democracy within the country to state pressure or to close them down entirely. For Surkov (2008: 93), "To assimilate freedom, you have to extract the essence and utility from foreign experience and not chew, with the tragic mien of a hired human rights defender, the wrappers and price lists of imported democracy." A conception of sovereignty as strong, centralized control, rather than popular sovereignty or sovereignty as authorized by the people, has become predominant (Ziegler, 2012: 407).[18]

The Russian government frequently applies such a reading of sovereignty to R2P. In the 2012 General Assembly informal dialogues on R2P, for example, Russian officials noted that

> it is our belief that the paramount obligation for protecting the responsibility of one's own population lies with the state. The role of the international community amounts, first and foremost, to providing the necessary assistance to the state in implementing this duty.[19]

Thus, Baranovsky and Mateiko (2016: 52) argue that "Russia fully agrees with and consistently emphasises the R2P first pillar.... Moscow does not dispute the very basic idea of the first pillar and within this logic has usually supported references to this pillar in UNSC resolutions." However, Russia has pushed this to also include its citizens beyond its own borders and in direct tension with the understandings of sovereignty that the government has argued in favor of at the international level.

This tension affects how the Russian government asserts that R2P should be applied. As Averre and Davis (2015: 821) note,

> Moscow is prepared to support the concept of R2P but calls for the strict interpretation of the 2005 WSO document: the idea of states' responsibility to protect their populations from the 'four crimes' with international support. A reliance on pillars 1 and 2 underpins arguments from Russia....

But Allison (2017: 525) adds that it is not that Russia necessarily opposes Pillar Three, rather it is adamant that collective action and the potential use of force "depends on UNSC authorization." Baranovksy and Mateiko (2016: 55) add that it "is against any 'mechanistic' approaches. It objects to introducing any formal criteria, as they are prone to political manipulation." As with Libya, Russia wants any Pillar Three usage to be within an arena in which they can control its usage.

Increasingly, Russian conceptions of sovereign equality also includes a narrative which reflects "the illegitimacy of imposed regime change" (Allison, 2017: 522). As Russian Deputy Permanent Representative Sergey Karev noted in the open debate on the Protection of Civilians in Armed Conflict in 2012, "practice has shown that invoking [the R2P] concept with what initially appeared to be noble goals often leads to interference in the international affairs of sovereign States and to violent regime change."[20] In the 2012 informal interactive dialogue on the R2P, they similarly noted that the use of coercive measures is an extreme measure which should prompt the responsible state to implement its obligations, "not supplant … its role in so doing" and that the third pillar is not only the most contradictory but that examples from practice showed that its application "may be for distorted goals."[21] In 2013, they added that "We cannot agree with attempts to base military action against Syria on narrow concepts of so-called 'humanitarian intervention.' "[22]

As Ralph and Gifkins (2017) have argued, the inclusion of the "Assad must go" rhetoric by France, the US and UK within Council deliberations on Syria linked those debates to the earlier Libyan intervention. But, as discussed further below, this has also been used by the government to defend its actions in Ukraine as a response to an illegitimate coup against the Yanukovych government. In Crimea, the intervention occurred in order "not to let ultranationalist forces organise another bloody 'maidan' "[23] and those "who opposed the coup" had "turned to Russia for help in defending their rights and lives."[24] Similarly, with respect to Syria, the Foreign Ministry has argued that "It would have been unacceptable to allow Syria to fall into the fate of Iraq or Libya, which were invaded, which in turn led to the destabilisation in the Middle East."[25]

Russia's privileged interests and the issue of intervention

This authoritarian impulse underpins a contradictory, exceptionalist reading of sovereignty by Russian authorities, which gives two grounds on which Russia can negate the traditional protection of non-interference in their own perceived interests while strongly avowing that other states should abide by it. This leads, as Ziegler has argued, to coercive diplomacy through which Russia "seeks to create a new multilateral balance of power in the regional, if not the global order." But this use, Ziegler notes, is limited: "Russia's coercive diplomacy has been applied along the country's periphery, and beyond that to Syria, but not much further" (Ziegler, 2018). But such privileging of one's own citizens or ethnic groups is not a return to norms against sovereign interference; instead it marks a much older tradition from the nineteenth century of sovereign violation.

This language appeared with the Russo-Georgian War in 2008. As then President Dmitry Medvedev argued following its conclusion, "protecting the lives and the dignity of Russian citizens, wherever they may be, is the raison d'être of the Russian state."[26] In addition, Medvedev argued that there are "regions in which Russia has privileged interests," regions that "are home to countries with which we share special historical relations" (cited in Allison, 2008: 1168). Lavrov similarly argued that the domestic constitution in effect trumped international norms:

> [U]nder the Constitution [the President] is obliged to protect the life and dignity of Russian citizens, especially when they find themselves in the armed conflict.... According to our Constitution there is also responsibility to protect – the term which is very widely used in the UN when people see some trouble in Africa or in any remote part of other regions. But this is not Africa to us, this is next door. This is the area, where Russian citizens live. So, the Constitution of the Russian Federation, the laws of the Russian Federation make it absolutely unavoidable to us to exercise responsibility to protect.[27]

This conception of privileged interests has marked Russia's interventions in both Crimea and southeastern Ukraine and in support of the Syrian government. Russia's involvement in Ukraine began following the Euromaidan protests in Kiev which led to the collapse of the Viktor Yanukovych government. The Crimean Peninsula, while part of Ukraine, hosted large numbers of Russian troops. Following protests by Russian speakers in Crimea in late February 2014 who opposed recognition of the new Ukrainian government, Russian troops seized government buildings and then held a referendum on joining Russia. The referendum itself was widely criticized as a fraud, however international protests including sanctions levied by the United States and European Union failed to stop the annexation.[28] Russia's justifications for their actions very much prioritized the need to protect the Russian-speaking population (Cooley, 2014) while, at the same time, using very similar arguments to those that Western states had deployed in support of recognizing Kosovo's independence (Burai, 2016: 69). As President Putin argued,

> what worries the citizens of Ukraine, both Russian and Ukrainian, and the Russian-speaking population … is this uncontrolled crime. Therefore, if we see such uncontrolled crime spreading to the eastern regions of the country, and if the people ask us for help … we retain the right to use all available means to protect those people
>
> (cited in Stafford and Dzelyte, 2014)

It was also a claim which the government sought to root in history. As Putin declared in an address in March 2014, "Crimea has always been an integral part of Russia in the hearts and minds of people."[29] Allison notes that Putin's central claim in Crimea is "very consistent," reflecting a "right of self-determination" (Allison, 2017: 525), yet this is a right to be used instrumentally by the Russian government, and certainly not a right to be extended to groups within Russia itself.

The Russian government also took advantage of the turmoil in Ukraine following the collapse of the government to support separatist movements in southeastern Ukraine, which have now formed two self-declared republics, the Donetsk and Luhansk People's Republics respectively. Here, Russian language has been more circumspect, in part because the Russian government generally denies their direct involvement.[30] Vladimir Putin has admitted that Russia had military intelligence officers in Ukraine, however, he insisted that this was not the same as regular troops.[31] The general academic consensus, as Clem (2017: 597) notes, is that from July 2014 "Russia was simply not prepared to allow the Ukrainian government to crush the separatist insurrection in the Donbas, and accordingly, took direct military action itself to insure" their survival.

Even so, rhetoric with respect to the separatist movements has similarly been framed by the Russian government through the lens of interests and protection of Russian speakers.[32] Lavrov noted in an April 2014 interview that "if our interests, our legitimate interests, the interests of Russians have been attacked directly, like they were in South Ossetia for example, I do not see any other way but to respond in full accordance with international law."[33] Putin similarly noted in a 2015 interview that "We proceed from only one thing, which is we cannot abandon the people who live in the southeast of the country to nationalists to eat them up" including not only ethnic Russians but also Russian speakers.[34]

Finally, while Russia had supported the Syrian government from the start of its civil war in 2011, in 2015 the government made the deliberate decision to commit military troops to the conflict. Here, there was a slower pattern of escalation. The Russian government had frequently referred to the Syrian government's responsibility to protect their own population. Thus, in July 2012 Foreign Minister Sergei Lavrov noted that "We have repeatedly said that the regime has the primary responsibility to ensure the safety of its citizens and the safety of Syria."[35] Further, throughout the early years of the conflict, the Russian government sought to downplay any likelihood of their own involvement in the conflict. In November 2012, Lavrov noted that "of course, no involvement of Russia in armed conflict can be considered."[36] Even by 2015, Lavrov would note that "we cannot assume responsibility for developments in a sovereign, even if friendly, country."[37]

When Russia began air strikes in September 2015, Putin argued that it was not only in respect to a request from Syria, but that they were supporting the Syrian military "in its legitimate fight with terrorist groups."[38] Russia routinely invokes a frame that it is there "at the request of its legitimate government only after a serious threat of the seizure of Damascus by terrorists emerged"[39] and to assist Syria in returning "to peaceful life and reconstruction"[40] while denying civilian deaths as parts of either an "information war" or a "hoax."[41] However, their air strikes have been widely condemned for directly attacking and allegedly killing over 6,000 civilians, as well as attacking civilian objects including medical facilities which are prohibited by international humanitarian law.[42] And, while no claim to protect Russian citizens can easily be made[43] Medvedev has argued that "to fulfil a limited, specific mission that is related to protecting our national interests."[44]

This does not mean we should expect such use in every case. Natasha Kuhrt (2014: 105), for example, notes that in the case of Kyrgyzstan in 2010, even though the state called for an intervention, Russia instead characterized it as an internal affair, sending only humanitarian aid and medical supplies. She suggests that this was because there was no clear objective to an intervention and little appetite among "other Central Asian leaders for an intervention."

What is clear, though, is that Russia has a strong conception of its privileged interests in its region and it is willing to forcibly abrogate the sovereignty of weaker states to pursue these interests. Russia seeks, with limited success, to legitimate such actions in terms of responsibility to Russian citizens and state rights under international law and it continues to advocate sovereignty as equality and non-interference in cases that do not concern it. These are claims that are not widely accepted internationally. An effort by the UN Security Council to argue the Russian supported referendum in Crimea would not have validity as it was not authorized by Ukraine was vetoed by Russia but had gained the support of all the other Council members with the exception of China.[45] A similar General Assembly resolution saw 99 states voted in favor, 82 abstain, and only 11 countries support Russia in rejecting the resolution (Allison, 2017: 531).

Conclusion

All of the above highlights that Russia sees itself as a great power that should be accorded recognition of its status and is resentful when such recognition is not forthcoming. Russia advocates sovereign equality and non-interference but will ignore these principles when they would limit Russia's actions. This has been the case recently closest to home in the sphere of Russian 'privileged interests,' in Georgia, Crimea and Ukraine but it can also be seen in Russia's unilateral decision to start bombing Syria in support of the Assad regime. It is clear that the conception of sovereignty that Russia employs is at odds with the conception of sovereignty as international responsibility that underpins Pillar Three of the R2P doctrine, which it regards with suspicion as a possible cover for Western interventions.

As we have shown, issues of national identity are, as they have so often been for Russia, playing an important role today (Neumann and Pouliot, 2011; Zarakol, 2010). We see a hardening of nationalist discourse accompanying increasingly authoritarian government, with domestic critics threatened, linked to 'Western' influences, and sometimes killed. A more closed conception of sovereignty as control is predominant and, as a result, the diffusion of R2P norms through domestic institutions seems unlikely at the moment.

As we have also noted, while Russia asserts the value of the existing *international* order, namely the post-World War II 'equalitarian' order, this coexists with an increasingly direct rejection of the liberal *world* order in which the US and its allies have been dominant. Instead, the rules-based order that Russia supports (and sometimes ignores) stresses sovereign rights and support for international law through the UN system, particularly the Security Council. It also hierarchically privileges the protection of its own citizens (as well as the broader category of ethnic Russians and Russian speakers) as well as its interests over the norms of the R2P. When it comes to these issues, therefore, Russia has no concerns with engaging in norm violation, even at significant international cost.

Notes

1 Many thanks to Heidi Stubbs Holdal and Liam Moore for research assistance.
2 UN General Assembly, World Summit Outcome Document, (A60/L, September 15, 2005): 31. Also see the GA consensus Resolution of September 2009 (A/Res/63/308, September 14, 2009).
3 Ban Ki-moon, "Implementing the Responsibility to Protect: Report of the Secretary-General", *United Nations General Assembly*, Sixty-third session, A/63/677, para. II, 2009; (Bellamy, 2015: 167).
4 UN Security Council, S/RES/1973, March 17, 2011. There have also been suggestions that Vladimir Putin, then Russia's prime minister, opposed the abstention. See Clifford J. Levy and Thom Shanker "In Rare Split, Two Leaders in Russia Differ on Libya." *New York Times*, March 21, 2011.
5 A complete list of Security Council resolutions on the Syrian crisis is available at: www.securitycouncilreport.org/un-documents/syria/
6 Bloomfield argues that Pillar Three represents the "most controversial element" of the R2P norm but does not suggest that by itself it is a norm (Bloomfield, 2016: 327). Subsequently, he notes that the R2P may be a complex norm or, following an early draft of Orchard's work, a regime with a range of components at different levels of institutionalization, but generally retains the view that R2P is a single norm (Bloomfield, 2016).
7 S/PV.5319, December 9, 2015: 19.
8 UN Digital Library Security Council Voting Data. https://digitallibrary.un.org/record/574114?ln=en
9 Ministry of Foreign Affairs of the Russian Federation, "К ситуации в Кении", February 1, 2008. www.mid.ru/web/guest/maps/ke/-/asset_publisher/Ekuq3mezVhOy/content/id/350778 (No official English translation available, translated via google translate) and Ministry of Foreign Affairs of the Russian Federation, "Concerning Situation in Kenya," Feb 29, 2008. www.mid.ru/en/web/guest/maps/ke/-/asset_publisher/Ekuq3mezVhOy/content/id/347110. See also (Junk, 2016: 59)
10 UN (2011). Security Council Demands End to Violence in Côte d'Ivoire, Imposing Sanctions against Former President and Urging Him to "Step Aside", in Resolution 1975, SC/10215, March 30, 2011. www.un.org/press/en/2011/sc10215.doc.htm
11 Associated Press, "Russia lashes out at UN military action in Côte d'Ivoire," Associated Press, April 6, 2011. See also (Bellamy and Williams, 2011: 834–836).
12 This view is expressed by Vladislav Surkov who portrayed the West as wanting Russia to be weak: "... the West encouraged the weakness and muddle-headedness that we showed at that time" (Surkov, 2008: 90; Tsygankov, 2014: 25). On differing approaches to foreign policy in Russia at this time see Ziegler (2012: 410–411).
13 Ministry of Foreign Affairs of the Russian Federation, "Concept of the Foreign Policy of the Russian Federation," February 12, 2013. www.rusemb.org.uk/in1/
14 Ministry of Foreign Affairs of the Russian Federation, "Concept of the Foreign Policy of the Russian Federation," December 1, 2016. www.mid.ru/en/web/guest/foreign_policy/official_documents/-/asset_publisher/CptICkB6BZ29/content/id/2542248

15 President of Russia, "Speech and the Following Discussion at the Munich Conference on Security Policy," February 10, 2007. http://en.kremlin.ru/events/president/transcripts/24034

16 Ministry of Foreign Affairs of the Russian Federation, "Concept of the Foreign Policy of the Russian Federation," Feb 12, 2013. www.rusemb.org.uk/in1/

17 Ministry of Foreign Affairs of the Russian Federation, "Concept of the Foreign Policy of the Russian Federation," December 1, 2016. www.mid.ru/en/web/guest/foreign_policy/official_documents/-/asset_publisher/CptICkB6BZ29/content/id/2542248

18 As Ziegler notes, the West is not the only "other" here. The concept of democracy aspired to under Boris Yeltsin is also regarded as leading to chaos: "Morozov rightly observes that 'the identity of Putin's Russia crucially depends on the negation of Yeltsin's 'democracy' as a period of chaos and destruction'" (Morozov, 2008: 156, cited in Ziegler, 2012: 411).

19 Permanent Mission of the Russian Federation to the United Nations "Statement to the General Assembly Informal, Interactive Dialogue on the 'Responsibility to Protect: Timely and Decisive Response,'" September 5, 2012. http://responsibilitytoprotect.org/Russia%20Statement%20_Transcribed_.pdf

20 Sergey Karev, "Open debate on the Protection of Civilians in Armed Conflict," United Nations Security Council, June 25, 2012. http://responsibilitytoprotect.org/Statement%20by%20Russian%20Federation%20POC%20debate(1).pdf

21 Permanent Mission of the Russian Federation to the United Nations "Statement to the General Assembly Informal, Interactive Dialogue on the 'Responsibility to Protect: Timely and Decisive Response'", September 5, 2012.

22 Permanent Mission of the Russian Federation to the United Nations "Statement to the Informal Interactive Dialogue on the Responsibility to Protect at the General Assembly," Wednesday, September 11, 2013. http://responsibilitytoprotect.org/Russia%2013.pdf

23 Ministry of Foreign Affairs of the Russian Federation, "Comment by the official representative of the Ministry of Foreign Affairs of Russia, Alexander Lukashevich, regarding the 'statements of facts' by the U.S. Department of State about the situation in Ukraine," March 6, 2014. www.mid.ru/en/kommentarii/-/asset_publisher/2MrVt3CzL5sw/content/id/71994

24 Vladimir Putin, "Address by President of the Russian Federation," March 18, 2014. http://en.kremlin.ru/events/president/news/20603. Sergey Lavrov similarly referred to "an unconstitutional coup in Kiev in February 2014" in a 2019 speech: Ministry of Foreign Affairs of the Russian Federation, "Foreign Minister Sergey Lavrov's speech at the Terra Scientia National Educational Youth Forum, Solnechnogorsk," August 15, 2019. www.mid.ru/en/web/guest/meropriyatiya_s_uchastiem_ministra/-/asset_publisher/xK1BhB2bUjd3/content/id/3756067

25 Ministry of Foreign Affairs of the Russian Federation, "Foreign Ministry statement in connection with Russia's veto of the French-proposed UN Security Council draft resolution on Syria on October 8, 2016," Oct 9, 2016. www.mid.ru/en/press_service/spokesman/official_statement/-/asset_publisher/t2GCdmD8RNIr/content/id/2494622

26 Dmitry Medvedev, "Transcript of the Meeting with the Participants in the International Club Valdai," September 12, 2008. http://archive.kremlin.ru/eng/speeches/2008/09/12/1644_type82912type82917type84779_206409.shtml. See also (Allison, 2008: 1167).

27 The Ministry of Foreign Affairs of the Russian Federation "Interview by Minister of Foreign Affairs of the Russian Federation Sergey Lavrov to BBC, Moscow," August 9, 2008. https://argentina.mid.ru/documents/3018403/9266181/russian_foreign_policy_11e.pdf

28 Steven Lee Myers and Ellen Barry, "Putin Reclaims Crimea for Russia and Bitterly Denounces the West." *New York Times*, March 18, 2014.

29 Ibid.
30 See for example Tass, "Russia blasts US assessment of events in Ukraine's southeast," April 17, 2014. https://tass.com/russia/728304
31 Shaun Walker, "Putin admits Russian military presence in Ukraine for first time." *Guardian*, December 17, 2015. www.theguardian.com/world/2015/dec/17/vladimir-putin-admits-russian-military-presence-ukraine
32 Tom Miles, "U.N. finds growing signs of Russian involvement in Ukraine war." Reuters, June 1, 2015. www.reuters.com/article/us-ukraine-crisis-un-idUSKBN0OH2SK20150601; Maksymilian Czuperski, John Herbst, Eliot Higgins, Alina Polyakova and Damon Wilson, "Hiding in Plain Sight: Putin's War in Ukraine." Atlantic Council, May 2015.
33 BBC News, "Ukraine crisis: Russia 'to respond if its interests' attacked," April 23, 2014. www.bbc.com/news/world-europe-27124453
34 Moscow Times, "Putin Vows to Protect Russians in Southeastern Ukraine from Nationalists," December 21, 2015. www.themoscowtimes.com/2015/12/21/putin-vows-to-protect-russians-in-southeastern-ukraine-from-nationalists-a51285
35 Russian Ministry of Foreign Affairs, "Speech and answers of the Minister of Foreign Affairs of Russia S.V. Lavrov to the questions of mass media during the press conference after the meeting of 'Action Group' regarding Syria and Geneva on 30 June 2012," July 1, 2012. www.mid.ru/en/press_service/minister_speeches/-/asset_publisher/7OvQR5KJWVmR/content/id/150786
36 Russian Ministry of Foreign Affairs, "Response of the Minister of Foreign Affairs of Russia S.V. Lavrov to the question of the newspaper «Arguments and Facts» on the Syrian issues," November 28, 2012. www.mid.ru/en/press_service/minister_speeches/-/asset_publisher/7OvQR5KJWVmR/content/id/132856
37 Russian Ministry of Foreign Affairs, "Sergey Lavrov's address at the second inter-Syrian consultative meeting in Moscow, April 9, 201 [*sic*]," Apr 9, 2015. www.mid.ru/en/press_service/minister_speeches/-/asset_publisher/7OvQR5KJWVmR/content/id/1155620
38 Patrick J. McDonnell, W.J. Hennigan and Nabih Bulos, "Russia launches airstrikes in Syria amid U.S. concern about targets." *Los Angeles Times*, September 30, 2015. www.latimes.com/world/europe/la-fg-kremlin-oks-troops-20150930-story.html
39 Russian Ministry of Foreign Affairs, "Foreign Ministry statement in connection with Russia's veto of the French-proposed UN Security Council draft resolution on Syria on October 8, 2016," October 9, 2016. www.mid.ru/en/press_service/spokesman/official_statement/-/asset_publisher/t2GCdmD8RNIr/content/id/2494622
40 Russian Ministry of Foreign Affairs "Statement by the Foreign Ministry," July 5, 2018. www.mid.ru/en/press_service/spokesman/official_statement/-/asset_publisher/t2GCdmD8RNIr/content/id/3288522
41 Amnesty International, "'Civilian Objects were Undamaged': Russia's Statements on Its Attacks in Syria Unmasked," December 23, 2015. www.amnesty.org/en/documents/mde24/3113/2015/en/
42 See ibid.; Syrian Network for Human Rights, "On the 3rd Anniversary of Russia's Intervention in Syria, SNHR Unveils an Incident Database for International Law Violations," September 30, 2018. http://sn4hr.org/blog/2018/09/30/52709/
43 Though in 2012 the government did note that a large Russian community had lived in Syria and that while "many of our citizens have been forced to return to Russia …. We closely monitor the situation will inform on any changes that affect the interests of Russian citizens." Ministry of Foreign Affairs of the Russian Federation, "Response of the Minister of Foreign Affairs of Russia S.V. Lavrov to the question of the newspaper «Arguments and Facts» on the Syrian issues," November 28, 2012. www.mid.ru/en/press_service/minister_speeches/-/asset_publisher/7OvQR5KJWVmR/content/id/132856
44 Dmitry Medvedev, "Dmitry Medvedev's interview with Time magazine," February 15, 2016. http://government.ru/en/news/21790/
45 UN Security Council Draft Resolution S/2014/189, March 15, 2014.

References

Acharya, A. (2004). How Ideas Spread: Whose Norms Matter? Norm Localization and Institutional Change in Asian Regionalism. *International Organization,* 58, 239–275.

Allison, R. (2008). Russia Resurgent? Moscow's Campaign to "Coerce Georgia to Peace." *International Affairs,* 84, 1145–1171.

Allison, R. (2017). Russia and the Post-2014 International Legal Order: Revisionism and Realpolitik. *International Affairs,* 93, 519–543.

Averre, D. and Davies, L. (2015). Russia, Humanitarian Intervention and the Responsibility to Protect: The Case of Syria. *International Affairs*, 91, 813–834.

Baranovsky, V. and Mateiko, A. (2016). Responsibility to Protect: Russia's Approaches. *The International Spectator,* 51, 49–69.

Bellamy, A.J. (2009a). *Responsibility to Protect.* Malden, MA: Polity.

Bellamy, A.J. (2009b). *Responsibility to Protect: The Global Effort to End Mass Atrocities.* Cambridge: Cambridge University Press.

Bellamy, A.J. (2011). Libya and the Responsibility to Protect: The Exception and the Norm. *Ethics & International Affairs,* 25, 263–269.

Bellamy, A.J. (2015). The Responsibility to Protect Turns Ten. *Ethics & International Affairs,* 29, 161–185.

Bellamy, A.J. and Williams, P.D. (2011). The New Politics of Protection? Côte d'Ivoire, Libya and the Responsibility to Protect. *International Affairs,* 87, 825–850.

Betts, A. and Orchard, P. (2014). Introduction: The Normative Institutionalization-Implementation Gap. *In:* Betts, A. and Orchard, P. (eds.) *Implementation and World Politics: How International Norms Change Practice*, 1–26. Oxford: Oxford University Press.

Bloomfield, A. (2016). Norm Anti-preneurs and Theorising Resistance to Normative Change. *Review of International Studies,* 42, 310–333.

Burai, E. (2016). Parody as Norm Contestation: Russian Normative Justifications in Georgia and Ukraine and Their Implications for Global Norms. *Global Society,* 30, 67–77.

Busby, J.W. (2010). *Moral Movements and Foreign Policy.* Cambridge: Cambridge University Press.

Claes, J. (2012). Protecting Civilians from Mass Atrocities: Meeting the Challenge of R2P Rejectionism. *Global Responsibility to Protect,* 4, 67–97.

Clem, R.S. (2017). Clearing the Fog of War: Public Versus Official Sources and Geopolitical Storylines in the Russia-Ukraine Conflict. *Journal of Eurasian Geography,* 58, 592–612.

Cooley, A. (2014). *Ukraine Insta-Symposium: Russia's Rule-Breaking as Power Politics* [Online]. *OpinioJuris*. Available from: http://opiniojuris.org/2014/03/07/russias-rule-breaking-power-politics/

Cortell, A.P. and Davis, J.W.J. (2005). When Norms Clash: International Norms, Domestic Practices, and Japan's Internalisation of the GATT/WTO. *Review of International Studies,* 31, 3–25.

Evans, G.J. (2008). Russia, Georgia and the Responsibility to Protect. *Amsterdam Legal Forum,* 1, 25–28.

Fukuyama, F. (2006). *The End of History and the Last Man.* New York: Simon and Schuster.

Gifkins, J. (2012). The UN Security Council Divided: Syria in Crisis. *Global Responsibility to Protect,* 4, 377–393.

Glanville, L. 2016. Does R2P Matter? Interpreting the Impact of a Norm. *Cooperation and Conflict*, 51, 184–199.

Ikenberry, G.J. (2013). The Liberal International Order and its Discontents. *In:* Friedman, R., Oskanian, K. and Pardo, R.P. (eds.) *After Liberalism? The Future of Liberalism in International Relations*, 91–102. Houndmills: Palgrave.

Junk, J. (2016). Bringing the Non-Coercive Dimensions of R2P to the Fore: The Case of Kenya. *Journal of Global Security*, 30, 54–66.

Kanet, R.E. (2015). The Failed Western Challenge to Russia's Revival in Eurasia? *International Politics*, 52, 503–522.

Kuhrt, N. (2014). Russia, the Responsibility to Protect and Intervention. *In:* Fiott, D. and Koops, J. (eds.) *The Responsibility to Protect and the Third Pillar: Legitimacy and Operationalization*, 97–114. Houndmills, Basingstoke: Palgrave MacMillan.

Kurowska, X. (2014). Multipolarity as Resistance to Liberal Norms: Russia's Position on Responsibility to Protect. *Conflict, Security & Development*, 14, 489–508.

Morris, J. (2013). Libya and Syria: R2P and the Spectre of the Swinging Pendulum. *International Affairs*, 89, 1265–1283.

Neumann, I.B. and Pouliot, V. (2011). Untimely Russia: Hysteresis in Russian-Western Relations over the Past Millennium. *Security Studies*, 20, 105–137.

Orchard, P. (2014). Implementing a Global Internally Displaced Persons Protection Regime. *In:* Betts, A. and Orchard, P. (eds.) *Implementation and World Politics: How International Norms Change Practice*, 105–123. Oxford: Oxford University Press.

Panke, D. and Petersohn, U. (2012). Why International Norms Disappear Sometimes. *European Journal of International Relations*, 18, 719–742.

Ralph, J. and Gifkins, J. (2017). The Purpose of United Nations Security Council Practice: Contesting Competence Claims in the Normative Context Created by the Responsibility to Protect. *European Journal of International Relations*, 23, 630–653.

Reus-Smit, C. (2005). Liberal Hierarchy and the Licence to Use Force. *Review of International Studies*, 31, 71–92.

Sakwa, R. (2012). The Problem of "the International" in Russian Identity Formation. *International Politics*, 49, 449–465.

Sakwa, R. (2015). The Death of Europe? Continental Fates after Ukraine. *International Affairs*, 91, 553–579.

Shannon, V.P. (2000). Norms are What States Make of Them: The Political Psychology of Norm Violation. *International Studies Quarterly*, 44, 293–316.

Simmons, B.A. (2009). *Mobilizing for Human Rights: International Law in Domestic Politics.* Cambridge: Cambridge University Press.

Stafford, T. and Dzelyte, L. (2014). *Crimea and the Hijacking of the Responsibility to Protect* [Online]. London: Human Security Centre. Available from: www.hscentre.org/opinion/crimea-hijacking-responsibility-protect/

Surkov, V. (2008). Russian Political Culture: The View from Utopia. *Russian Social Science Review*, 49, 81–97.

Tsygankov, A.P. (2014). Contested Identity and Foreign Policy: Interpreting Russia's International Choices. *International Studies Perspectives*, 15, 19–35.

Welsh, J. (2013). Norm Contestation and the Responsibility to Protect. *Global Responsibility to Protect*, 5, 365–396.

Wiener, A. (2007). Contested Meanings of Norms: A Research Framework. *Comparative European Politics*, 5, 1–17.

Wiener, A. (2009). Enacting Meaning-in-use: Qualitative Research on Norms and International Relations. *Review of International Studies*, 35, 175–193.

Wiener, A. (2014). *A Theory of Contestation*. Berlin: Springer.

Zarakol, A. (2010). *After Defeat: How the East Learned to Live with the West*, Cambridge University Press.

Ziegler, C.E. (2012). Conceptualizing Sovereignty in Russian Foreign Policy: Realist and Constructivist Perspectives. *International Politics,* 49, 400–417.

Ziegler, C.E. (2018). Russian Diplomacy: Challenging the West. *Seton Hall Journal of Diplomacy and International Relations,* 19, 74–89.

Index

Page numbers in **bold** denote tables.

For Product Safety Concerns and Information please contact our EU representative GPSR@taylorandfrancis.com
Taylor & Francis Verlag GmbH, Kaufingerstraße 24, 80331 München, Germany

www.ingramcontent.com/pod-product-compliance
Lightning Source LLC
LaVergne TN
LVHW011131300926
849160LV00008B/604
9781032174747